Register Now for
to Your L

SPRINGER PUBLISHING COMPANY
CONNECT™

Your print purchase of *The Psychology of Oppression,* **includes online access to the contents of your book**—increasing accessibility, portability, and searchability!

Access today at:

**http://connect.springerpub.com/content/book/978-0-8261-7817-6
or scan the QR code at the right with your smartphone
and enter the access code below.**

EBWGCKLW

*Scan here for
quick access.*

If you are experiencing problems accessing the digital component of this product, please contact our customer service department at cs@springerpub.com

The online access with your print purchase is available at the publisher's discretion and may be removed at any time without notice.

Publisher's Note: New and used products purchased from third-party sellers are not guaranteed for quality, authenticity, or access to any included digital components.

LS

SPRINGER PUBLISHING COMPANY
View all our products at springerpub.com

BLACK PANTHER — MEN — AMERICAN QUESTION THE WOMEN'S
AUTHORITY. LOOKS AT THE WOMAN, ~~~~~ HE THINKS SHE LOOKS
WIERD.

— WOMEN — GENERAL, QUEEN, TECHNOLOGY ENGINEER
   FIGHTERS (SOULDERS)

The Psychology of Oppression

"DON'T WORRY DARLING" IS A SIFI MOVIE about a
man who tricks his life partner into a SIMULATION
THAT SIMULATES A "PERFECT" LIFE.
WOMAN - STAYS HOME ALL DAY, SHE COOKS & CLEANS
THE MAN - PRETENDS TO WORK OR WE DON'T KNOW WHAT THEY
DO, BUT THEY ARE GONE ALL DAY. THE MEN COME BACK HOME

E. J. R. David, PhD, obtained his bachelor's degree in psychology from the University of Alaska Anchorage (2002) and master of arts (2004) and doctoral (2007) degrees in clinical–community psychology from the University of Illinois at Urbana–Champaign. Dr. David is an associate professor of psychology at the University of Alaska Anchorage, his primary duties being with the PhD program in clinical–community psychology that has a rural, cultural, and indigenous emphasis. He has published theoretical and empirical works on internalized oppression or colonial mentality, including *Brown Skin, White Minds: Filipino -/ American Postcolonial Psychology* and *Internalized Oppression: The Psychology of Marginalized Groups* (Springer Publishing Company). Dr. David is also a contributor to *Psychology Today,* periodically writing about the psychology of race, ethnicity, and culture. Dr. David was the 2007 recipient of the American Psychological Association (APA) Society for the Psychological Study of Ethnic Minority Issues (Division 45) Distinguished Student Research Award "for his significant contribution in psychological research related to ethnic minority popula-tions." In 2012, he was honored by the APA Minority Fellowship Program (MFP) with the Early Career Award in Research for Distinguished Contributions to the Field of Racial and Ethnic Minority Psychology, citing his "outstanding scientific contributions and the application of this knowledge toward the improved mental and physical well-being of people of color." In 2013, he was chosen to receive the Asian American Psychological Association Early Career Award for Distinguished Contributions to Research. In 2014, he was honored by the Alaska Psychological Association with the Cultural Humanitarian Award for Exemplary Service and Dedication to Diversity, and in 2015 he was inducted as a Fellow by the Asian American Psychological Asso-ciation for "unusual and outstanding contributions to Asian American psychology."

Annie O. Derthick, PhD, earned her PhD in clinical–community psychology with a rural, cultural, and indigenous emphasis from the University of Alaska Anchorage, where her dissertation included the production of one of the first quantitative mea-sures of microaggressions against women while documenting the predictive power of sexist microaggressions in women's mental health. In general, her research and clinical interests relate to the psychological impact of oppression and discrimination. Dr. Derthick is currently working as a licensed psychologist at a clinic for the uninsured and underserved, where she works with members of marginalized and disenfran-chised communities utilizing a liberation psychotherapy framework to address the complex relationship between psychological well-being and a divisive, oppressive socio–political–historical–cultural–economic context for sexual- and gender-minority groups, immigrants and refugees, and non–English-speaking people. Dr. Derthick is a frequently invited presenter, trainer, and workshop facilitator in academic and community settings, where she discusses the clinical implications of interpersonal and systemic oppression for individuals and communities and ways to address systemic injustice in individual treatment.

The Psychology of Oppression

E. J. R. David, PhD, and Annie O. Derthick, PhD

SPRINGER PUBLISHING COMPANY

Copyright © 2018 Springer Publishing Company, LLC

All rights reserved.

No part of this publication may be reproduced, stored in a retrieval system, or transmitted in any form or by any means, electronic, mechanical, photocopying, recording, or otherwise, without the prior permission of Springer Publishing Company, LLC, or authorization through payment of the appropriate fees to the Copyright Clearance Center, Inc., 222 Rosewood Drive, Danvers, MA 01923, 978-750-8400, fax 978-646-8600, info@copyright.com or on the Web at www.copyright.com.

Springer Publishing Company, LLC
11 West 42nd Street
New York, NY 10036
www.springerpub.com

Acquisitions Editor: Debra Riegert
Compositor: S4Carlisle Publishing Services

ISBN: 9780826178169
ebook ISBN: 9780826178176

17 18 19 20 21 / 5 4 3 2 1

The author and the publisher of this Work have made every effort to use sources believed to be reliable to provide information that is accurate and compatible with the standards generally accepted at the time of publication. The author and publisher shall not be liable for any special, consequential, or exemplary damages resulting, in whole or in part, from the readers' use of, or reliance on, the information contained in this book. The publisher has no responsibility for the persistence or accuracy of URLs for external or third-party Internet websites referred to in this publication and does not guarantee that any content on such websites is, or will remain, accurate or appropriate. *Another one.*

Library of Congress Cataloging-in-Publication Data

Names: David, E. J. R. (Eric John Ramos), author. | Derthick, Annie O.,
  author.
Title: The psychology of oppression / E.J.R. David, PhD and Annie O.
  Derthick, PhD.
Description: New York : Springer, [2017] | Includes bibliographical
  references and index.
Identifiers: LCCN 2017026481 | ISBN 9780826178169 | ISBN 9780826178176 (ebook)
Subjects: LCSH: Marginality, Social--Psychological aspects. | Oppression
  (Psychology) | Intergroup relations. | Social justice.
Classification: LCC HM1136 .D38 2017 | DDC 305.5/6--dc23
LC record available at https://lccn.loc.gov/2017026481

Contact us to receive discount rates on bulk purchases.
We can also customize our books to meet your needs.
For more information please contact: sales@springerpub.com

Printed in the United States of America.

For Malakas, Kalayaan, Kaluguran, and the other children of the world. May your generation continue to strive for a just, harmonious, and healthy world.

—E. J. R. David

For the 65.3 million forcibly displaced people worldwide and all those seeking refuge from oppression. I pray that you find safe harbor.

—Annie O. Derthick

Contents

Preface

Think back to when you were around 4 or 5 years old, when you were just beginning your formal education. Do you remember learning about basic math such as counting to 10? Do you remember being taught how to do simple addition and subtraction? Do you also remember being introduced by your teacher to the basic principles of science? In addition to science and math, do you also remember being taught some aspects of history (e.g., presidents, revolutionary war) and civics (e.g., government, taxes), perhaps as early as the first grade? For many of us, especially those of us raised in the United States, we were exposed to these topics early in our lives because our society considers science, math, and social studies as "core" to our education and to what would make us well-rounded, well-informed, and successful human beings who care about and contribute to our society.

Over the past few years, however, our society has drifted toward emphasizing just math and the natural sciences. For example, government funding for the social studies disciplines (i.e., art, history, religion, philosophy, social sciences such as psychology, political science, and sociology) has been decreased and even eliminated, while funding for the areas of science, technology, engineering, and math (STEM) has been dramatically increased (e.g., Zakaria, 2015). While the STEM fields are definitely important, we hold the position that **social studies**—"the integrated study of the social sciences and humanities to promote civic competence" and help people "make informed and reasoned decisions for the public good as citizens of a culturally diverse, democratic society in an interdependent world" (National Council for the Social Studies, 1994, p. 3)—is just as important for creating a well-functioning, thriving, and healthy society. This is because, for a society to function well and be healthy, we believe that the society must be just and, thus, strive to be free of oppression. Well, the topics of oppression and social justice are primarily in the realm of the humanities and social sciences—the realm of social studies. Therefore, our society needs to better appreciate social studies—the forgotten core—because learning about oppression and striving for social justice should be core components of people's education for them to be caring, kind, and compassionate members of society.

Oppression is the antithesis of, and greatest threat to, justice. Thus, oppression is a significant barrier to a society's quest to be well and healthy. Oppression has been a defining concept of human history, and it continues to define our modern-day reality, yet few people understand oppression and its widespread, serious implications. In the United States, for instance, we see today the importance of social justice for a society's well-being as clearly as perhaps at any other time in our history. When we were writing this book, there were daily reminders of oppression and injustice, such as Black and Brown peoples' continued struggles against police brutality, mass incarceration, and the systemic devaluation of their lives. There is continued discrimination against women, lesbian, gay, bisexual, transgender, and queer people, immigrants, and Muslims. Our indigenous brothers and sisters in Standing Rock are still resisting the continued colonization of their lands. We have seen rights (e.g., Voting Rights Act, Immigration Act of 1965) that various social groups took decades to fight for and achieve be taken away almost instantaneously. We hear terms such as "microaggressions," and we see oppression in various levels and manifestations continuing to dominate our lives. These current events clearly show that oppression continues to be pervasive in our society, and so our modern-day society is unjust. Therefore, our contemporary society is unhealthy. Indeed, the value of social studies is very much needed now, given the pressing societal issues we are facing today.

To do our little part in making oppression and social justice education more central, core, or fundamental in our world—at least in our own discipline of psychology—we draw heavily from the various social studies disciplines to write what we hope is an accessible, "scholarly light" book on oppression. This book provides a basic introduction to the psychology of oppression that we hope will be useful in making oppression and social justice education more accessible to more people. The first three chapters focus on the fundamentals of oppression, as we provide brief overviews of *what* oppression is (Chapter 1), *who* experiences oppression (Chapter 2), and *where* and *when* oppression has taken place (Chapter 3). In the next three chapters we discuss some of the layers and complexities of oppression, as we cover *how* oppression may be expressed blatantly or subtly and overtly or covertly (Chapter 4), *how* oppression exists and operates on different levels (Chapter 5), and *how* oppression influences peoples' well-being and health (Chapter 6). In Chapters 7 through 9, we discuss *why* oppression exists and continues to persist throughout history (Chapter 7), and *what we can do* to address oppression in both clinical (Chapter 8) and community (Chapter 9) contexts. Finally, we close the book with some suggestions about *future psychological work* on oppression across research, clinical, and community contexts (Chapter 10). With the currently tenuous conditions in the United States and of its relationship with the rest of the world, we feel that this book is very timely, as it may reach and inform a wider range of people about various forms of oppression and how they influence peoples' **psychological experiences**—how they think, feel, and behave in relation to themselves, others who are like them (e.g., same cultural group, same country), and others who are not like them.

Essentially, we believe that all of us in this very diverse world need to have at least a basic understanding of oppression—the existing power inequalities and resulting dynamics between different groups of people—in order to create a more just, harmonious, and healthy world. We believe that understanding social group oppression, having a commitment to combatting bias at the interpersonal, institutional, and internalized levels, and striving toward achieving social justice should be core values for all people. We feel that this is an important core foundation for all of us to have—similar to how we regard science and math—in order to create a better world. We hope our book helps in our collective efforts to make this happen.

Thank you for supporting the book and we hope you find it useful.

E. J. R. David and Annie O. Derthick

REFERENCES

National Council for the Social Studies. (1994). *Expectations of excellence: Curriculum standards for social studies.* Washington, DC: Author.

Zakaria, F. (2015). *In defense of a liberal education.* New York, NY: W. W. Norton.

Acknowledgments

Maraming salamat, dakal a salamat, enaa' baasee' to my wife—Margaret—and our children—Malakas, Kalayaan, and Kaluguran—for giving me connectedness, strength, freedom, and love. I dedicate every day to you.

I am also eternally grateful to Dr. Sumie Okazaki for accepting me into graduate school, and to Dr. Kevin Nadal for being a brother and a role model over the past 15 years. I also thank Anissa Hauser, Dr. Claudia Lampman, Dr. John Petraitis, and the rest of the Psychology Department at the University of Alaska Anchorage for giving me the autonomy to write books such as this one. Gratitude also goes to Stephanie Drew, Mindy Chen, Debra Riegert, and the rest of Springer Publishing Company for appreciating the need for this book.

Finally, as always, special acknowledgment and appreciation also go to my Nanay, Tatay, Ate Ellen, Bonz, Jass, and Alex for always being there for me; the Vinas, Ebue, Concepcion, Rochon, Danner, Morse, Olin, Hoffman, Shaw, David, Clemente, Pangilinan, Ocampo, Dimson, De Leon, and Abad families for being my family; my Alaska and Busko Boys for always having my back; the Nageak, Harcharek, Fuller, and Baksis families for seeing something valuable in me when no one else did; and the Barrow High School Whalers and the entire community of Utkiagvik, Alaska, for giving this lost boy a chance and some direction.

Maraming salamat, dakal a salamat, enaa' baasee', quyanaqpak, many thanks, and *mabuhay kayong lahat!*

—E. J. R. David

I want to thank Dr. E. J. R. David for inviting me to join my voice with his in this book. As my mentor and advisor, you have helped me find that voice. Thank you for teaching me, believing in me, and finding value in what I have to say. I am forever indebted to you for sharing your wisdom with me and continuing to be a source of support as you have become my friend. I am inspired by you every day. Thank you for what you have given to me and for what you give to the world.

When we started writing this book, the first African American president was in office, and it seemed impossible that the first woman would not be elected. And even though we knew we had many battles still left to fight, I felt hopeful about the future and excited about the changes that were occurring in our country. However, over the last few months as we pushed to get this book finished, things have changed. Our new president has openly disparaged women, people of color, immigrants, people with disabilities, and the poor, and has attacked freedom of speech and freedom of the press—all before he was even elected. Since his election, he has challenged freedom of religion and has turned our country's back on the most vulnerable in the world—refugees. The hope and optimism I felt growing over the last few years have been replaced with fear and sadness. So because of these current events, I want to thank those people—and groups of people—who are speaking up and demanding justice. I want to thank every person who has marched, who has written his or her representatives, who has organized a protest, who has held a sign, and who has lit a candle in the name of peace and justice. I feel a collective voice rising, saying "this is not normal, and we don't have to accept it!" Thank you to everyone who continues to fight on the side of right and good and who continues to show up. You have been my source of strength during the last few months; you have been my hope.

Finally, I want to thank my wife, Kris Pitts, who lives fearlessly. You challenge me, teach me, and inspire me to live my truth. Thank you for loving me; I am a better version of me because you do.

—Annie O. Derthick

CHAPTER 1

Oppression 101: An Overview

Black Lives Matter. It is a movement that has gained widespread recognition for fighting against the oppression of Black Peoples. Through television, radio, newspapers, magazines, social media, and perhaps by just walking or driving around in any city, it is very likely that most of us have already been exposed to #BlackLivesMatter in some form. Therefore, we have already been witness to one of the more powerful, remarkable, and recognizable movements against oppression in the history of the United States.

As many of us may already know, the Black Lives Matter movement is just one of many organizations that have fought against the oppression of Black Peoples. For instance, there's the National Association for the Advancement of Colored People founded by a group led by W. E. B. DuBois in 1909, the Southern Christian Leadership Conference led by Martin Luther King Jr. in 1957, and the Organization of Afro-American Unity founded by Malcolm X in 1964. There is also the Underground Railroad, a network of individuals—including Harriet Tubman—who helped Black Peoples escape slavery in the 1800s. We can even go all the way back to the 1600s and find records of people and organizations who were calling for the abolition of African slavery. The fact that groups have been fighting against the oppression of Black individuals ever since the beginning of the United States makes it clear that the oppression of Black Peoples has been going on throughout American history (Bailey, Williams, & Favors, 2014).

Similarly, oppression in its many forms has also been going on throughout human history worldwide. We see examples of oppression from biblical stories (e.g., the enslavement of Israelites) to colonization of indigenous peoples (e.g., Gonzalez, Simard, Baker-Demaray, & Iron Eyes, 2014; Lewis, Allen, & Fleagle, 2014; Salzman & Laenui, 2014) and the subjugation of women (e.g., Bearman & Amrhein, 2014), all the way to the denial of equal rights for lesbian, gay, bisexual, transgender, and queer (LGBTQ) individuals (e.g., Nadal & Mendoza, 2014) and the marginalization of people with disabilities (e.g., Watermeyer & Gorgens, 2014). Oppression has been so omnipresent and widespread in our world (discussed in more detail in Chapter 3) that it is very likely that all of us have witnessed oppression, experienced oppression, inflicted oppression, felt the negative consequences of oppression, or all of the above.

Despite its pervasiveness and harmful impacts, however, it seems as though many of us still do not have a clear understanding of oppression, its many manifestations, and its consequences. Many of us may have heard of racism, sexism, and even heterosexism or homophobia (more specific forms of oppression are discussed in Chapter 2), but do not see the need to address them—believing that such "isms" are not legitimate concerns and are just products of some people's ideological movement toward "political correctness"—thereby failing to understand that "isms" are oppressive and are therefore harmful. Even among those of us who are familiar with specific "isms" and agree that they are social ills that need to be addressed, many seem to not see that the core commonality between these various forms of "isms" is that they are problematic precisely because they are oppressive. This seems to be the case for the field of psychology, as a simple search on PsycINFO—the largest database of psychology-related scholarly literature—using "racism," "sexism," and "heterosexism or homophobia" as keywords produced 6,647, 2,137, and 1,709 hits, respectively (as of July 14, 2016). On the other hand, the keyword "oppression" produced only 1,822 hits, seemingly failing to recognize that racism, sexism, heterosexism, and other "isms" fall under the broader concept of oppression. Indeed, oppression in all of its forms, complexities, and effects seems to remain an especially vague, unclear, and misunderstood concept to many of us.

So to begin the book, this opening chapter provides a brief overview of oppression, its many forms and manifestations, and why we need to pay attention to it, while also outlining the coverage of such topics in the other chapters.

■ WHAT IS OPPRESSION? A STATE AND A PROCESS

For those of us with a background in psychology, we might remember from our introductory course that a basic definition of psychology is something like *the scientific study of people's thoughts, emotions, and behaviors.* Therefore, the field of psychology is interested in all the factors—whether they be physiological or biological, social, cultural, environmental, perhaps even spiritual—that may influence how people think, feel, and act. The multitude and complexity of factors that influence our psychological experiences may lead our thoughts, emotions, and behaviors to become distorted, inaccurate, and biased. In psychology, we refer to these distorted thoughts and beliefs that may lead to unfair behaviors as *stereotypes, prejudice,* and *discrimination* (discussed in more detail later). Stereotypes, prejudice, and discrimination are concepts that have been studied extensively; for instance, a search on the PsycINFO database on these keywords resulted in 2,768, 6,962, and 5,267 hits, respectively—even way more than the large psychological literature on specific "isms"! In other words, the field of psychology has done plenty of work on how people's thoughts, attitudes, emotions, and behaviors may become biased! One of the many things we have learned about these concepts is that all of us have these erroneous beliefs and biases about our fellow human beings. In turn, these inaccurate perceptions and unfair treatments of certain groups of people may lead to the creation of a society that generally favors or benefits some people while systematically degrading and subjugating others. This unfair process of aiding some people while harming others and the resulting condition of inequality between people is **oppression.**

A dictionary definition of oppression is "Unjust or cruel exercise of authority or power especially by the imposition of burdens; the condition of being weighed down; an act of pressing down; a sense of heaviness or obstruction in the body or mind" (*Merriam-Webster Third International Edition*). As we can see, this definition suggests that in addition to oppression being a condition in which there is inequality between groups, oppression is also a process that enacts or maintains the state of oppression.

Similarly, the abundant definitions for oppression in the scholarly literature (e.g., Barker, 2003; Collins, 1993; Davis, 2002; Deutsch, 2006; Freire, 1970; Frye, 1983; Gil, 1994; Johnson, 2000a, 2000b; Prilleltensky & Gonick, 1996; Turner, Singleton, & Musick, 1984; Young, 1990) all center on the notion that groups of people have unequal power (**oppression as a condition or state**) and the more dominant or privileged groups use their power to exert violence on, exploit, marginalize, and inferiorize the dominated groups (**oppression as a process or act**). For example,

Asymmetric power refers to a relationship between two individuals in which one, the powerful person, has control over the outcomes of the other, the subordinate, but not vice versa

psychologists Prilleltensky and Gonick (1996) conceptualize oppression as follows: *Subordinate - treat or regard as of lesser importance than something else*

> . . . oppression entails a state of asymmetric power relations characterized by domination, subordination, and resistance, where the dominating persons or groups exercise their power by restricting access to material resources and by implanting in the subordinated persons or groups fear or self-deprecating views about themselves. . . . Oppression, then, is a series of asymmetric power relations between individuals, genders, classes, communities, nations, and states. (pp. 129–130)

Consistent with these definitions, we offer the following:

> Oppression occurs when one group has more access to power and privilege than another group, and when that power and privilege is used to maintain the status quo (i.e., domination of one group over another). Thus, oppression is both a state and a process, with the state of oppression being an unequal group access to power and privilege, and the process of oppression being the ways in which inequality between groups is maintained. (David & Derthick, 2014, p. 3)

The process, exercise, or enactment of oppression can take the form of imposition and deprivation. According to Hanna, Talley, and Guindon (2000), **oppression by imposition or force** is "the act of imposing on . . . others . . . a label, role experience, or set of living conditions that is unwanted, needlessly painful, and detracts from physical or psychological well-being . . . (such as) demeaning hard labor, degrading job roles, ridicule, and negative media images and messages that foster and maintain distorted beliefs" (p. 431). In the case of colonialism, for example, colonizers hold power and privilege over the colonized or indigenous peoples in that colonizers are more likely to be in positions of power because the colonizers' characteristics (e.g., the language they speak, the type of knowledge they hold, the type of expertise they have, their mannerisms, the way they dress) are more generally accepted and valued (e.g., the colonizers' characteristics are seen by many people as the standard or the definition of a "qualified" leader, so people are more likely to vote for people with such characteristics). In turn, these positions of power are often used to impose a certain belief about acceptable definitions of "important knowledge," degrading indigenous worldviews, knowledge, and expertise while propagating a distorted and dehumanizing public perception of indigenous culture (e.g., as backward, uncivilized, or "old fashioned" and no longer relevant) that operates to keep indigenous peoples subjugated.

Even further, oppression can also be enacted by deprivation. According to Sue (2010), **oppression by deprivation** "involves depriving people of desired jobs, an education, healthcare, or living conditions necessary for physical and mental well-being . . . [such as] food, clothing, shelter, love, respect, social support, or self-dignity" (p. 7). An example of this is when colonizers deprive indigenous peoples of the right to govern themselves or when colonizers limit the power of indigenous peoples' tribal government, basically treating indigenous peoples as deserving less than what colonizers are allowed to do. Therefore, the process of oppression—enacted through imposition and deprivation—essentially operates to preserve the status quo which is a state of oppression.

▪ ALWAYS REMEMBER: "OPPRESSION" HAS TWO Ps

In addition to understanding that oppression is both a state and a process and that the process of oppression can be done through imposition and deprivation, it is also very important to clarify two key and necessary components of oppression—*Power* and *Privilege.* By its very definition oppression does not exist if there is no power and privilege inequalities between people. **Power** may be defined as people's access to resources that enhance their chances of getting what they need in order to lead safe, productive, fulfilling lives. It is the capacity to exert force, influence, or control over one's environment—which includes other people, organizations, and institutions—in order to get what one wants. Power also includes the system of individuals, institutions, and cultural norms, standards, and assumptions that support, justify, legitimize, and protect certain worldviews and ways of doing. The ideal, of course, is for all people and groups to have equal power; however, this is not the reality. Some groups of people—like Americans—have more capacity to control or influence their environment to get the resources they want than other groups of people—like people in Somalia, for example. Indeed, Americans have more power, clout, and influence than almost everyone else in the world as the United States is widely regarded as a "world leader," its military being considered as the "most powerful in the world," and its president being often regarded as "the leader of the free world." ← concept

The existing inequality of power between groups gives some people privileges that others do not have. For instance, just by being an American and possessing an American passport give one the privilege to travel pretty much anywhere in the world with relative ease, whereas Somali people (and people in many other countries) will need to go through a long and arduous process of obtaining approvals before being allowed to enter the United States (and other Western countries). **Privilege**, therefore, is unearned power that is only easily or readily available to some people simply as a result of their social group membership. It is a privilege for many European or White Americans, for example, to have their ancestors' histories (e.g., courses on "European History," "Western Civilization"), cultures (e.g., Greek mythology, Shakespearean literature), and worldviews (e.g., individualism, capitalism) validated as the standard, the norm, or as important and required knowledge on which social acceptance and admiration, educational achievement, economic opportunities, and social mobility are based. In other words, knowing and understanding such material (e.g., Western history, literature) and thinking a certain way (e.g., quickly, competitively) are parts of the dominant society's definition of "intelligent," "acceptable," or even "desirable," and what institutions consequently consider as the standard to which other people are measured (or tested) and forced to live up to. Privilege is enjoyed by a dominant group—whether they are aware of their privileges or not, whether they want it or not, and whether they are well intentioned or not—giving them economic, political, social, and cultural advantages at the expense of members of marginalized groups.

■ WHAT IS A SOCIAL GROUP, AND WHO ARE OPPRESSED?

Another way to think about the process or enactment of oppression is when a group of people make it difficult or even impossible for other groups of people to reach their human potential. In other words, oppression is when a social group in power dehumanizes other social groups and keeps them that way (Freire, 1970). This could mean treating oppressed social groups in a degrading or undignified manner (i.e., oppression by imposition or force) or denying them equal rights, privileges, protections, and opportunities that groups in power have, enjoy, and benefit from. Therefore, oppression is essentially injustice (state) and it creates or maintains injustice (process), a vicious cycle—an unjust system—that perpetually ensures that people will have unequal power and privileges based solely on their social group membership. So what, then, is a social group? According to noted scholar Iris Marion Young (1990), a **social group** is

> . . . a collective of persons differentiated from at least one other group by cultural forms, practices, or way of life. Members of a group have a specific affinity with one another because of their similar experience or way of life, which prompts them to associate with one another more than with those not identified with the group, or in a different way. (p. 43)

Using this definition, we can easily see that there are many types of social group categorizations (e.g., by race, sex, age, sexual orientation, abilities, national origin) and, thus, oppression based on group membership may also come in various forms (e.g., racism, sexism, ageism, heterosexism, ableism, xenophobia). The next question, then, is how do we determine which group is privileged and which group is oppressed in each of the social group categorizations that exist?

There is not one clear, perfect, or one-size-fits-all way of determining whether a social group is oppressed or not. This is primarily because power structures and dynamics may vary *between* societies or countries. For example, a dominant social group in one society (e.g., the Tagalog people in the Philippines hold power over the other ethnic groups in the country) may be a marginalized group in another (e.g., Tagalog people are marginalized in the United States). Even further, power structures and dynamics may vary between the diversity of contexts that may exist *within* a single society or country. For example, a dominant social group in one specific context (e.g., Chinese Americans in a neighborhood that is considered to be the Chinese ethnic enclave of a city, like many Chinatowns) may be a marginalized group in a more macrolevel or larger perspective of the same society (e.g., Chinese Americans are still not represented in city or state governance).

Nevertheless, one useful framework to help guide us as we think about the power dynamics between social groups is Marilyn Frye's (1983) 5-point criteria. According to Frye, the first criterion to help us determine if the social group to which a person belongs is oppressed is that *there must be restrictions, barriers, or limitations on the person's freedoms*. In the case of LGBTQ people, for example, there are limitations in their freedoms to have a family in terms of whom they are allowed to love and marry, and if they are allowed to adopt children. Second, *the restrictions, barriers, and limitations must be harmful* and the harm outweigh any potential benefits incurred as a result of those same restrictions. Staying with the same example, although people may argue that being single and not having children may present some benefits to LGBTQ people (e.g., no children to look after), the fact still remains that LGBTQ people are not given the same freedom to make such decisions (i.e., decision to get married or not, have children or not). Also, in a more direct manner, there are benefits to being married and having children (e.g., tax benefits, visitation rights in hospitals, "next of kin" recognitions) that are denied to LGBTQ individuals because of the restrictions. Third, *the restrictions, barriers, and limitations must be imposed protected, and justified by a social structure or institution.* We see this in our current society with various forms of laws, policies, and cultural norms that restrict LGBTQ people's rights. Fourth, *the restrictions, barriers, and limitations must be suffered by people simply because of their social group membership.* This is clearly the case for LGBTQ individuals who are marginalized, ridiculed, discriminated against, and even demonized (or pathologized) simply because of who they are. Finally, the fifth criterion is that *there must be a separate social group that maintains the status quo of oppression and who benefits from the imposed restrictions, barriers, and limitations.* In our LGBTQ example, non-LGBTQ people who impose their ideas of relationships and families and deny equal freedoms and rights to LGBTQ people benefit from such a system of oppression because the "normal" family structure is validated as "acceptable" and the "standard."

Combining Frye's 5-point criteria for identifying oppressed groups with Hays's (2003) influential **ADDRESSING** (*a*ge, *d*isability, *r*eligion, *e*thnicity or race, *s*exual orientation, *s*ocial class, *i*ndigenous heritage, *n*ational origin, *g*ender or sex) framework for understanding our social identities and where we are in relation to other people, Table 1.1 summarizes the most commonly seen social group categorizations, specifying the privileged (or dominant) and oppressed (or marginalized) groups for each category.

■ A VICIOUS SYSTEM: LEVELS AND MANIFESTATIONS OF OPPRESSION

Oppression can exist and operate in the *interpersonal, institutional, and internalized levels* (discussed in more detail in Chapter 5). Interpersonal oppression can happen between individuals such as when a White person hurriedly locks her car door when she sees a Black person approaching (e.g., Steele, 2010); between groups such as when heterosexual people refer to something that is dumb, stupid, not cool, or undesirable as

TABLE 1.1 Pamela Hays's ADDRESSING Framework: A Model of Cultural Influences and Their Relationship to Power and Privilege in the United States

Social Group Categorization	Privileged or Dominant Groups	Oppressed or Marginalized Groups
Age	Early and middle adulthood	Children, adolescents, and elders
Disability	Temporarily able-bodied	People with disabilities
Religion	Christians	Muslims, Jews, other non-Christians, agnostics, atheists
Ethnicity or race	European or White Americans	People of color
Sexual orientation	Heterosexual people	Lesbian, gay, bisexual, asexual people
Social class	Middle and upper class	Poor and working class
Indigenous heritage	Nonnative or non-Indigenous	Native, Indigenous, aboriginal peoples
National origin	U.S. born	Immigrants, refugees, asylees
Gender or sex	Male	Female, transgender people, intersex

Source: Adapted from Hays (2003).

[handwritten annotations: "so basically, everyone else"; "So basically, a white boy."]

"so gay" (e.g., Nadal, 2013); and even within groups such as when more Americanized Latinx derogatorily refer to less Americanized Latinx as "paisa" or "ghetto" (Hipolito-Delgado, Gallegos Payan, & Baca, 2014). As can be deduced from these examples, **interpersonal oppression** is driven by and expressed as stereotypes, prejudices, and discrimination. Briefly, **stereotypes** are defined as specific beliefs about a group, such as general descriptions of what members of a particular group look like, how they behave, or their abilities. As such, stereotypes are (over)generalized *cognitive* representations of how members of a group are similar to one another and different from members of other groups. **Prejudice** refers to the attitudes, feelings, or *affective* components of our perceptions about members of certain social groups. The emotions or affect we attach to certain groups may be positive or negative and may be conscious or nonconscious. **Discrimination** is the *behavior* that results from a person's stereotypes and prejudices. In other words, when one's actions are driven by biased beliefs and attitudes against a certain group of people, then one is discriminating against that particular group (e.g., racial discrimination, gender discrimination). An easy way to remember these is: *Biased CAB,* wherein C is cognition for stereotypes, A is affect for prejudice, and B is behavior for discrimination. Biased CAB, therefore, stands for biased cognition, biased affect, and biased behavior and, in many cases, this is the kind of oppression—the interpersonal-level type that often comes out as stereotypes, prejudices, and discriminatory behaviors—that people have in mind when talking about specific forms of oppression such as racism, sexism, heterosexism, and others.

Keep in mind, however, that a necessary component of oppression is power and privilege (as discussed in the previous section of "Always remember: oPPression has two Ps"). So just because people may hold certain stereotypes and prejudices that may lead them to behave in a discriminatory manner against some groups of people, their biased thoughts, attitudes, and actions are not oppression unless they are also members of the dominant group that holds power and privileges that other groups do not have. For example, just because an Asian American person may think that all White people are untrustworthy, may be turned off by White people's assertiveness, and therefore choose to avoid being around White people, this does not mean that the Asian American person is oppressing (more specifically, racially oppressing or is racist against) White people because White people hold more power and privileges in the United States than Asian Americans (e.g., Millan & Alvarez, 2014). In other words, as summarized in Table 1.1 and in the previous section on "What is an oppressed social group?," an Asian American person may hold stereotypes and prejudices against White people that may lead the person to discriminate against White people, and this is problematic, but the Asian American person is not oppressing White people because White people are the dominant and privileged group. Simply disliking or favoring someone based on their social group membership is problematic but is not automatically oppression; the individual's biased opinions or behaviors must be backed up, legitimized, protected, and supported by sociopolitical institutions, policies, norms, standards, or assumptions—power and privilege—for the stereotypical beliefs, prejudiced attitudes, and discriminatory behaviors to become interpersonal oppression. An easy way to remember this is *Interpersonal Oppression = Biased CAB+PP*, with PP representing power and privilege.

Even further, it is also important to note that oppression is not always consciously inflicted by ill-intentioned, evil, powerful, and privileged people and the systems, institutions, or policies they create. In many cases, especially in our modern times, even well-intentioned people and the systems, institutions, and policies they develop and uphold may still inadvertently and unknowingly end up dehumanizing other people, limiting other people's access to resources, and constraining other people's freedoms (unconscious, unintentional, and subtle forms of oppression are discussed in more detail in Chapter 4). Because oppression may be very subtle and unnoticed, oppressive rules, standards, norms, habits, symbols, and assumptions can eventually become widely accepted and unquestioned leading to the creation and maintenance of oppressive organizations and institutions. Thus, oppression can also exist and operate at the institutional level through laws, policies, and "normative" assumptions and practices that marginalize and inferiorize groups of people (Jones, 1997). If interpersonal oppression can be conceptualized as when stereotypes, prejudices, and discrimination are expressed by individuals toward other individuals, we can conceptualize **institutional oppression** as when stereotypes, prejudices, and discrimination are expressed—whether intentionally or unintentionally or even well intentionally, consciously or unconsciously, and overtly or covertly—through organizations' or institutions' policies, laws, regulations, assumptions, standards, cultural norms, and practices. Institutional oppression can be seen through laws (e.g., laws that limit women's freedoms to make decisions about their own bodies), policies (e.g., New York Police Department's "Stop and Frisk" policy), physical environments (e.g., public buildings and venues that are not accessible by wheelchair), and social norms and conventions (e.g., the standard use of the term "maternity leave" to refer to a parent taking time off work due to pregnancy and giving birth).

Interpersonal and institutional oppression are linked and they feed off of each other. Stereotypes, prejudices, and discriminatory behavior may lead to the establishment of organizations that have policies, procedures, and practices that in turn reflect, legitimize, and protect those stereotypes, prejudices, and discriminatory behaviors. Such institutionalized unfairness can then shape people to think, feel, and behave in ways that are consistent with the created standards, norms, culture, and climate. Eventually, people may no longer even see that their climate and the beliefs, attitudes, and practices it encourages are oppressive—equating "right" with policies, laws, regulations, and standard operating procedures—forgetting that just because something is "legal" or consistent with the law does not necessarily mean that it is right, fair, or just. In essence, individuals may use their access to power and privilege to impose their worldviews on the oppressed, enforcing the social, political, and systematic denial of resources to the oppressed which, in turn, is used to justify the oppressive behaviors or individuals.

In addition to oppression existing and operating in interpersonal and institutional levels, there is also internalized oppression. As alluded to earlier, oppression may be overt or covert, with contemporary forms of oppression being more subtle than and not as blatant as oppression of the past (Dovidio, Gaertner, Kawakami, & Hodson, 2002; Pierce, Carew, Pierce-Conzalez, & Willis, 1978; Sears, 1988; Sue, 2010; Sue et al., 2007; Thompson & Neville, 1999). Although not as blatant, clear, and obviously brutal as oppressions of the past (e.g., apartheid, Jim Crow laws, regarding homosexuality as a mental disorder), contemporary forms of oppression are still dangerous for oppressed individuals. The fact that modern forms of oppression occur at a subtle, often unconscious, and unintentional level often leads oppressed individuals to experience *attributional ambiguity*, which is when we cannot confidently conclude that we experienced oppression and when we cannot clearly identify the perpetrator of oppression (Sue et al., 2007). In other words, because modern-day oppression is often enacted subtly, unconsciously, and even well intentionally, it is more difficult to determine if comments, behaviors, laws, policies, or assumptions are influenced by some type of social group bias. Thus, people who experience contemporary oppression may frequently dismiss or minimize their experiences and lead them to self-blame: "Oh, it's my fault, I'm just being too paranoid and oversensitive." *SELF-BLAME* This line of reasoning is dangerous because it might lead us to learn to tolerate oppression or even internalize oppression. When one cannot identify and confront the source of oppression, the anger may be directed inwardly and at others who remind the oppressed of themselves, a condition known as "internalized oppression" (David, 2013, 2014). Using Lipsky's (1977) definition, internalized oppression is the "turning upon ourselves, upon our families, and upon our own people the distress patterns that result from the . . . oppression of the (dominant) society" (p. 6). In these ways, internalized oppression is linked to interpersonal and institutional oppression, and all three levels of oppression feed off of each other and work together to perpetuate oppression. All three are components of the vicious and seemingly inescapable **system of oppression.**

Figure 1.1 pictorially summarizes the different forms, levels, and manifestations of oppression and their relationships with each other.

WHY SHOULD WE CARE ABOUT OPPRESSION?

In the field of psychology, there is abundant literature on *self-concept*, which is how we perceive ourselves and the characteristics we have

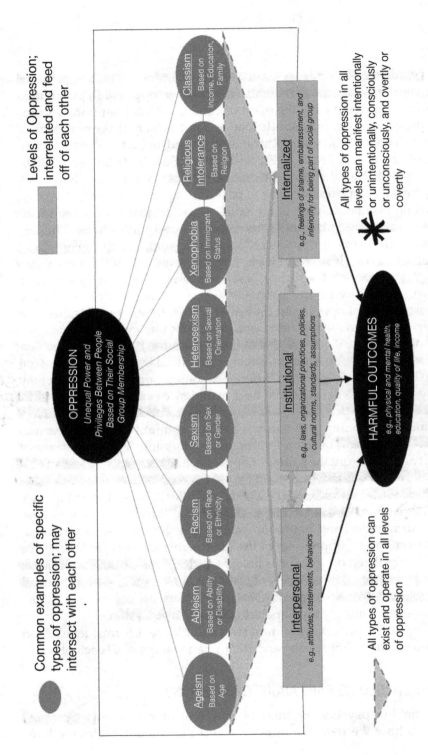

Common examples of specific
types of oppression; may
intersect with each other

Levels of Oppression;
interrelated and feed
off of each other

OPPRESSION
*Unequal Power and
Privileges Between People
Based on Their Social
Group Membership*

Ageism
Based on
Age

Ableism
Based on Ability
or Disability

Racism
Based on Race
or Ethnicity

Sexism
Based on Sex
or Gender

Heterosexism
Based on Sexual
Orientation

Xenophobia
Based on Immigrant
Status

**Religious
Intolerance**
Based on
Religion

Classism
Based on
Income, Education,
Family

Interpersonal
e.g., attitudes, statements, behaviors

Institutional
*e.g., laws, organizational practices, policies,
cultural norms, standards, assumptions*

Internalized
*e.g., feelings of shame, embarrassment, and
inferiority for being part of social group*

HARMFUL OUTCOMES
*e.g., physical and mental health,
education, quality of life, income*

All types of oppression can
exist and operate in all levels
of oppression

All types of oppression in all
levels can manifest intentionally
or unintentionally, consciously
or unconsciously, and overtly or
covertly

FIGURE 1.1   The different forms, levels, and manifestations of oppression.

(e.g., Baumeister, 1999). Similarly, there is also an abundance of litera-ture on *self-esteem*, which is how positively or negatively we evaluate the characteristics we have (e.g., Blascovich & Tomaka, 1993; Rosenberg, 1965). Indeed, self-concept and self-esteem have been some of the more core topics in the field of psychology, with such keywords producing 41,674 and 23,748 hits on PsycINFO, respectively. However, psycholo-gy's understanding of the self and self-esteem has been incomplete in that it is overly individualistic; that is, our understanding of the self and self-esteem has been focused primarily on the individual component. This individualistic bias is perhaps influenced by the invisible Western privilege the majority of psychological theorists and researchers hold that led to their individualistic worldviews coming through in their work. Some scholars (Tajfel & Turner, 1986) have noted that although we are all individuals, all of us are also social beings who are part of social groups and the social groups to which we belong also have characteristics of their own. Therefore, in addition to having an individual component to our self-concept, we also have a collective component to our self-concept. Even further, if individual self-esteem is how we evaluate our personal characteristics, *collective self-esteem* is how we evaluate the characteristics of the social groups to which we belong. The research literature on col-lective self-esteem (i.e., only 275 hits on PsycINFO!) has lagged behind research on personal self-esteem, but the research does suggest that both individual and collective self-esteem are important contributors to our mental health and psychological well-being.

Therefore, one pathway through which oppression can harm indi-viduals and communities is by damaging how people perceive and feel about their social groups—that is, oppression may damage their collective self-esteem (the psychological and mental health implications of oppression are discussed in more detail in Chapter 6). In other words, oppression of a particular social group may lead its members to see their group as inferior, not as valuable, not as good, not as attractive, or not as worthy as the dominant group. Thus, oppressed individuals may begin to have poor evaluations of the characteristics of their social group (e.g., the language, the beliefs, the cultures, the traditions, the typical physical appearance, the food). Even worse, some individuals may even begin to view their social group membership as an inescapable curse. And because social group membership is an important part of individuals' self-concepts, oppression then can damage one's mental health and psychological well-being. Even further, given that oppression may negatively affect not just individuals' perceptions of themselves but also how they perceive other people, the groups to which they belong, other marginalized social groups, and the dominant groups, oppression therefore has the potential to also damage families, communities, and societies. This potential to have widespread and devastating impact is probably the most important reason why we need to understand oppression and its many consequences, and figure out ways to address oppression in the interpersonal, institutional, and internalized levels.

Indeed, there is a large and growing body of psychology research that consistently shows how oppression in all of its levels—interpersonal, institutional, and internalized—and in all of its manifestations—conscious or unconscious, intentional or unintentional or even well intentional, and overt or covert—is detrimental in a variety of ways. As depicted toward the bottom of Figure 1.1, research suggests that oppression may lead to various negative and harmful social, educational, and health consequences. This is consistent with the assertion of psychologists Prilleltensky and Gonick (1996) who argued that the "asymmetric power relations (between social groups) lead to conditions of misery, inequality,

---

TABLE 1.2   A Partial List of the Characteristics of Oppression

- Oppression is both a *process* and a *state.*
- Oppression as a *state* or *condition* is when there is inequality of power and privileges between groups.
- Oppression as a *process* or *enactment* is when dominant groups use their power and privilege to constrain the humanity of oppressed groups, and therefore maintain the existing inequalities between groups.
- Oppression as a process or enactment can be done through *imposition* or *deprivation.*
- There need to be *unequal power* and *privilege* (the two Ps) between groups for oppression to exist.
- Power and privilege inequalities must be seen and defined from a *systems-level perspective.*
- Oppression can be *intentional* or *unintentional.*
- Oppression can be *overt* or *covert.*
- Oppression can be *conscious* or *unconscious.*
- Oppression can exist and operate in three levels: *interpersonal, institutional,* and *internalized.*
- There are various *specific types of oppression* (e.g., age, disability, religion, race or ethnicity, sexual orientation, social class, indigenous heritage, national origin, gender).
- Oppression is *widespread* and has various *negative health and social impacts.*

exploitation, marginalization, and social injustice" (pp. 129–130). Thus, given the widespread and devastating consequences oppression has had and continues to have on human beings throughout the world, there is a desperate need for all of us to understand (major theories on why oppression happens are discussed in Chapter 7) and address oppression in all of its forms, manifestations, and complexities (promising clinical and community approaches to addressing oppression are discussed in Chapters 8 and 9).

To this end, we close this opening chapter with Table 1.2 that presents a summary of what oppression is and its many forms, manifestations, and consequences that we hope you will find useful as you go through the rest of the book.

REFERENCES

Bailey, T.-K. M., Williams, W. S., & Favors, B. (2014). Internalized racial oppression in the African American community. In E. J. R. David (Ed.), *Internalized oppression: The psychology of marginalized groups* (pp. 137–162). New York, NY: Springer Publishing.

Barker, R. L. (2003). *The social work dictionary* (5th ed.). Washington, DC: National Association of Social Workers Press.

Baumeister, R. F. (Ed.). (1999). *The self in social psychology*. Philadelphia, PA: Psychology Press (Taylor & Francis).

Bearman, S., & Amrhein, M. (2014). Girls, women, and internalized sexism. In E. J. R. David (Ed.), *Internalized oppression: The psychology of marginalized groups* (pp. 191–226). New York, NY: Springer Publishing.

Blascovich, J., & Tomaka, J. (1993). Measures of self-esteem. In J. P. Robinson, P. R. Shaver, & L. S. Wrightsman (Eds.), *Measures of personality and social psychological attitudes* (3rd ed., pp. 115–160). Ann Arbor, MI: Institute for Social Research.

Collins, P. H. (1993). Toward a new vision: Race, class and gender as categories of analysis and connection. *Race, Sex and Class, 1*(1), 25–45.

David, E. J. R. (2013). *Brown skin, white minds: Filipino -/ American postcolonial psychology (with commentaries)*. Charlotte, NC: Information Age Publishing.

David, E. J. R. (Ed.). (2014). *Internalized oppression: The psychology of marginalized groups*. New York, NY: Springer Publishing.

David, E. J. R., & Derthick, A. O. (2014). What is internalized oppression, and so what? In E. J. R. David (Ed.), *Internalized oppression: The psychology of marginalized groups* (pp. 1–30). New York, NY: Springer Publishing.

Davis, K. E. (2002). *Expanding the theoretical understanding of oppression*. Alexandria, VA: Council on Social Work Education.

Deutsch, M. (2006). A framework for thinking about oppression and its change. *Social Justice Research, 19*(1), 7–41.

Dovidio, J. F., Gaertner, S. L., Kawakami, K., & Hodson, G. (2002). Why can't we just get along? Interpersonal biases and interracial distrust. *Cultural Diversity & Ethnic Minority Psychology, 8,* 88–102. doi:10.1037/1099-9809.8.2.88

Freire, P. (1970). *Pedagogy of the oppressed*. New York, NY: Continuum.

Frye, M. (1983). *The politics of reality: Essays in feminist theory*. Trumansburg, NY: The Crossing Press.

Gil, D. G. (1994). Confronting social injustice and oppression. In F. G. Reamer (Ed.), *The foundations of social work knowledge*. New York, NY: Columbia University Press.

Gonzalez, J., Simard, E., Baker-Demaray, T., & Iron Eyes, C. (2014). The internalized oppression of North American indigenous peoples. In E. J. R. David (Ed.), *Internalized oppression: The psychology of marginalized groups* (pp. 31–56). New York, NY: Springer Publishing.

Hanna, F. J., Talley, W. B., & Guindon, M. H. (2000). The power of perception: Toward a model of cultural oppression and liberation. *Journal of Counseling and Development, 78,* 430–446. doi:10.1002/j.1556-6676.2000.tb01926.x

Hays, P. A. (2003). *Addressing cultural complexities in practice: A framework for clinicians and counselors*. Washington, DC: American Psychological Association.

Hipolito-Delgado, C., Gallegos Payan, S., & Baca, T. I. (2014). Self-hatred, self-doubt, and assimilation in Latina/o communities. In E. J. R. David (Ed.), *Internalized oppression: The psychology of marginalized groups* (pp. 109–136). New York, NY: Springer Publishing.

Johnson, A. G. (2000a). *Privilege, power and difference.* Boston, MA: McGraw-Hill.

Johnson, A. G. (2000b). *The Blackwell dictionary of sociology: A user's guide to sociological language* (2nd ed.). Malden, MA: Blackwell Publishers.

Jones, J. M. (1997). *Prejudice and racism* (2nd ed.). New York, NY: McGraw-Hill.

Lewis, J., Allen, J., & Fleagle, E. (2014). Internalized oppression and Alaska native peoples: "We Have to Go Through the Problem." In E. J. R. David (Ed.), *Internalized oppression: The psychology of marginalized groups* (pp. 57–82). New York, NY: Springer Publishing.

Lipsky, S. (1977). Internalized oppression. *Black Re-emergence, 2*(1–3), 5–10.

Millan, J. B., & Alvarez, A. N. (2014). Asian Americans and internalized oppression: Do we deserve this? In E. J. R. David (Ed.), *Internalized oppression: The psychology of marginalized groups* (pp. 163–190). New York, NY: Springer Publishing.

Nadal, K. L. (2013). *That's so gay!: Microaggressions and the lesbian, gay, bisexual, and transgender community.* Washington, DC: American Psychological Association.

Nadal, K. L., & Mendoza, R. J. (2014). Internalized oppression and the lesbian, gay, bisexual, and transgender community. In E. J. R. David (Ed.), *Internalized oppression: The psychology of marginalized groups* (pp. 227–252). New York, NY: Springer Publishing.

Pierce, C., Carew, J., Pierce-Conzalez, D., & Willis, D. (1978). An experiment in racism: TV commercials. In C. Pierce (Ed.), *Television and education* (pp. 62–88). Beverly Hills, CA: Sage.

Prilleltensky, I., & Gonick, L. (1996). Polities change, oppression remains: On the psychology and politics of oppression. *Political Psychology, 17*, 127–148. doi:10.2307/3791946

Rosenberg, M. (1965). *Society and the adolescent self-image.* Princeton, NJ: Princeton University Press.

Salzman, M., & Laenui, P. (2014). Internalized oppression among Pacific Island peoples. In E. J. R. David (Ed.), *Internalized oppression: The psychology of marginalized groups* (pp. 83–108). New York, NY: Springer Publishing.

Sears, D. O. (1988). Symbolic racism. In P. Katz & D. Taylor (Eds.), *Eliminating racism: Profiles in controversy* (pp. 53–84). New York, NY: Plenum Press.

Steele, C. M. (2010). *Whistling Vivaldi: How stereotypes affect us and what we can do.* New York, NY: W. W. Norton.

Sue, D. W. (Ed.). (2010). *Microaggressions and marginality: Manifestations, dynamics, and impact.* Hoboken, NJ: Wiley.

Sue, D. W., Capodilupo, C. M., Torino, G. L., Bucceri, J. M., Holder, A. M. B., Nadal, K. L., & Esquilin, M. (2007). Racial microaggressions in everyday life. *American Psychologist, 62,* 271–286. doi:10.103770003-066X.624.271

Tajfel, H., & Turner, J. C. (1986). The social identity theory of intergroup behavior. In S. Worchel & W. Austin (Eds.), *Psychology of intergroup relations.* Chicago, IL: Nelson-Hall.

Thompson, C. E., & Neville, H. A. (1999). Racism, mental health, and mental health practice. *The Counseling Psychologist, 27,* 155–223. doi:10.1177/0011000099272001

Turner, J. H., Singleton Jr., R., & Musick, D. (1984). *Oppression: A socio-history of Black-White relations in America.* Chicago, IL: Nelson-Hall Publishers.

Watermeyer, B., & Gorgens, T. (2014). Disability and internalized oppression. In E. J. R. David (Ed.), *Internalized oppression: The psychology of marginalized groups* (pp. 253–280). New York, NY: Springer Publishing.

Young, I. M. (1990). *Justice and the politics of difference.* Princeton, NJ: Princeton University Press.

Convention - a way in which something is usually done, especially within a particular area or activity.

Reflexive process - directed or turned back on itself.

CHAPTER 2

Who We Be: Historically and Contemporarily Oppressed Social Groups

As human beings, each one of us is unique. There is not another human being on the entire planet who is exactly the same as you, me, us! Even for those of us who have identical or monozygotic twins—which means that they are genetically the same—there are still many differences between them and their siblings (e.g., Bouchard, Lykken, McGue, Segal, & Tellegen, 1990; Lykken, 2006; Torgersen & Janson, 2002; Vernon, Jang, Harris, & McCarthy, 1997). There might be similarities in physical traits, personalities, interests, dislikes, preferences, abilities, chosen careers, hobbies, lifestyles, and even intelligence levels, but there is no 100% match across all dimensions. Indeed, each one of us is most definitely one of a kind!

Human beings, however, are social creatures—even Aristotle said so! Therefore, *although we are all unique individuals, all of us are also parts of social groups*. What is perhaps the most basic social group we have is our family. Some of us have what may be considered the conventional family—biological father, mother, and siblings. Some of us may be the only child. Some of us may have been adopted by another family. Some of us may have been raised by a single parent. Some of us may have been raised by older siblings, aunts, uncles, grandparents, or other extended family members. Some of us may have two fathers or two mothers. Some of us may have grown up with friends or with caregivers in the foster care system, or with other children in adoption homes. Regardless of our family history, composition, and situation, all of us have some level of meaningful and influential connection (regardless of whether such connection is positive/pleasant or negative/unpleasant) with at least another human being.

Another example of a basic social group we have is biological sex; we are categorized very early on in our lives—even as early as when our biological mothers are halfway through their pregnancy with us (16–20 weeks)—as to what our biological sex is! Even further, we are socialized to learn very early on in life what our biological sex is (e.g., male, female, intersex); that other people are like us while others are not like us; and what expectations, roles, and behaviors being of a particular sex entails. This early socialization about the various differences between different kinds of people extends to other dimensions besides biological sex, as research (Quintana, 1998) suggests that we begin to notice basic differences between social groups such as skin and hair color by the time we are 3 years old! Thus, it is clear that *we are all parts of social groups regardless of whether we want to be or not, or whether we are aware of it or not, because societal forces put us in certain social groups!* Indeed, according to Aristotle in his classic work *The Politics,* "Society is something that precedes the individual."

As we learned in Chapter 1, however, society does not regard and treat all social groups equally (process of oppression), resulting in some social groups having advantages and privileges that other social groups do not have (state of oppression). And just as we are socialized to see differences between people at an early age, it also seems to be the case that we are socialized to attach different values to such differences early in our lives. For instance, research suggests that as early as 3 to 4 years old we begin to make overgeneralizations about groups of people and begin to attach societal messages (positive and negative) about them and the characteristics we have learned to assume that they have (Quintana, 1998). In other words, *stereotypes and prejudices, which may be conceptualized as mental schemas or general patterns of organizing the world into categories and the relationships between such categories, tend to develop early in our lives.* Thus, not only are we all inherently parts of social groups, we are also socialized into a state and process of social group oppression right from the get-go. To this end, using the social group categories outlined by Hays's (2003) ADDRESSING framework (introduced in Chapter 1, Table 1.1) and guided by Frye's (1983) 5-point criteria for identifying oppressed groups (summarized in Table 2.1), we now provide brief overviews of oppressed social groups—focusing primarily on the U.S. context—to help us better situate and understand the concepts, issues, and examples that are discussed in the later chapters of the book. Let us begin with an overview of peoples of color (POC).

TABLE 2.1   Frye's (1983) 5-Point Criteria for Identifying Oppressed Social Groups

A social group may be oppressed if all of the following criteria are met.

1. There must be restrictions, barriers, or limitations on the freedoms (e.g., where to live, where to go to school, whom to marry, getting a job and type of job, learning their heritage language, practicing their religion, following their cultural traditions) of people who identify with the social group (e.g., ethnic group).

2. The restrictions, barriers, and limitations must be harmful and that the harm outweigh any potential "benefits" that may be incurred as a result of those same restrictions (e.g., not learning one's heritage language and culture contributes to the potential permanent loss of the language and culture, which is a harm that outweighs any temporary "benefit" that being assimilated may bring).

3. The restrictions, barriers, and limitations must be imposed, protected, and justified by a social structure or institution (e.g., English-only policies, absence of courses in school curriculum about one's heritage language, ethnicity, and culture).

4. The restrictions, barriers, and limitations must be suffered by people simply because of their social group membership (e.g., one's heritage language, ethnicity, and culture are not valued as equal to other languages, ethnicities, and cultures to also warrant inclusion in curriculum).

5. There must be a separate social group that maintains the status quo of oppression and that benefits from the imposed restrictions, barriers, and limitations (e.g., people whose heritage language is English resist other languages, impose their notions of what is important to be included in school curriculum, and they benefit from such a system because it is their language, culture, and values that are regarded and validated as important and "the standard").

■ PEOPLES OF COLOR

POC compose a substantial and growing portion (approximately 38%) of the U.S. population, with African Americans composing 12%, Latinas/os composing 17%, Asian Americans composing 5%, Native Americans and Alaska Natives composing 0.9%, Native Hawaiians and other Pacific Islanders composing 0.2%, and Mixed Race individuals composing 3% (Humes, Jones, & Ramirez, 2011). As you may have guessed, POC are individuals who identify with a racial group other than White, and *the oppression that POC experience—***racism** *or oppression that is based on race—is what we most often think of when we think of oppression.* So what do we mean by race? **Race** is a sociocultural concept wherein certain characteristics, values, and behaviors are associated with groups of people who are perceived to have biological or physiological (e.g., skin color, facial features) similarities. For example, people from China, Korea, Japan, the Philippines, India, and other Asian countries are racially categorized—or **racialized**—by society as the "Asian race" because such individuals are perceived to have biological similarities that define them and separate them from other racial groups like "Black," "White," or "Hispanic." Racial categories and the definitions for who goes into which category are determined by society, more specifically by the dominant people or groups of society. Thus, racial categories and definitions can change and have changed. For instance, the U.S. Census's definition of "Asian" has changed over time from exclusively referring to East Asians (i.e., Chinese, Korean, Japanese) to also include Filipinos, Indians, and other Asians, attesting to how race is a human-made—or sociocultural—concept.

It is important to note that although race is based on perceived biological similarities, there is actually no biological basis for racial categorizations, as research shows *there are greater genetic differences between people within the same racial group than there are genetic differences between people across racial groups* (Jorde & Wooding, 2004). However, just because race is not a biological construct and is instead a sociocultural one does not mean that race and racism are not real. As we will see in the later chapters (primarily Chapters 3–5), POC are subjected to second (or even lower) class status and their characteristics are associated with inferiority, undesirability, or stereotypical (uncomplex, incomplete, untrue) representations. In other words, people are regarded and treated very differently as a function of how society perceives their racial group membership and what attitudes society attaches to their racial group.

Another term that people often use interchangeably with race is **ethnicity**, which is a group of people who share similar physical and cultural characteristics. Ethnic groups are composed of people who hold the same worldview, speak the same language, or trace their roots to the same geographic location (e.g., country, province). Thus, ethnicity is a combination of race and culture. Staying with the example of "Asian" as a race, the different groups of people within this racial category who share a similar worldview, language, or geographic roots (e.g., Chinese, Korean, Japanese, Filipino, Indian) are the different ethnicities of the racial group. By definition, then, ethnic groups of color in the United States have different cultures (e.g., language, ways of doing things) than the dominant group. Such *cultural differences are often in opposition to the dominant culture, especially subjecting ethnic groups of color to the processes of oppression.*

■ INDIGENOUS PEOPLES

One specific group in the POC category is indigenous peoples. In the United States, **indigenous peoples** include Native Americans, Alaska Natives, Native Hawaiians, Polynesians or Pacific Islanders (e.g., Chamorros of Guam, Samoans in American Samoa), and the Taino people of Puerto Rico. Currently, there are approximately 5.2 million people in the United States who identify as Native American or Alaska Native, and approximately half a million people who are Native Hawaiian or Pacific Islander (Humes et al., 2011). Although indigenous peoples are often racialized together (e.g., Native Americans, Alaska Natives, Native Hawaiians, and Other Pacific Islanders), it is important to remember that *these umbrella categories are composed of very diverse groups of people with different histories, cultures, languages, ways of living, and worldviews.* For example, there are 565 federally recognized Native American tribes in the United States (Gonzalez, Simard, Baker-Demaray, & Iron Eyes, 2014). Also, Alaska Natives are composed of at least five different language groups (Aleut/Alutiiq, Athabascan, Inupiat, Yup'ik, and Tlingit/Haida/Tsimshian), and there are even more variations within each of the five major language groups (e.g., Koyukon Athabascan, Denai'na Athabascan, Gwich'in Athabascan; Langdon, 1989). The umbrella term Pacific Islanders also encompasses different peoples with very different cultures and histories (e.g., Samoan, Tongan, Fijian, Chamorro).

In addition to facing modern-day oppression based on their race, ethnicity, or culture—just like other POC—indigenous peoples also deal with the **legacies of colonialism.** For example, colonialism led to the forceful and violent loss of ancestral lands, sovereignty, language, and culture for many indigenous peoples, all of which research is showing to have created **historical trauma** (discussed in more detail in Chapter 6) that has been passed on to later generations (Brave Heart, 2003). *Historical trauma, in turn, may be contributing to the many issues facing indigenous peoples today such as alcohol and drug use, domestic violence, depression, and suicide* (e.g., Duran & Duran, 1995). Also, for many indigenous peoples, colonialism is not over at all and is still happening today with Puerto Rico, Guam, and American Samoa still being U.S. colonies, with Native Hawaiians still resisting the encroachment of outsiders on their lands and with Alaska Native and Native American tribes still fighting the U.S. government to respect their sovereignty and to stop taking away native lands and resources (e.g., Standing Rock protests, the Arctic National Wildlife Refuge drilling controversy). Thus, *indigenous peoples have been facing and resisting oppression—even genocide—for centuries!*

IMMIGRANTS, REFUGEES, AND ASYLEES

Another significant portion of the POC population is foreign-born individuals. In total, around 13% of the U.S. population was born in another country and came into the United States as immigrants, refugees, or asylees. Briefly, **immigrants** are people born in one country and who later moved to another country to live there permanently. Unlike most immigrants who are assumed to have voluntarily left their home countries under their own will, **refugees** were forced to leave their home countries because of racial, religious, political, or some other social group persecution in their home countries (United Nations High Commissioner on Refugees [UNHCR], 2012). Similarly, **asylees** are people who claim persecution in their home countries, but unlike refugees, their claims have yet to be verified. Once their claims are evaluated and verified, asylees gain refugee status (UNHCR, 2012). There are approximately 16.5 million refugees and asylees worldwide (UNHCR, 2010), with approximately 1.8 million settling in the United States since 1980, when formal U.S. refugee resettlement programs began. Refugees and asylees are consistently found to face alarmingly high rates of mental health concerns (e.g., Fox & Tang, 2000; Thabet & Vostanis, 2000).

Although significant portions of the foreign-born population are POC, not all immigrants, refugees, or asylees are POC. In fact, *46% of America's foreign-born population identify as White!* For example, people may be shocked to learn that 53% of Mexican immigrants in the United States identify as White. Even further, 45% and 87% of U.S. immigrants from El Salvador and Cuba, respectively, are White (Grieco, 2010). Thus, *although all foreign-born people may deal with discrimination based on ethnicity or culture (e.g., language, religion), non-POC immigrants may not face the same level of racism as POC immigrants because non-POC immigrants may still pass as White.* Nevertheless, all foreign-born individuals deal with significant and possibly traumatic life events—especially refugees and asylees—as they leave behind their home countries, their families and support network, and their cultural ways of being and doing. In addition, they are faced with a variety of challenges in their new country such as learning a new language, new culture, new customs, new habits, and new ways of living and surviving—a process of adjustment that is referred to as **acculturative stress** (Berry, 2003). In an oppressive context, immigrants, refugees, and asylees are vulnerable as they may be forced to abandon—or at least compromise—their heritage culture (e.g., language, religious beliefs) in order to have access to various services, benefits, and opportunities. Even worse, such forced assimilation may not even be an "option" in societies that hold strong anti-immigrant (e.g., the perception that immigrants steal jobs, lower wages, free-load off the government, bring in drugs) and anti-refugee or anti-asylee (e.g., the fear that refugees and asylees are terror threats) sentiments, wherein foreign-born individuals are simply unwelcomed, kept out, or kicked out. Thus, immigrants, refugees, and asylees have to deal with both *premigration and postmigration stressors* (Porter & Haslam, 2005) that influence all aspects of their psychological experiences.

▪ GIRLS AND WOMEN

Beyond POC, another undervalued social group is girls and women. Although not a numerical minority—as approximately half of the U.S. and the world population is girls and women—this social group is historically and contemporarily oppressed in that they have been and are still struggling to be regarded and treated equally as boys and men. In other words, girls and women have been subjected to **sexism**, which is oppression that is based on their sex (Klonoff & Landrine, 1995; Matteson & Moradi, 2005), and this type of oppression has been happening for generations. Briefly, **sex** is a biologically based categorization of human beings as either male, female, or intersex (people who are born with external sex organs or sex chromosomes that are not easily identifiable as female or male). A closely related construct is **gender**, which is what our society deems appropriate or inappropriate for us based on our sex. In the United States and many other societies around the world, gender is almost automatically assigned at birth as either "boy" or "girl" based on the baby's sex (even intersex babies are often assigned a gender at birth or early in life), and this (limited binary) gender assignment is where (problematic) notions of masculinity and femininity come in, with masculine or "manly" traits being regarded as suitable only for boys and feminine or "girly" traits being regarded as suitable only for girls. Through **gender socialization** in our families, our schools, the media, and our institutions, we learn very early in our lives the roles, behaviors, and values that society considers appropriate or inappropriate for men or boys and what society considers appropriate or inappropriate for women or girls (Butler, 1990; Nadal, 2010; West & Zimmerman, 1987).

How society regards females (e.g., as physically or biologically weaker than males) and what society attaches to being a girl or a woman (e.g., emotionally fragile, dependent on men, sexually or romantically attracted only to men) are very different from how society regards males and what society attaches to being a boy or a man. *Although limiting to both genders, as males are also not allowed to have "feminine" traits, the differences clearly benefit or advantage males (or boys and men).* For instance, in the United States, the definition of what makes a "successful" person such as being assertive, ambitious, competitive, strong-willed, and self-reliant are characteristics that are typically attached to being a man and, therefore, are taught to and encouraged for boys (e.g., Bearman & Amrhein, 2014). Even further, such traits and attributes that society regards as admirable and desirable are deemed positive only if possessed or displayed by boys or men. For example, instead of being admired by society, a woman who is assertive, strong-willed, or independent is often regarded as "bossy," "inflexible," or even a "bitch." This differential and unequal regard of girls and boys, and of women and men, are expressed in various levels (e.g., interpersonally, institutionally) and sectors (e.g., education, leadership positions) in societies throughout the world.

■ LESBIAN, GAY, BISEXUAL, TRANSGENDER, QUEER, AND/OR QUESTIONING (LGBTQ) PEOPLE

According to scholars (e.g., Nadal & Mendoza, 2014), approximately 4% of adults in the United States identify as lesbian, gay, bisexual, or transgender. This is similar to the estimate found for adolescents, as one study reported that approximately 5% of middle school students identify as lesbian, gay, bisexual, or transgender (Shields et al., 2013). Some studies also show that although people may not identify as lesbian, gay, bisexual, or transgender, approximately 8% still reported having engaged in same-sex sexual behavior, and 11% still acknowledged having same-sex sexual or romantic attraction (Gates, 2011). These numbers are probably underestimates of the actual percentage of LGBTQ individuals, people who have engaged in same-sex sexual behavior, or people who are attracted to same-sex people but deny the attraction because of the negative stigma attached to such identities, behaviors, and feelings. Indeed, society's limited but strongly entrenched and institutionalized conceptualizations of sex and gender—as well as society's expectation (or demand) that sex and gender must match (i.e., cisgender)—put the LGBTQ community in a very vulnerable state of oppression based on its social group membership (i.e., **heterosexism** or **homophobia**), as *LGBTQ individuals occupy the full matrix of combinations and intersections between sex, sexual orientation, gender identity, and gender expression.*

Briefly, **sexual orientation** is "an individual's sense of personal and social identity based on one's sexual attractions (and) behaviors expressing those attractions" (Nadal & Mendoza, 2014, p. 230), whereas **gender identity** is a person's sense of identification as a boy/man, girl/woman, neither, or both. Thus, LGB individuals are people whose sexual orientations do not fit society's expectations based on their gender identity. Further, a person's **gender expression**—how one follows or not follows society's expectations of how boys/men and girls/women should look and behave—may or may not match one's gender identity. For example, a female (sex) person may identify as a woman (gender identity) and be gender-conforming (gender expression) in that she lives in a way that is mostly consistent with what society expects of women (e.g., wears dresses, wears makeup), while being sexually and romantically attracted only to women (sexual orientation). Another example is a male person may identify as a man and be gender nonconforming in expression (e.g., wears makeup, wears women's clothes), while being sexually and romantically attracted to both men and women. A person may also be biologically male (sex) but identify as a woman (gender identity), in which case the person may identify as transgender. It should be noted, however, that being transgender does not automatically imply a certain sexual orientation. Indeed, transgender people may be heterosexual, gay, lesbian, or bisexual. For instance, a transgender woman (i.e., sex is male, gender identity is woman) may identify as heterosexual because she is sexually and romantically attracted only to men. In addition to the transgender identity, other people may also identify as gender queer, gender questioning, gender nonconforming, Two Spirit, transsexual, or others. *It is important to refer to people with the term or identity—and the pronouns (e.g., he, she, they)—that they prefer* (Nadal, 2013).

▪ PEOPLE WITH DISABILITIES

In the United States, approximately 13% of the general population might be having "serious difficulty" with hearing, seeing, concentrating, remembering, making decisions, walking, climbing stairs, self-care (e.g., dressing, bathing), or living independently (e.g., doing errands, eating) (Erickson, Lee, & von Schrader, 2017). Worldwide, a study by the World Health Organization (2011) suggests that approximately 16% of adults (data collected from 59 countries) might be experiencing "significant functional difficulties," and an additional 2.2% of adults might be having "very significant functional difficulties." These estimates translate to a total of approximately 820 million people worldwide who are living with either "significant" or "severe" functional difficulties. Because of the aging population, prolonged wars, and stressful environments, *the numbers of people who may be considered as having disabilities are bound to increase over the years* (Braddock & Parrish, 2001). Scholars have estimated that the average person who lives up to 75 years will spend approximately 13 years of his or her life with functional limitation (Marks, 1999), making living with disability a more common reality for people than the dominant but mythical view that people with disabilities are rare, weird, strange, anomalous, nonnormal, or even "abnormal" (Davis, 2002; Watermeyer & Gorgens, 2014).

The fact that our institutions (e.g., "normal" policies and operating procedures) and infrastructures (e.g., roads, vehicles, buildings) are not designed for people with disabilities in mind puts people with disabilities especially vulnerable to exploitation and oppression. For instance, people with cognitive difficulties may be unknowingly rushed or pressured—and, thus, manipulated—even by well-meaning people to make certain decisions due to assumed "normal protocol" or "standard operating procedures" (e.g., medical staff assuming that all people can read and comprehend quickly the information on medical consent forms). Another example is that people with mobility difficulties may face more barriers in getting to meetings that significantly influence their lives and well-being (e.g., court hearings, job interviews, school) because of societal assumptions that all people should be able to drive a car, take public transportation, climb stairs, or other "normal" forms of transportation (e.g., riding a bike, walking). Further, it is also undeniable that *the dominant societal worldview is that having a disability means a person is broken, wrong, inferior, wretched, or damaged instead of more accurately seeing disability as another dimension of human diversity like race, ethnicity, sexual orientation, or gender.* Such an inferiorizing perception of disability leads to other "ideas, practices, institutions, and social relations that presume able-bodiedness" (Chouinard, 1997, p. 380), all of which create a system of **ableism**—the type of social group oppression that dehumanizes, devalues, and marginalizes people with disabilities and renders them invisible.

■ NON-CHRISTIAN PEOPLE

It may come as a surprise to many, but approximately 30% of the U.S. population is not Christian (Pew Research Center, 2015a). In other words, a significant portion of people in the United States—3 out of every 10—are agnostic, atheist, Jewish, Muslim, Buddhist, Hindu, Sikh, Baha'i, Taoist, Unitarian, or even "nothing in particular." Nevertheless, *people who report Christianity as their religion hold a disproportionate amount of power and privilege in the United States.* For example, although only around 70% of the U.S. population is Christian, approximately 92% of U.S. Senate and House representatives are Christian (Pew Research Center, 2015b). Further, all U.S. presidents—100%—have been Christians. Even further, Christian practices and traditions (e.g., Christmas is considered a national holiday) as well as established institutions (e.g., preponderance of Christian schools) are normalized and accepted throughout the United States, whereas the acceptance of and opportunities to observe other religions' practices (e.g., building a mosque in certain areas, removing the phrase "under God" in the pledge of allegiance to accommodate U.S. citizens who are atheists or do not believe that there is a God) are often met with resistance.

Worldwide, only around 30% of people are Christian (Pew Research Center, 2015c). However, 56% of the world's millionaires report Christianity to be their religion (Frank, 2015). Another example is the G8 countries—the countries considered to be the world's "Great Powers" (Kirton, 1989)—which is a group composed of the United States, Canada, France, United Kingdom, Italy, Germany, Russia, and Japan. Although there are 196 countries in the world, these 8 countries alone account for approximately 60% of the world's gross domestic product. Also, although these eight countries account for only around 15% of the world's population, they possess approximately 65% of the world's wealth (Shorrocks, Davies, & Lluberasis, 2013)! Except for Japan, where the dominant religions are Shinto and Buddhism, the other seven countries in the G8 are predominantly Christian countries. And if we take out Japan, the *seven predominantly Christian countries still possess 56% of the world's wealth despite accounting for only around 13% of the world's population, further supporting the notion that Christianity is the dominant religion in the world in terms of power, privilege, and influence.*

▪ OTHER VULNERABLE SOCIAL GROUPS (YOUTH, OLDER ADULTS, POOR AND WORKING CLASS)

Similar to the case of non-Christians worldwide, although people who are poor or working class are not numerical minorities—as there are significantly more of them than people in higher classes—people who are poor or working class are often not the ones who are in positions of power and influence. Thus, people who are poor or working class may struggle with **classism**—oppression based on socioeconomic class—in that they are frequently unheard, disregarded, and exploited by the upper-middle class. Typically, **upper-middle-class** people in the United States are those who are highly educated, who work white-collar jobs, and who live in households with an annual income of $100,000 or above. In the United States, households with annual incomes of $100,000 or above compose around 20% of the population (U.S. Census Bureau, 2012). Thus, 80% of the population may be considered as either **people who are poor or working class** (or lower-middle class). *Although accounting for only around 20% of the U.S. population, upper-middle-class and upper-class families own approximately 88% of the country's wealth,* with the top 1% of the population (**upper class**) possessing around 37% of the country's wealth (Wolff, 2010)! Such an extreme imbalance in wealth distribution supports the notion that upper-middle-class and upper-class people hold a disproportionate amount of power, privilege, and influence over poor and working-class people.

Finally, two other social groups that face oppression are older adults and youth. Although there is no widely accepted age definition for older adults and youth, it may be assumed that they collectively compose a significant portion of the population and, thus, may not necessarily be a numerical minority. Indeed, even if we simply use the U.S. government's definitions of below 18 years of age for **youth** and 65 years of age or above for **older adults**, people in these age ranges still compose approximately 37% of the country's population (Howden & Meyer, 2011). It is important to note, however, that societies and cultures may define older adults and youth as encompassing wider age ranges. The United Nations Educational, Scientific, and Cultural Organization (2016), for example, has a definition of youth that goes up to 24 years of age while still acknowledging that some cultures may consider people who are up to 35 years of age as youth. Nevertheless, regardless of whether older adults and youth are numerical minorities or not, it is the case that *many youth and older adults may be vulnerable to exploitation because they are often powerless and voiceless when it comes to making decisions that may significantly impact their lives.* For example, typical lifespan developmental factors may present physical (e.g., older adults may develop mobility difficulties, youth may be physically overpowered) or cognitive (e.g., older adults may be more forgetful, youth may not be able to make well-reasoned judgments) limitations on youths' and older adults' participation, and thus, their perspectives, realities, and well-being may not be accurately represented and considered by others who are in the "prime" of their lives (i.e., **early to middle adulthood,** approximately 20 to 60 years of age).

▪ THE INTERSECTIONALITY REALITY

Now that we have gone over some background and contextual information about oppressed social groups, it should be clear that *social group oppression is widespread and that some type of social group oppression is experienced by the majority of people in the United States. In fact, some type of social group oppression is faced by most people on Earth!* To this end, try to do a little self-assessment. Do you see yourself identifying with any of the oppressed social groups? Do you see yourself identifying with more than one of them? For example, perhaps being a Black, lesbian woman who is a refugee is part of your identity? Or perhaps you are an immigrant who also identify as belonging to an indigenous group that was colonized by the United States and, thus, have also been "forced" to come to the United States? Even further, do you see yourself identifying with at least one socially oppressed group and at least one dominant group? For instance, maybe you identify as a White, Muslim, upper-middle-class man who is visually impaired? Or perhaps you identify as an Alaska Native Christian woman who is considered an older adult? These examples speak to the simultaneous existence of multiple social identities within people, which is what **intersectionality** (Crenshaw, 1989) is about. For some people, intersectionality is the existence of multiple oppressed social identities within themselves and how they, consequently, face and grapple with multiple forms of social group oppression. For others, intersectionality includes the overlap of a privileged identity (or identities) with an oppressed one (or several), forcing them to grapple with how power hierarchies (or inequalities) between social groups may exist and operate within one's own self.

In contemporary United States, we see many examples of inter-sectionality reflected in highly publicized events or issues. For instance, we see prejudice toward foreigners such as immigrants, refugees, and asylees—**xenophobia**—intersect with racism in how society grapples with the topic of Latina/o/x or Mexican immigration. Another example is the intersections of xenophobia, racism, and **islamophobia**—prejudice against Islam or people who follow the Muslim religion—in the U.S. decision to accept or not accept immigrants, refugees, and asylees from predominantly Muslim countries in the Middle East and Africa. Another example is the perpetrator of the Isla Vista shooting in 2014—a mixed race (White and Asian) heterosexual man—where we see the intersections of racism and sexism (or **misogyny**, seeing women as less than human) as contributing to the crime. And finally, with the Pulse nightclub massacre in 2016, we see the intersections of xenophobia, racism, islamophobia, and homophobia (or heterosexism) in society's narratives about the perpetrator and his potential motives. Overall, *the notion of intersectionality seems to be a more accurate reflection of the reality that multiple social identities do exist simultaneously within people and that these identities may interact with each other in very complex ways to influence psychological experiences (i.e., our thoughts, attitudes, and behaviors toward ourselves and others).*

REFERENCES

Bearman, S., & Amrhein, M. (2014). Girls, women, and internalized sexism. In E. J. R. David (Ed.), *Internalized oppression: The psychology of marginalized groups* (pp. 191–226). New York, NY: Springer Publishing.

Berry, J. W. (2003). Conceptual approaches to acculturation. In K. Chun, P. Balls-Organista, & G. Martin (Eds.), *Acculturation: Advances in theory, measurement, and applied research* (pp. 17–37). Washington, DC: American Psychological Association Press.

Bouchard, T. J., Jr., Lykken, D. T., McGue, M., Segal, N. L., & Tellegen, A. (1990). Sources of human psychological differences: The Minnesota Study of Twins Reared Apart. *Science, 250*(4978), 223–228.

Braddock, D., & Parrish, S. (2001). An institutional history of disability. In G. Albrecht, K. Seelman, & M. Bury (Eds.), *Handbook of disability studies* (pp. 11–68). Thousand Oaks, CA: Sage.

Brave Heart, M. Y. (2003). The historical trauma response among natives and its relationship with substance abuse: A Lakota illustration. *Journal of Psychoactive Drugs, 35*(1), 7–13.

Butler, J. (1990). *Gender trouble: Feminism and the subversion of identity.* New York, NY: Routledge.

Chouinard, V. (1997). Making space for disabling difference: Challenges ableist geographies. *Environment and Planning D: Society and Space, 15,* 379–387.

Crenshaw, K. W. (1989). Demarginalizing the intersection of race and sex: A black feminist critique of antidiscrimination doctrine, feminist theory and antiracist politics. *The University of Chicago Legal Forum, 140*, 139–167.

Davis, L. J. (2002). *Bending over backwards: Disability, dismodernism, and other difficult positions.* New York: New York University Press.

Duran, E., & Duran, B. (1995). *Native American postcolonial psychology.* Albany: State University of New York Press.

Erickson, W., Lee, C., & von Schrader, S. (2017). *Disability statistics from the American Community Survey (ACS).* Ithaca, NY: Cornell University Yang-Tan Institute (YTI). Retrieved from http://www.disabilitystatistics.org

Fox, S., & Tang, S. (2000). The Sierra Leonean refugee experience: Traumatic events and psychiatric sequelae. *Journal of Nervous and Mental Disease, 188*, 490–495.

Frank, R. (2015). *The religion of millionaires.* Retrieved from http://www.cnbc.com/2015/01/14/the-religion-of-millionaires-.html

Frye, M. (1983). *The politics of reality: Essays in feminist theory.* Trumansburg, NY: The Crossing Press.

Gates, G. J. (2011). *How many people are lesbian, gay, bisexual, and transgender?* Los Angeles: The Williams Institute, University of California at Los Angeles. Retrieved from http://williamsinstitute.law.ucla.edu/wp-content/uploads/Gates-How-Many-People-LGBT-Apr-2011.pdf

Gonzalez, J., Simard, E., Baker-Demaray, T., & Iron Eyes, C. (2014). The internalized oppression of North American indigenous peoples. In E. J. R. David (Ed.), *Internalized oppression: The psychology of marginalized groups* (pp. 31–56). New York, NY: Springer Publishing.

Grieco, E. M. (2010). *Race and Hispanic origin of the foreign-born population in the United States: 2007.* Washington, DC: U.S. Census Bureau. Retrieved from https://www.census.gov/prod/2010pubs/acs-11.pdf

Hays, P. A. (2003). *Addressing cultural complexities in practice: A framework for clinicians and counselors.* Washington, DC: American Psychological Association.

Howden, L. M., & Meyer, J. A. (2011). *Age and sex composition: 2010.* Retrieved from http://www.census.gov/prod/cen2010/briefs/c2010br-03.pdf

Humes, K. R., Jones, N. A., & Ramirez, R. R. (2011). *Overview of race and Hispanic origin: 2010.* Retrieved from https://www.census.gov/prod/cen2010/briefs/c2010br-02.pdf

Jorde, L. B., & Wooding, S. P. (2004). Genetic variation, classification and 'race'. *Nature Genetics, 36,* 28–33. doi:10.1038/ng1435

Kirton, J. (1989). *Contemporary concert diplomacy: The seven-power summit and the management of international order.* Retrieved from http://www.g8.utoronto.ca/scholar/kirton198901/kcon1.htm

Klonoff, E. A., & Landrine, H. (1995). The schedule of sexist events: A measure of lifetime and recent sexist discrimination in women's lives. *Psychology of Women Quarterly, 19,* 439–472.

Langdon, S. J. (1989). *The native people of Alaska.* Anchorage, AK: Greatland Graphics.

Lykken, D. T. (2006). The mechanism of emergenesis. *Genes, Brain, and Behavior, 5*(4), 306–310.

Marks, D. (1999). *Disability: Controversial debates and psychosocial perspectives.* London, England: Routledge.

Matteson, A. V., & Moradi, B. (2005). Examining the structure of the schedule of sexist events: Replication and extension. *Psychology of Women Quarterly, 29,* 47–57.

Nadal, K. L. (2010). Gender roles. In S. Goldstein & J. Naglieri (Eds.), *Encyclopedia of child behavior and development* (pp. 687–690). New York, NY: Springer.

Nadal, K. L. (2013). *That's so gay!: Microaggressions and the lesbian, gay, bisexual, and transgender community.* Washington, DC: American Psychological Association.

Nadal, K. L., & Mendoza, R. J. (2014). Internalized oppression and the lesbian, gay, bisexual, and transgender community. In E. J. R. David (Ed.), *Internalized oppression: The psychology of marginalized groups* (pp. 227–252). New York, NY: Springer Publishing.

Pew Research Center. (2015a). *America's changing religious landscape.* Retrieved from http://www.pewforum.org/2015/05/12/americas-changing-religious-landscape

Pew Research Center. (2015b). *Faith on the hill: The religious composition of the 114th congress.* Retrieved from http://www.pewforum .org/2015/01/05/faith-on-the-hill/2

Pew Research Center. (2015c). *The future of world religions: Population growth projections, 2010–2050.* Retrieved from http://www .pewforum.org/2015/04/02/religious-projections-2010-2050

Porter, M., & Haslam, N. (2005). Predisplacement and postdisplacement factors associated with mental health of refugees and internally displaced persons: A meta-analysis. *Journal of the American Medical Association, 294*(5), 602–612.

Quintana, S. M. (1998). Children's developmental understanding of ethnicity and race. *Applied and Preventive Psychology, 7,* 27–45.

Shields, J. P., Cohen, R., Glassman, J. R., Whitaker, K., Franks, H., & Bertolini, I. (2013). Estimating population size and demographic characteristics of lesbian, gay, bisexual, and transgender youth in middle school. *Journal of Adolescent Health, 52*(2), 248–250. doi:10.1016/j.jadohealth.2012.06.016

Shorrocks, A., Davies, J., & Lluberasis, R. (2013). *Global wealth report 2013.* Zurich, Switzerland: Credit Suisse. Retrieved from https:// thenextrecession.files.wordpress.com/2013/10/global-wealth -report.pdf

Thabet, A., & Vostanis, P. (2000). Post-traumatic stress disorder reactions in children of war: A longitudinal study. *Child Abuse & Neglect, 24,* 291–298.

Torgersen, A. M., & Janson, H. (2002). Why do identical twins differ in personality: Shared environment reconsidered. *Twin Research, 5*(1), 44–52.

United Nations Educational, Scientific, and Cultural Organization. (2016). *What do we mean by "youth"?* Retrieved from http://www .unesco.org/new/en/social-and-human-sciences/themes/youth/ youth-definition

United Nations High Commissioner for Refugees. (2010). *Statistical yearbook 2009: Trends in displacement, protection and solutions.* Geneva, Switzerland: Author.

United Nations High Commissioner for Refugees. (2012). *Who we help.* Retrieved from http://www.unhcr.org/pages/49c3646c11c.html

U.S. Census Bureau. (2012). *Section 13: Income, expenditures, poverty, and wealth.* Retrieved from https://www.census.gov/prod/2011pubs/12statab/income.pdf

Vernon, P. A., Jang, K. L., Harris, J. A., & McCarthy, J. M. (1997). Environmental predictors of personality differences: A twin and sibling study. *Journal of Personality and Social Psychology, 72*(1), 177–183.

Watermeyer, B., & Gorgens, T. (2014). Disability and internalized oppression. In E. J. R. David (Ed.), *Internalized oppression: The psychology of marginalized groups* (pp. 253–280). New York, NY: Springer Publishing.

West, C., & Zimmerman, D. H. (1987). Doing gender. *Gender & Society, 1,* 125–151.

Wolff, E. N. (2010). *Recent trends in household wealth in the United States: Rising debt and the middle-class squeeze—An update to 2007.* Annandale-on-Hudson, NY: Levy Economics Institute. Retrieved from http://www.levyinstitute.org/pubs/wp_589.pdf

World Health Organization. (2011). *World report on disability.* Geneva, Switzerland: Author. Retrieved from http://www.who.int/disabilities/world_report/2011/en

CHAPTER 3

This chapter will discuss some examples of social group oppression through time - focusing on U.S. History

History Is Now! Historical and Contemporary Oppression

$\rightarrow$

Imagine the following scenario: Approximately 850,000 African American men are captured and held against their will. For many years—decades even—they are all forced to work without pay. The only "benefit" they receive is food and a place to sleep. The forced and unpaid labor they provide benefits others, mostly wealthy White families. If they are able to get away, they are shunned by society and treated forever as criminals. Are you still with us? Now, as you imagine this scenario, of what does it remind you? Does it make you think of real-life examples in the United States? Does the scenario lead you to think of a particular period in U.S. history? If the scenario led you to think of African American slavery in the United States during the 1600s to the 1800s, then great—you know U.S. history pretty well! However, if the scenario led you to think about the current state of the U.S. prison system, then great—you have a pretty good understanding of our contemporary society! Indeed, according to law professor and civil rights activist Michelle Alexander's (2012) groundbreaking book *The New Jim Crow: Mass Incarceration in the Age of Colorblindness*, our modern-day criminal justice system essentially operates in the same oppressive manner as the institution of slavery! In fact, based on Dr. Alexander's work, we have learned that there are more African American men in the U.S. criminal justice system (i.e., in prison, probation, parole) now than the number of Black men who were enslaved in 1850—approximately 10 years before the American Civil War (which has as its main cause the issue of slavery) and a period in history that may arguably be considered as the height of slavery!

We start Chapter 3 with this brief mind exercise to get us thinking about history as well as our modern-day realities and how they may be similar and even linked. We do this because it is important for all of us to know and remember the truth that oppression is a core component of the history and contemporary reality of the United States (and arguably, the world). We all need to acknowledge the reality that the United States was founded on oppression, thrived because of oppression, and is currently one of the most powerful nations (if not the most powerful) in the world because of oppression. Further, we also want to emphasize that it is important to know history not just to merely know it, but also to see how history's legacies continue to persist and significantly affect people today! We cannot just simply forget history or regard it as "long over with" and "move on." To this end, now that we have a basic understanding of oppression (Chapter 1) and the various social groups that are subjected to oppression (Chapter 2), this chapter discusses some examples of social group oppression through time, focusing mostly on the United States. Let us start with historical oppression.

[handwritten margin notes: "history is important.", "CANNOT FORGET HISTORY!", "CANNOT Move on!"]

■ NOTABLE CASES OF HISTORICAL OPPRESSION

When we think of oppression, most of us will probably think of racial oppression. And when racial oppression is brought up, particularly in history, the example of African American slavery is most likely to come to mind. According to scholars (e.g., Clarke, 1991; Du Bois, 1998), the **system of chattel slavery** from the early 1600s to around 1863 that treated Black people as property and inferior objects is the "most diabolical form of mental and physical torture experienced by any one group" (Bailey, Williams, & Favors, 2014, p. 139). Black people experienced brutal forms of oppression that included lynchings and other forms of executions, beatings, whippings, rape, and various forms of physical (e.g., starvation) and psychological (e.g., forced separation from family) violence. The dehumanization of Black people continued even after chattel slavery was abolished, as the United States legalized segregation between White people and people of color (mostly Black people) during the 1896 *Plessy v. Ferguson* Supreme Court ruling. This period of state-sanctioned racial segregation—known popularly as the **Jim Crow era**—lasted until around the 1950s to the 1960s. During the Jim Crow era, the degradation, inferiorization, and dehumanization of Black people continued under the illusion that—although separated—they had "equal" access to opportunities (e.g., education, jobs), resources (e.g., schools, bank loans, neighborhoods), and facilities (e.g., transportation, recreation) as White people. The reality, however, is that Black people were systematically discriminated against and unfairly treated in all aspects of society including employment and promotion decisions, college admissions, quality of neighborhood schools, housing opportunities, and the legal system.

Other groups of non-White people who experienced brutal forms of racial oppression are Native Americans, Alaska Natives, Native Hawaiians, and other indigenous peoples who were colonized. European settlers forcefully (e.g., through war, broken treaties) took over indigenous peoples' ancestral lands to exploit the natural resources and claim power and control over them (e.g., Gonzalez, Simard, Baker-Demaray, & Iron Eyes, 2014; Lewis, Allen, & Fleagle, 2014; Salzman & Laenui, 2014). During colonialism, European colonizers also imposed their worldviews, values, and ways of doing things on the indigenous peoples. Simultaneous to this, the indigenous peoples, their cultures, and their ways of doing things are regarded as inferior or uncivilized, creating a rationale for putting domination and oppression into practice. In other words, once a clear contrast has been established between the supposedly superior or civilized Western ways and the supposedly inferior, uncivilized, or savage ways of the indigenous peoples, the Western colonizers have essentially created a justification for why they need to "teach," train, civilize, enlighten, or help the indigenous peoples (Fanon, 1965). Focusing specifically on the U.S. context, for example, Native Americans (ca. late 1800s) and Alaska Natives (ca. early- to mid-1900s) were forced to attend boarding schools to shed them of their indigenous ways and assimilate them into the Western or European ways. It is clear, then, that in addition to policies and actions that attempted to physically exterminate indigenous peoples (e.g., war, mass executions, spreading of disease), there were also government-sanctioned efforts to eradicate indigenous peoples' worldviews, languages, and ways of doing things. Thus, beginning with colonialism, history shows that indigenous peoples faced physical and cultural genocide.

Speaking of genocide, the most well-known historical example of it is the **Jewish Holocaust**—the genocide that Jews were subjected to by Nazi Germany during World War II (ca. 1930s to 1940s). Under Adolf Hitler's regime, Germany regarded Jews as inferior and their characteristics were associated with negativity (e.g., untrustworthy, greedy). According to the United States Holocaust Memorial Museum (2017), German Jews were required to follow strict curfews, prohibited from going to many areas, forbidden from using public transportation, restricted from accessing food and other basic necessities, forced to relinquish their property (e.g., radios, cameras, bicycles, electrical appliances, businesses, and homes),

Eugenics movement-the scientifically erroneous & immoral theory of "racial improvement" & "planned breeding". Eugenicists worldwide believed that they could perfect human beings & eliminate so-called social ills through genetics & heredity

forced to perform unpaid labor, deported out of Germany, and unjustly jailed in internment camps, leading to the mass murder of approximately 6 million Jews. In addition to Jews, other people who were also viewed as genetically inferior and "racially undesirable"—such as individuals with mental illness, people with intellectual or physical disabilities, people with alcohol and drug addictions, and homosexual people—were subjected to such systemic oppression as well. For example, scholars have estimated that around 300,000 people with disabilities were also massacred in Nazi death camps during World War II (e.g., Marks, 1999; Ravaud & Stiker, 2001), clearly showing that Hitler was largely influenced by the principles of the **eugenics movement** that began in the late 1800s to inferiorize, marginalize, and eradicate differently abled people (e.g., forced sterilization of people with mental and physical disabilities) (Watermeyer & Gorgens, 2014).

Similar to the incarceration of Jews and other "undesirables" during World War II, approximately 120,000 Americans who had Japanese ancestry were also forcibly removed from their homes and jailed by the U.S. government in concentration camps after Pearl Harbor was attacked by Japan. The **Japanese American incarceration** during the early 1940s was portrayed as necessary in order to protect national security as Americans of Japanese ancestry were automatically regarded as potential threats or spies. However, later investigations by the U.S. government itself revealed that there was no evidence of disloyalty from Japanese Americans and that the U.S. government's actions during World War II were instead based on racism (Maki, Kitano, & Megan Berthold, 1999). The U.S. racism against Asians goes back even further in history, with the **Chinese Exclusion Act** of 1882 being a prime example, as it was the first law implemented to prevent a specific ethnic group from immigrating to the United States (Lee, 2015). These examples with Asians—along with the long list of laws, policies, and instances that reflect strong **anti-Mexican sentiments** throughout U.S. history (e.g., Mexican Repatriation during 1929 to 1939 that forcefully deported approximately 1 million people of Mexican descent, 60% of whom were U.S. citizens; Balderrama & Rodriguez, 2006; Carrigan & Web, 2003; Molina, 2014)—clearly show that American xenophobia (i.e., fear of foreigners, immigrants, or people from other countries) has existed for centuries! Indeed, there are countless examples of how immigrants in the United States were not allowed to become citizens (e.g., Nationality Acts of 1790 and 1870 that limited the right to naturalization only to "free whites" or those with "African descent") and, therefore, were not afforded the same legal protections and rights as others such as owning property and voting.

JAPANESE AMERICAN INCARCERATION!

Speaking of not being regarded as full citizens and consequently not having the right to own property and vote, peoples of color and immigrants were not the only ones who were subjected to such restrictions at one point or another in U.S. history. For centuries since the founding of the United States in 1776, women in the country—including White women—were also not treated as equal citizens as White men. For example, led by the **women's suffrage movement**, it was not until 1920 with the 19th Amendment to the U.S. constitution that women gained full voting rights. (*Note*: Non-White women, however, still faced plenty of barriers that prohibited them from voting and, in many cases, were still not allowed to vote at all.) In addition to voting rights, women at one point or another in U.S. history were not allowed to go to school, own and manage property in their own name, remarry, or even choose not to be married or not have children without losing rights or being scorned by society. Thus, women's right to choose what they want to do with their own bodies (e.g., have children or not) and lives (e.g., get married or not, own property, go to school, run for political office) have been restricted in various ways (e.g., through varying laws, norms, and inferiorizing stereotypes about married and unmarried women, women with and without children, women with children out of wedlock, women who are widowed or divorced, women who choose to remarry and those who do not) throughout the history of the United States (Boylan, 2015).

Having the right to choose what one wants to do with one's own body is also a long-standing historical issue for people who are lesbian, gay, bisexual, transgender, or queer (LGBTQ). During the 1800s, for example, gay and transgender people in the United States were often arrested and convicted of sodomy—a "sexual act usually involving anal or other copulation . . . involving two men" (Nadal & Mendoza, 2014, p. 232). The **criminalization of homosexuality** through the existence of **sodomy laws** continued in the United States until 2003 when the U.S. Supreme Court finally ruled that sodomy laws are unconstitutional. In addition to not having rights over one's own body, what LGBTQ individuals want to do with their lives has also been historically limited by society. For example, President Dwight Eisenhower issued an executive order in 1953 that prohibited homosexuals from any form of federal employment, including military service (Nadal & Mendoza, 2014). Moreover, Executive Order 10450 also required private contractors doing business with the federal government to fire their gay and lesbian employees (Johnson, 2004). Even further, the basic constitutional rights of LGBTQ people in the United States were also historically threatened. For instance, it was not until 1958 that the U.S. Supreme Court formally protected the First Amendment rights of LGBTQ people, when it ruled that *One: The Homosexual Magazine*—a lesbian, gay, and bisexual publication—may be delivered via U.S. mail. Thus, similar to peoples of color, people with disabilities, and women, LGBTQ people have also been excluded and marginalized for centuries and have faced various forms of oppression throughout history (for comprehensive reviews of the historical oppression of LGBTQ people, see Johnson, 2004; Nadal, 2013).

■ SOME EXAMPLES OF CONTEMPORARY OPPRESSION

You may have noticed that many, if not all, of the historical examples of oppression discussed in the previous section are still happening today in one form or another (see Table 3.1 for some examples of how historical oppression is linked to contemporary oppression). How such forms of oppression are expressed in policies and laws, how they are written about and talked about, and how they are enacted or implemented today in our contemporary times may be different, but they are nevertheless rooted in the same kinds of oppression! For example, many folks today may be

TABLE 3.1 Some Examples of How Historical Oppression Is Linked to Contemporary Oppression

Historical	Contemporary
Colonization of Native Americans	Standing Rock and tribal sovereignty issues
Colonization and involvement in other countries	Immigration, refugee, and asylee issues
Eugenics movement	Continued marginalization and inferiorization of people with disabilities
Chattel slavery and Jim Crow era	Mass incarceration and state-sanctioned killings of African Americans
Denial of voting rights	Voter suppression efforts
Limitations on women's rights	Limitations on reproductive rights
Persecution of Japanese Americans	Persecution of Muslims, South Asians, Sikhs, and Arabs
Anti-Mexican and anti-Asian sentiments	Immigration and border issues
Criminalization of homosexuality	Denial of equal rights for lesbian, gay, bisexual, and transgender people

familiar with LGBTQ individuals' continued fight for **marriage rights**. Society's continued resistance to same-sex relationships and unions is just another manifestation of how LGBTQ people are regarded as immoral, abnormal, and unacceptable. Thus, LGBTQ people's rights to choose what they want to do with their own bodies and lives are still restricted by society today (see Nadal, 2013, for a comprehensive discussion of contemporary oppression—such as microaggressions—faced by LGBTQ individuals). Similarly, women today are still fighting for their rights to make decisions for themselves and their own bodies, as can be easily seen through the continued debates on **reproductive rights**. For example, although the U.S. Supreme Court decision on *Roe v. Wade* in 1973 gave women the right to make their own decisions regarding abortion, intense national deliberations continue today about reversing such a decision. Even further, there are also ongoing pressures from many people and organizations to take away women's rights to choose whether or not to start a family; access or use contraceptives; receive sex education in public schools; and access or use reproductive health services (for a more comprehensive discussion of the current state of reproductive rights in the United States, see Center for Reproductive Rights, 2017). These examples show that women's rights to make decisions about their own bodies and other factors that may significantly affect their lives (e.g., whether or not to have children) are still constantly threatened to be taken away.

Many people today may also consider the issue about voting rights as a thing of the past. Indeed, due to the efforts of Martin Luther King Jr. and many other leaders of the **civil rights movement**, the **Voting Rights Act of 1965** eliminated many voting barriers for peoples of color (e.g., banned the use of literacy tests, protection of voting rights for non-English-speaking citizens) and poor people (e.g., elimination of poll taxes). However, we need to realize that there are still many people today who are either prohibited from voting or face more barriers to voting simply because of their social group membership. For example, people who are on parole or probation cannot vote and—as discussed previously—Black people are overrepresented among those who are on parole or probation. Thus, Black people are disproportionately affected by current voting laws. Another example is the U.S. Supreme Court's 2013 decision that struck down the heart of the Voting Rights Act by allowing states to change their election laws without the need for federal approval. Such a decision allowed states to create voter identification laws and other policies (e.g., fewer polling places, narrower voting hours, limited early voting and absentee voting policies) that make it more difficult for some social groups (e.g., peoples of color, immigrants, elders, people who are poor or working class) to exercise their right to vote. Thus, many social groups today are still facing barriers to voting, evidence that **voter suppression** continues to be an issue in our contemporary society (Roth, 2016).

We also see in today's society the widespread **religious persecution** of people who are Muslims, which is similar to the kind of persecution that Jews were subjected to during World War II. For example, since 9/11, the U.S. government has implemented surveillance programs based on people's religion and national origin (Iyer, 2015). The National Security Entry-Exit Registration System (NSEERS) that required males who are over 16 years of age from 25 predominantly Muslim countries in Asia and Africa to register with the Department of Homeland Security, for instance, was in effect until December 2016! More recently, just 1 month after NSEERS was discontinued, a January 2017 Executive Order banned people from seven predominantly Muslim countries in the Middle East and Africa—including people who are legal residents of the United States (i.e., "Green Card" holders)—from coming into the country. The issue of islamophobia is also linked to the widespread **xenophobia or anti-immigrant/refugee/asylee sentiments** that we are still seeing today. Indeed, we see how anti-immigrant/refugee/asylee sentiments extend beyond Muslims to other non-White groups as well, such as Mexicans and Asians. For instance, there's the proposed "Wall" to be built on the southern U.S. border to keep "bad hombres" out, and—between 2009 and 2016 during Barack Obama's presidency—the United States deported and separated more people from their families (over 2.5 million people) than any other administration in history (U.S. Department of Homeland Security, 2016)! Further, we have also seen **increased hate crimes** against Asians (e.g., Bharath, 2017) who are perpetually perceived as foreigners and who are often told to "go back to your country," with the recent murder of Srinivas Kuchibhotla—a man born in India—being a tragic example of such prevalent xenophobia (e.g., Eligon, Blinder, & Najar, 2017).

The long-standing debates about immigration and borders are interesting because people tend to forget that a big piece of the puzzle is U.S. colonialism and **foreign policy**. Many people in the United States seem to forget that the country extended its reach beyond its own "borders" to colonize other lands (e.g., the Philippines, Puerto Rico, Texas) or meddle with other countries' affairs (e.g., Honduras, El Salvador, Guatemala, and Nicaragua during the Contra War in the 1980s; Iraq, Iran, and Afghanistan during the Gulf War in the 1990s and currently; the Vietnam War from the 1950s to 1970s). As Mexican American actor Eva Longoria,

Neo colonialism - the continuation or reimposition of imperialist rule by a state (usually a former colonial power) over another nominally independent state (usually, a former colony)

whose family is from Texas—which was part of Mexico—once said: "My family didn't cross the border. The border crossed us." Similarly, it has become popular for many immigrants in the United States to utter the phrase "We are here, because you were there!" to succinctly explain their presence in the country. Indeed, the continued colonialism of the United States and **intrusion in other countries** tend to destabilize such countries (e.g., exploiting their resources, creating no law and order that leads to civil wars, bad economy, poverty, and extreme violence), forcing people from such countries to want—or in the case of refugees and asylees, need—to emigrate to the United States. Thus, the immigration, refugee, or asylee issue that is currently facing the United States is linked to the U.S. historical interference, colonization, or continued exploitation (or **neocolonialism**) of other countries! Further, colonialism is related to the immigration and border issue because many people who are in power today (White people, the United States) seem to forget the truth that they are also immigrants to these lands and that they stole these lands from its indigenous peoples through colonialism. In fact, we must realize that the colonization of Native peoples' ancestral lands and the exploitation of their land's resources are still happening today within the United States (e.g., Standing Rock)!

Another example of historical oppression that is still taking place in modern-day United States is the **devaluation of Black lives**. Although slavery, lynchings, segregation, and other blatant forms of race-based maltreatments and injustice may be considered by many people to be "things of the past," contemporary events and data suggest that the institutionalized devaluation of Black lives is still happening today. For instance, the tragic deaths of Oscar Grant, Trayvon Martin, Mike Brown, Eric Garner, Tamir Rice, Freddie Gray, Sandra Bland, Laquan McDonald, Keith Lamont Scott, Philando Castile, Samuel Dubose, and Terence Crutcher—along with seemingly endless stories of many other Black individuals who were unjustly harassed, imprisoned, or killed by law enforcement officers—have brought intense national attention to state-sanctioned racism once again. These devastating stories are real-life representations of research findings showing that Black people are the victims in 26% of all police shootings even though Black people make up only around 14% of the country's population (Center on Juvenile and Criminal Justice, 2014). These tragedies are also consistent with recent research by Goff, Jackson, Di Leone, Culotta, and DiTomasso (2014), who found that police officers tend to perceive Black boys (10 years of age and younger) as older than they really are and as more threatening than

White boys. Even further, the same research team found that police are more likely to dehumanize Black boys (e.g., associate them with apes), perceive them as guilty, and use violence on them. Moreover, the continued criminalization of Black people is clearly seen in the current state of the U.S. criminal justice system, where Black are people overrepresented in prisons. For example, although Black males compose only around 14% of the U.S. male population, Black men compose 60% of the male prison population (Alexander, 2012)! The same can be said about Black women; although composing only around 13% of the U.S. female population, Black women make up 30% of the female prisoners in the country (The Sentencing Project, 2007).

■ SCIENCE AND OPPRESSION → disability

A discussion of the systemic oppression of social groups throughout history is not complete without acknowledging the role that science itself has played in such oppression. This is because many of the conventions (e.g., quantification, measurement) and assumptions (e.g., tendency to look for intra-individual, usually biological, factors to explain phenomena) of science have been instrumental in oppressing—and justifying the oppression—of various social groups. Perhaps the best example of this is how scientific measurement and medicalization was used to literally position people with disabilities on the margins or outside of "normal," hence reinforcing the notion that people with disabilities are abnormal, strange, weird, or anomalous. As Watermeyer and Gorgens (2014) eloquently explained:

> The growth of the eugenics movement occurred alongside the 20th century's burgeoning medicalization of disability . . . Eugenic principles and biological medicine combined in policies of enforced sterilization of, in particular, intellectually impaired persons that . . . lasted well into the second half of the century . . . for many decades eugenic principles were championed by liberal voices in Europe and the United States . . . disabled and nondisabled alike were becoming ever more subject to an ideology of medical measurement that positioned all in some relation to a statistical normalcy. (p. 257)

Thus, it is clear that the scientific and medical communities have played significant roles in the othering, inferiorization, and dehumanization of people with disabilities.

Another example of how social group oppression was carried out under the guise of science and medicine is the infamous **Tuskegee Syphilis Study**, which was a study by the U.S. Public Health Service that sought to document the natural progression of untreated syphilis (Jones, 1981). Between 1932 and 1972, approximately 400 poor, uneducated African American men with syphilis in rural Alabama unknowingly took part in the study. Here we mean "unknowingly" in two ways: (a) they thought they were simply getting free medical care and had no idea they were participating in a study; and (b) they were never told that they had syphilis. Perhaps even more egregious is that, even though penicillin had become known as an effective treatment for syphilis by 1947—and although it had become standard practice to prescribe penicillin by that time—the U.S. government researchers still purposefully withheld treatment from the study participants. Even further, the researchers actively worked to keep participants from accessing syphilis treatment through other ways (e.g., seeing other providers and doctors where they lived). As a result, hundreds of poor African American people—the study participants along with their spouses, children, and other family members—had their physical and psychological well-being significantly affected (i.e., syphilis deaths, spouses who contracted syphilis, children born with syphilis, stress associated with carrying syphilis).

A more recent example of social group oppression being carried out under the guise of "objective" science is *The Bell Curve* (Hernstein & Murray, 1994). Using what seems like rigorous scientific data and analyses, this controversial book promoted the notion that non-White people—primarily Black people—are less intelligent and genetically inferior to White people. According to scholars (Graves, 2003; Graves & Johnson, 1995), **The Bell Curve** is a case of scientific racism as it uses questionable data analytic methodologies, fails to consider theories and data that contradict the authors' hypotheses, and makes bold policy recommendations that aligned with racist beliefs (e.g., dismantling programs designed to address social inequalities). The American Psychological Association also published a task force report (Neisser et al., 1996) and several other critiques (e.g., Rushton, 1997) that questioned the scientific merit and conclusions of the book. Even further, the Southern Poverty Law Center (2017)—which monitors hate groups and extremists in the United States—has classified one of the authors, Charles Murray, as a White nationalist who "has become one of the most influential social scientists in America, using racist pseudoscience and misleading statistics to argue that social inequality is caused by the genetic inferiority of the black and Latino communities, women, and the poor."

Similar to *The Bell Curve*, the **Barrow Alcohol Study** (Foulks, 1989) is another example of a scientific endeavor that perpetuated racist and negative stereotypes about a group of people—in this case against the Inupiat people of Alaska. Back in the early 1980s, researchers from Philadelphia were contracted by the North Slope Borough (local government of Barrow) to study alcohol abuse and alcohol use–related violence in the community. After data were collected and the results analyzed, however, a press release was disseminated and a press conference was conducted without input, representation, and knowledge of the Barrow community. Based on the press conference and press release, *The New York Times* ran a front-page story with the headline "Alcohol Plagues Eskimos" (Sobel, 1980). This article stated that the Inupiats of Alaska's North Slope were essentially committing suicide by alcoholism and called their entire society alcoholic.

In addition to destroying the community's trust with researchers, the reckless and disrespectful release of information without the community's knowledge and consent further propagated inferiorizing stereotypes against Alaska Native peoples (e.g., drunks).

Within the scientific field of psychology itself, we see that there was a time when psychological science was used to "legitimately" pathologize groups of people. For instance, in the 1800s, science and medicine were used to pathologize Black slaves' desire to be free. Indeed, a condition called **Drapetomania** (Cartwright, 1851) was a diagnosis given by doctors to Black slaves who tended to run away from their masters. It was a condition that was included in medical books and scientific journals and for which doctors developed treatments (White, 2002). Another example of how psychological science has been used to oppress certain social groups is the official regard of **homosexuality as a disorder** by the American Psychiatric Association in their *Diagnostic and Statistical Manual (DSM)* until as recently as 1973 (Drescher, 2015). However, it should be noted that the psychological and medical communities' pathologization of homosexuality continued with the inclusion of **Sexual Orientation Disturbance** and **Ego Dystonic Homosexuality** as disorders in later editions of the *DSM* (American Psychiatric Association, 1980). Even further, the *DSM* continued to legitimize the use of conversion therapies to cure homosexuality. Thus, it was not until 1987 that homosexuality completely disappeared from the *DSM* (American Psychiatric Association, 1987). Despite the depathologization of homosexuality, the most current

Science & medical communities causing oppression ↓

DSM still has **gender identity disorder** and **gender dysphoria** (American Psychiatric Association, 2013), which are examples of how the scientific and medical communities continue to pathologize transgender people.

More generally worldwide, we see the scientific and medical communities' wide-ranging tendency to look for individual-level factors to explain phenomena as potentially oppressive, because such a narrow perspective may lead to a failure to see that—many times—the root causes of problems are factors outside the individual such as oppression. Thus, in cases wherein oppression is the cause of the problem, the tendency to look for intra-individual factors may inadvertently maintain oppressive systems (because they remain unchallenged and unquestioned) and to blame individuals (or groups) for the problems they are experiencing. For example, the World Health Organization (WHO; 2011) has recently expressed concern about the widespread use of **skin-whitening products** in various countries worldwide, such as in China, the Philippines, Malaysia, Mali, Nigeria, Senegal, South Africa, South Korea, and Togo. However, the WHO framed the issue as simply a mercury problem, failing to consider that oppression—specifically worldwide racial oppression— is why non-White people have developed a desire to have lighter skin tones! That is, the WHO has implied that so long as mercury is eliminated from skin-whitening products, then having a desire to have lighter skin tones and using skin-whitening products are not problematic (David & Derthick, 2014)!

▪ FACING OUR OPPRESSIVE REALITY

As you can see, oppression has been happening throughout history and is still happening today, even (perhaps especially) in the United States! To know that oppression was, has been, and is still a core component of the United States (and the world) is a sobering—perhaps even devastating— but necessary realization. Another depressing but essential truth is that the cases of oppression we discussed in this chapter are not even all of it! That is, this chapter is not even close to being an exhaustive review of various types of social group oppression in U.S. history. Even further, we also see that the scientific enterprise too has been used as a tool to legitimize the oppression of people and justify the continued oppression of people! Therefore, it should be clear by now that many social groups have experienced historical oppression and continue to face contemporary forms of systemic oppression today.

ee These experiences of oppression have happened at both interpersonal and institutional levels (discussed in Chapter 5), and the literature suggests that they are related to various modern-day disparities in education, incarceration, socioeconomic status, and health (discussed in Chapter 6). Oppression is not a new problem, and it is not an easy problem to address (discussed in Chapters 8 and 9) largely because people in power and established institutions tend to prefer the maintenance of the status quo, of what is familiar and comfortable, and be resistant to change (discussed in Chapter 7). Even further, it is difficult to address oppression because it continues to evolve across time and adapts to changing zeitgeists and norms—like a constantly moving target (discussed in Chapter 4). Nevertheless, as disheartening as it may be to realize that oppression is so widespread, complex, and difficult to tackle, we must remain steadfast in our efforts to resist it, eliminate it, and address its negative consequences. To this end, instead of being paralyzed by its enormity and complexity, we humbly suggest that we should face our oppressive reality and continue to learn more about oppression as such knowledge may help us in our collective efforts to create a more just, fair, and healthy society. Let us now move on to Chapter 4.

[handwritten: ↑ Good for research paper; why we must face our history of oppression. We can view the changes of oppression.]

REFERENCES

Alexander, M. (2012). *The new Jim Crow: Mass incarceration in the age of colorblindness*. New York, NY: The New Press. *[handwritten: Look up these References to see if they fit Research Paper]*

American Psychiatric Association. (1980). *Diagnostic and statistical manual of mental disorders* (3rd ed.). Washington, DC: Author.

American Psychiatric Association. (1987). *Diagnostic and statistical manual of mental disorders* (revised 3rd ed.). Washington, DC: Author.

American Psychiatric Association. (2013). *Diagnostic and statistical manual of mental disorders* (5th ed.). Arlington, VA: American Psychiatric Publishing.

Bailey, T.-K. M., Williams, W. S., & Favors, B. (2014). Internalized racial oppression in the African American community. In E. J. R. David (Ed.), *Internalized oppression: The psychology of marginalized groups* (pp. 137–162). New York, NY: Springer Publishing.

Balderrama, F. E., & Rodriguez, R. (2006). *Decade of betrayal: Mexican repatriation in the 1930s*. Albuquerque: University of New Mexico Press.

Bharath, D. (2017). Rise in crimes targeting Asian Americans leads to new anti-hate website. *The Orange County Register.* Retrieved from http://www.ocregister.com/articles/hate-741806-people-crimes.html

Boylan, A. M. (2015). *Women's rights in the United States: A history in documents.* New York, NY: Oxford University Press.

Carrigan, W. D., & Web, C. (2003). The lynching of persons of Mexican origin or descent in the United States, 1848 to 1928. *The Journal of Social History, 37*(2), 411–438. doi:10.1353/jsh.2003.0169

Cartwright, S. A. (1851). Report on the diseases and physical peculiarities of the Negro race. *The New Orleans Medical and Surgical Journal, 11,* 691–715.

Center for Reproductive Rights. (2017). *2016 state of the states: A pivotal time for reproductive rights.* New York, NY: Author. Retrieved from https://www.reproductiverights.org/sites/crr.civicactions.net/files/documents/USPA_StateofStates_11.16_Web_Final.pdf

Center on Juvenile and Criminal Justice. (2014). *Who are police killing?* Retrieved from http://www.cjcj.org/news/8113

Clarke, J. H. (1991). *Notes for an African world revolution: Africans at the crossroads.* Trenton, NJ: Africa World Press.

David, E. J. R., & Derthick, A. O. (2014). What is internalized oppression, and so what? In E. J. R. David (Ed.), *Internalized oppression: The psychology of marginalized groups* (pp. 1–30). New York, NY: Springer Publishing.

Drescher, J. (2015). Out of DSM: Depathologizing homosexuality. *Behavioral Sciences, 5*(4), 565–575.

Du Bois, W. E. B. (1998). *Black reconstruction in America: 1860-1880.* New York, NY: Free Press.

Eligon, J., Blinder, A., & Najar, N. (2017). Hate crime is feared as 2 Indian engineers are shot in Kansas. *The New York Times.* Retrieved from https://www.nytimes.com/2017/02/24/world/asia/kansas-attack-possible-hate-crime-srinivas-kuchibhotla.html?_r=0

Fanon, F. (1965). *The wretched of the earth.* New York, NY: Grove.

Foulks, E. F. (1989). Misalliances in the Barrow Alcohol Study. *American Indian and Native Alaska Mental Health Research, 2*(3), 7–17.

Goff, P. A., Jackson, M. C., Di Leone, B. A. L., Culotta, C. M., & DiTomasso, N. A. (2014). The essence of innocence: Consequences of dehumanizing Black children. *Journal of Personality and Social Psychology, 106*(4), 526–545.

Gonzalez, J., Simard, E., Baker-Demaray, T., & Iron Eyes, C. (2014). The internalized oppression of North American indigenous peoples. In E. J. R. David (Ed.), *Internalized oppression: The psychology of marginalized groups* (pp. 31–56). New York, NY: Springer Publishing.

Graves, J. L. (2003). *The emperor's new clothes: Biological theories of race at the millennium.* New Brunswick, NJ: Rutgers University Press.

Graves, J. L., & Johnson, A. (1995). The pseudoscience of psychometry and The Bell Curve. *The Journal of Negro Education, 64*(3), 277–294.

Hernstein, R. J., & Murray, C. (1994). *The Bell Curve: Intelligence and class structure in American life.* New York, NY: Free Press.

Iyer, D. (2015). *We too sing America: South Asian, Arab, Muslim, and Sikh immigrants shape our multiracial future.* New York, NY: The New Press.

Johnson, D. K. (2004). *The lavender scare: The cold war persecution of gays and lesbians in the federal government.* Chicago, IL: University of Chicago Press.

Jones, J. (1981). *Bad blood: The Tuskegee syphilis experiment.* New York, NY: Free Press.

Lee, J. H. X. (2015). *Chinese Americans: The history and culture of a people.* Santa Barbara, CA: ABC-CLIO.

Lewis, J., Allen, J., & Fleagle, E. (2014). Internalized oppression and Alaska native peoples: "We have to go through the problem." In E. J. R. David (Ed.), *Internalized oppression: The psychology of marginalized groups* (pp. 57–82). New York, NY: Springer Publishing.

Maki, M. T., Kitano, H. H. L., & Megan Berthold, S. (1999). *Achieving the impossible dream: How Japanese Americans obtained redress.* Urbana: University of Illinois Press.

Marks, D. (1999). Dimensions of oppression: Theorising the embodied subject. *Disability & Society, 14,* 611–626.

Molina, N. (2014). *How race is made in America: Immigration, citizenship, and the historical power of racial scripts.* Oakland: University of California Press.

Nadal, K. L. (2013). *That's so gay!: Microaggressions and the lesbian, gay, bisexual, and transgender community*. Washington, DC: American Psychological Association.

Nadal, K. L., & Mendoza, R. J. (2014). Internalized oppression and the lesbian, gay, bisexual, and transgender community. In E. J. R. David (Ed.), *Internalized oppression: The psychology of marginalized groups* (pp. 227–252). New York, NY: Springer Publishing.

Neisser, U., Boodoo, G., Bouchard, T. J., Boykin, A. W., Brody, N., Ceci, S. J., . . . Urbina, S. (1996). Intelligence: Knowns and unknowns. *American Psychologist, 51,* 77–101.

Ravaud, J. F., & Stiker, H. J. (2001). Inclusion/exclusion: An analysis of historical and cultural meanings. In G. Albrecht, K. Seelma, & M. Bury (Eds.), *Handbook of disability studies* (pp. 490–512). Thousand Oaks, CA: Sage.

Roth, Z. (2016). *The great suppression: Voting rights, corporate cash, and the conservative assault on democracy*. New York, NY: Crown.

Rushton, J. P. (1997). Race, IQ, and the APA report on The Bell Curve. *American Psychologist, 52*(1), 69–70.

Salzman, M., & Laenui, P. (2014). Internalized oppression among Pacific Island peoples. In E. J. R. David (Ed.), *Internalized oppression: The psychology of marginalized groups* (pp. 83–108). New York, NY: Springer Publishing.

Sobel, D. (1980, January 22). Alcohol plagues Eskimos. *The New York Times.* Retrieved from http://query.nytimes.com/gst/abstract .html?res=9C03EFD91538E732A25751C2A9679C94619FD6CF&legacy=true

Southern Poverty Law Center. (2017). *Charles Murray*. Retrieved from https://www.splcenter.org/fighting-hate/extremist-files/ individual/charles-murray

The Sentencing Project. (2007). *Women in the criminal justice system: Briefing sheets*. Retrieved from http://www.sentencingproject.org/ wp-content/uploads/2016/01/Women-in-the-Criminal-Justice -System-Briefing-Sheets.pdf

United States Holocaust Memorial Museum. (2017). Introduction to the Holocaust. *Holocaust Encyclopedia*. Retrieved from https://www .ushmm.org/wlc/en/article.php?ModuleId=10005469

U.S. Department of Homeland Security. (2016). *Yearbook of immigration statistics*. Retrieved from https://www.dhs.gov/immigration-statistics/yearbook

Watermeyer, B., & Gorgens, T. (2014). Disability and internalized oppression. In E. J. R. David (Ed.), *Internalized oppression: The psychology of marginalized groups* (pp. 253–280). New York, NY: Springer Publishing.

White, K. (2002). *An introduction to the sociology of health and illness*. Thousand Oaks, CA: Sage.

World Health Organization. (2011). *Mercury in skin lightening products*. Retrieved from http://www.who.int/ipcs/assessment/public_health/mercury_flyer.pdf

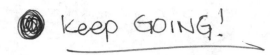

CHAPTER 4

The Evolution of Oppression: From Blatant to Subtle, to Blatant Again?

Most people in the United States can probably identify blatant forms of oppression. Consider Figure 4.1, for example, which is a photo that was taken at a softball field in Wellsville, NY, in November 2016. What do you think of it?

If you are like most people, when you see an image like Figure 4.1, you are likely to readily identify it as racist and inappropriate. This is because we have developed a consensus in our society about what is acceptable discourse in public and what is not, and for the most part, we have agreed that blatant, offensive rhetoric like this is unacceptable. In other words, we have established **social norms**—standards of acceptable and unacceptable attitudes and behaviors based on the values of one's group. In this case, we as a society have developed norms against the overt expression of discrimination. This has been demonstrated by experimental research. For instance, Crandall, Eshleman, and O'Brien (2002) examined people's expression of prejudice toward 105 different social groups (e.g., Black Americans, Native Americans, elderly people, Jews, homeless people, deaf people, gay soldiers, feminists, people on Medicare, racists, rapists, illegal immigrants, gang members, rednecks) and found that the participants adhered closely to social norms (i.e., socially expected behavior) when "expressing prejudice, evaluating scenarios of discrimination, and reacting to hostile jokes" (p. 359). That is, their findings seem to suggest that people tend to suppress prejudicial attitudes in order to conform to perceived social norms regarding the appropriateness (or inappropriateness) of expressing such prejudice.

Crandall et al.'s (2002) series of studies also suggest that as people mature and as cultural norms become increasingly negative toward blatant

FIGURE 4.1   Make America White again (Buncombe, 2016). Photo by Brian Quinn of the Wellsville Daily Reporter.

expressions of prejudices against various social groups (e.g., people of color, Muslims, people who are lesbian, gay, bisexual, transgender, and queer), people tend to "become motivated and skilled at suppressing inappropriate forms of prejudice" (p. 367). For example, if an adult public figure (whom we assume as "mature") in the year 2017 (a time in history when, presumably, there is a strong social norm against blatant oppression) said "Make America White again!" in a speech while wearing a shirt with a swastika on it, we can assume that many people would be outraged because such blatant expressions of oppression are not what we expect of a mature person in the year 2017. That is, such behavior is not in accordance with social norms! The social trend in the past few decades would suggest this outrage as research indicates that blatant forms of discrimination have decreased in frequency and intensity since the civil rights movement of the 1960s (e.g., Dovidio & Gaertner, 2000; McConahay, 1986; Steele, 1997; Sue & Sue, 2007; Sue et al., 2007). Indeed, scholars have described a general drift away from blatant forms of oppressive messages toward more subtle, covert, hidden, and difficult-to-detect expressions of hostility against marginalized social groups (Wong, Derthick, David, Saw, & Okazaki, 2013).

To this end, as we continue with our efforts to better understand social group oppression, this chapter provides an overview of how oppression has evolved over time due to changing social norms: from overt, blatant, obvious, and explicit forms to more covert, subtle, concealed,

"social group oppression"

and implicit forms—and perhaps back again. Let us begin with overt forms of oppression.

▪ OVERT OPPRESSION

Overt oppression can be defined as "unequal and harmful treatment of [marginalized groups] that is readily apparent" (Benokraitis & Feagin, 1986, p. 30). Many of the examples provided as historical oppression in Chapter 3 may be considered as overt forms of oppression, because many cases of oppression in the past are now perceived as blatant and clearly identifiable as oppression. For instance, the enslavement, lynchings, and beatings of Black people during the 1600s to the 1800s are clear examples of blatant—even brutal—racial oppression. Other examples of blatant oppression in history include the colonization and genocide of America's indigenous peoples, the segregation of public services during the Jim Crow era, "redlining" of neighborhoods (i.e., banks who automatically reject loans for properties that are located in predominantly Black neighborhoods, which are encircled in red ink on maps used by the banks), the apartheid in South Africa, the Jewish Holocaust, the Japanese American internment during World War II, the forced deportation of Mexican Americans in the 1930s, the use of conversion therapy to "cure" gay people of homosexuality, the prohibition of women from owning property and from voting, and the forced sterilization of people with disabilities.

Our use of historical examples for overt oppression is not to say, however, that blatant hostility toward various social groups no longer exists, as evidenced by the image we presented in the beginning of the chapter. Indeed, the Southern Poverty Law Center (SPLC), an organization that tracks and catalogues hate crimes, counted over 1,000 incidents of overt racist, sexist, xenophobic, homophobic, and transphobic incidents in just 1 month following the 2016 presidential election (SPLC, 2016). For example, immediately following the election, there were multiple incidents of students telling their peers (and even teachers) that they should be deported, groups of students chanting "Build the Wall!" to taunt their Latino/a classmates, people forcibly pulling off women's hijab, and dozens of hateful vandalisms that say things like "Black lives don't matter and neither does your vote!" Indeed, despite the general trend of decreased blatant oppression over the past few decades (Sue et al., 2007), reports like the one from SPLC seem to indicate that *overt and blatant oppression have potentially increased in recent months*. Comedian Aziz Ansari provided a lighthearted, yet poignant perspective on the apparent recent rise in overt forms of oppression when he performed on *Saturday Night Live* on January 21, 2017, explaining that the election of Donald Trump has most likely emboldened people to once again behave in overtly discriminatory ways toward others (Kelly, Schneider, King, & Briganti, 2017). As noted by Derthick (2015), it is important to note that these blatant forms of hostility occur frequently in the lives of people who are members of marginalized groups. For instance, 96% of African Americans (Klonoff & Landrine, 1999), 98% of Asian Americans (Alvarez, Juang, & Liang, 2006), and 99% of women (Klonoff & Landrine, 1995) report experiencing discrimination, and that these experiences are harmful (discussed in more detail in Chapter 6).

■ COVERT OPPRESSION

In the field of psychology and other social sciences, overt forms of oppression were the primary focus in studies related to oppression (e.g., prejudice, stereotypes, racism) until around the 1990s, when scholars began attempting to define and understand a trend they were noticing: society's seeming drift away from overt discrimination toward what researchers called "covert discrimination" (overt and covert oppression, along with other forms of oppression, are summarized in Table 4.1). By the 1990s, social norms seem to have changed toward regarding overt forms of discrimination as unacceptable, leading many people to hide or "cover" oppressive attitudes they may hold. Thus, many people may have resorted to **covert oppression**, which "involves engaging in unequal treatment of [members of marginalized groups] in a hidden or clandestine manner" (Swim & Cohen, 1997, p. 104). For example, modern-day companies or businesses might have an *overt* policy of nondiscrimination; that is, they may have written policies against discrimination and they may even claim to "value diversity." Nevertheless, such a company may still have supervisors who do not interview applicants with "ethnic-sounding" or female names. In this example, the supervisors or hiring authorities may not openly discuss this informal and personal policy; in fact they might pride themselves openly about their nondiscrimination practices! Nevertheless, their covert (and private) attitude and behavior—which occurs behind closed doors—are discriminatory in nature and perpetuate oppression by limiting access to certain jobs for members of marginalized social groups.

Empirical research suggests that covert discriminatory practices in various settings—such as in hiring decisions as described above—seem

TABLE 4.1   Different Manifestations of Oppression

Manifestation of Oppression	Brief Description
Overt	Blatant, obvious, clear, unambiguous (e.g., typically, historical oppression such as slavery, genocide, apartheid)
Covert	Hidden, concealed, covered, kept in secret or "behind closed doors" because oppression is socially unacceptable
Modern	Effortfully denied or qualified, justified or rationalized, and covered or hidden only from people who may be offended, but disclosed to people who are assumed to "get it" and are deemed "safe"; symbolic oppression
Subtle	Less obvious, less clear, less noticeable, and more easily justified, rationalized, or denied; More "in-group" preference as opposed to overt "out-group" hostility; aversive oppression
Implicit bias	Automatically activated oppressive thoughts and attitudes toward individuals because of their social group membership; may exist and operate outside of awareness, intention, or control, and may lead to oppressive behavior
Microaggressions	Intentional or unintentional statements, actions, and physical contexts (e.g., buildings, posters, flags) that communicate hostile, derogatory, inferiorizing, or "othering" messages about oppressed social groups; synthesized modern and subtle forms of oppression into a unified conceptual model

[handwritten annotation next to "Modern" row: —"Just a Joke"]

to be common. For instance, a study by Berterand and Mullainathan (2003) found that—although the contents of the fake resumes they sent to potential employers were identical—resumes with "White-sounding" names (e.g., Emily or Greg) received 50% more callbacks for interviews than resumes with "Black-sounding" names (e.g., Lakisha or Jamal). A similar example is research by Moss-Racusin, Dovidio, Brescoll, Graham, and Handelsman (2012) who found that job applicants for a laboratory manager position were rated as less competent and were offered a lower starting salary when the name on the application was a female name compared to when the name was male, even though the applications were identical! Another similar example is research by Oreopoulos (2011) and colleagues (Banerjee, Reitz, & Oreopoulos, 2017) who found that job applicants with "Anglo-sounding" names (e.g., Greg Smith, Emily Martin, Mathew Brown, Michael Wilson, Alison Johnson) were 28% to 39% more likely to get callbacks for interviews compared to applicants with "Asian-sounding" names (i.e., names of

Asian Indian, Pakistani, or Chinese origin such as Samir Sharma, Rabab Saeed, Chaudhry Mohammad, Maya Kumar, Xiuying Zhang, or Yong Zhang) even when all the qualifications listed on the job applications were the same across all applicants.

A MAN SAYING "Bitch", but doesn't want to seem SEXIST.

■ **MODERN OPPRESSION**

Similar to covert oppression, the term **modern oppression** refers to people hiding their prejudiced or oppressive attitudes and revealing them only in circumstances they consider as "safe" or when their biased behaviors could be attributed to something else other than discrimination based on social group membership (Swim & Cohen, 1997). An example of modern discrimination is when a male employee calls an assertive female supervisor a "bitch," but only in the presence of his male coworkers who he perceives will "get it." The male employee would likely not say this to his female supervisor's face, but feels comfortable to do so in private or in the presence of other people he considers as "safe" because he does not want to be perceived as sexist. In fact, he may even believe that sexism is wrong, but argue that sexism is no longer a problem today; thus, he may argue that this particular case with his supervisor is not sexism. The male employee may not see himself as sexist or his behavior as sexist, and instead might argue that his hostility was not about his female supervisor's gender even though the word "bitch" is specifically used to punish, humiliate, dehumanize, and target women—particularly women who embody confidence, assertiveness, decisiveness, and power.

example ↙

It is important to note that individuals who engage in modern forms of discrimination do so consciously and intentionally. They know that their behaviors may be considered as discriminatory and that they may contribute to the continued oppression of marginalized social groups, which is why they deliberately and effortfully attempt to hide, justify, or deny their actions. In other words, perpetrators of modern discrimination cover, rationalize, or even qualify ("I'm not racist but . . ." or "I don't have anything against gay people, but . . .") their actions because (a) they know their behavior is socially unacceptable; (b) they may be unaware of the oppressive nature of their words and behaviors; and/or (c) they conflict with what they say they believe (e.g., equality; Derthick, 2015; Swim & Cohen, 1997). For example, Annie remembers a time when some people with whom she was having dinner started remarking on the fireplace and how impressive the fire was—nicknaming the fireplace "Auschwitz." When Annie raised an objection and pointed out that Auschwitz is a symbol *oppression can be fixed if you just work hard enough & get yourself out of a bad situation*

of genocide against an entire race of people (Jews during the Holocaust) and that making jokes about it was not appropriate, the dinner guests first laughed off the accusation—assuming perhaps that Annie was "safe" and that she'll "get it." However, when Annie persisted, the dinner guests became angry, defensive, argued that they are not anti-Semitic, and that their nicknaming of the fireplace as Auschwitz was "just a joke."

A specific example of modern oppression is **symbolic oppression**, which is when prejudice against social groups is framed, not as bias against such social groups but instead as lack of adherence to traditional American values (Kinder & Sears, 1981). In the U.S. context, for instance, oppression is embedded in dominant societal morals and values such as individualism, self-reliance, and hard work, all of which are embodied by the common saying "pull yourself up by your bootstraps!" The sentiment behind this very American saying is that if you are experiencing difficulties in life, then you are responsible for rallying whatever resources you might have at your disposal and figuring out how to overcome any obstacles in your path. The premise of this "argument" is that all people have equal access to resources (with which they can avoid difficulties in the first place, if they make the right choices) and that all people face the same barriers or obstacles regardless of social group membership. Thus, in this case, symbolic oppression is when bias against certain social groups is framed as a lack of adherence to the American values of individualism, self-reliance, effort, determination, and hard work.

what fuels this way of thinking

Using racial oppression as an example, the assumption of modern oppressors is that a Black male has the same opportunity for success as does a White male. If the Black male experiences difficulties (e.g., being arrested), they are likely perceived as being due to poor choices he has made, with no regard for systemic racial oppression (e.g., police biases against Black people), *because modern oppression assumes that oppression is a thing of the past and is no longer a problem.* The assumption is that all a Black person needs to do in order to succeed is use whatever resources he has (pull himself up by his bootstraps) and stop depending on "handouts." Modern racists who use symbolic oppression may say something like "I'm not racist, but most Black people just need to go look for a job, work hard, and stop depending on food stamps," but only to people who they feel are "safe," would "get it," and not perceive them as racist. In this example, the modern racist has **qualified or denied** ("I'm not racist . . ."), **rationalized or justified** (i.e., reframed anti-Black bias as concern for loss of American values like hard work and self-sufficiency), and **partly covered** (i.e., disclosed only to "safe" people who will not perceive them as racist) their oppressive attitude, belief, and statement. Indeed, as Kinder and Sears (1981) explained, "Whites may feel that people should be rewarded on their merits, which in turn should be based on hard work and diligent services; hence, symbolic racism should find its most vociferous expression on political issues that involve 'unfair' government assistance to blacks" (p. 416) such as affirmative action policies, minority hiring practices, and programs that are designed to address social inequalities.

■ SUBTLE OPPRESSION

Similar to covert and modern oppression—both of which developed out of contemporary social norms that propagate the unacceptability of stereotypes, prejudices, and discriminatory behaviors based on social group membership—many forms of oppression today have evolved to become subtle. **Subtle oppression** involves "openly unequal and harmful treatment of [marginalized social groups]" which goes "unnoticed because it is perceived to be customary or normal behavior" (Swim & Cohen, 1997). Perpetrators of subtle discrimination often endorse beliefs in equality among different groups of people (often verbally), but their behaviors may nevertheless still be influenced by biases they may not even know they hold. Thus, although unintended—or perhaps sometimes even well intended—people may still end up behaving differently or unfairly toward people or groups against whom they hold biases.

For example, a study by Butler and Geis (1990) showed that while men and women reported holding equalitarian beliefs about male and female leaders, their nonverbal and unconscious behaviors suggested otherwise. In their experiment, the researchers asked participants to report the extent to which they may hold sex bias by indicating their level of agreement on statements such as "Although women may appear as qualified as men, they seldom are on matters that really count, and therefore should not receive the high salaries needed to attract the most competent men" and "Although women are as good or better than men at many occupations, group problem solving is not one of them." Then, the researchers had either a male or female lead a discussion group for the study participants who did not know that their nonverbal (e.g., facial expressions) behaviors toward their group leaders were being observed and recorded behind a one-way mirror. Butler and Geis found that participants reported no sex bias, even renouncing it. However, although male and female group leaders followed the exact same script during the discussions, the female leaders received fewer pleased and positive responses—and more displeased and negative responses—from the participants than male leaders offering the same contributions. Thus, research seems to suggest that female leaders—especially assertive ones—tend to elicit more negative reactions or less positive reactions from people than an equally competent male, even though the same people may (perhaps even genuinely or honestly) report that they believe in equality and that they hold no bias against women!

Another example of subtle sexism is a common occurrence described by Nancy Pelosi in the documentary *Miss Representation* (Abeles et al., 2011). She recalled how, when she was campaigning for office, she was asked by dozens of reporters and news outlets (perhaps even well intentioned) about who would take care of her children if she were elected. She said, "of course, it's one of those questions that I don't think a man has ever been asked when he is running for office." In this way, *subtle oppression differs from covert and modern oppression in that perpetrators of subtle oppression are often not aware their words or actions support discriminatory beliefs and practices.* Nevertheless, although it may be unintended (perhaps even well intended), subtle oppression still leads to different treatment of individuals because of their social group membership, invalidates marginalized social groups, dismisses their contributions and accomplishments, and limits their effectiveness in social, educational, and professional settings (Benokraitis, 1997; Nielsen, 2002; Watkins et al., 2006).

A specific example of subtle oppression is **aversive oppression**, when individuals express bias toward members of marginalized social groups through a tendency to feel disgust, fear, discomfort, and other negative emotions or attitudes, as opposed to automatically having more positive, happy, hopeful, and other pleasant feelings toward members of their own group (Dovidio & Gaertner, 2004). Thus, *aversive oppression may be understood as more "in-group" preference and "out-group" discomfort, instead of overt "out-group" derogation.* For example, patients may prefer a White doctor over a person of color, but if pressed to explain why, they may be unable to articulate what is motivating their preference. Another example is when White people—even those who vehemently claim to believe in equality and to be not racist—end up crossing to the other side of the street when they see that they are about to walk past peoples of color, or when they automatically clutch or hold their bags, purses, or belongings—or suddenly lock their vehicle's doors—when they see peoples of color approaching. Again, although it may operate outside of people's awareness and although it may be unintentional, aversive oppression still communicates—in a subtle, nonverbal, and less obvious manner—a message of hostility, discomfort, fear, or "otherness" to members of marginalized social groups.

■ IMPLICIT PREJUDICE

One way to think about aversive oppression, which is an example of subtle oppression, is through a social cognition lens. The social cognition literature in psychology suggests that there are two types of cognitions or thoughts—conscious and unconscious (Greenwald & Banaji, 1995). Conscious thoughts are ones that we are aware of, can control, manipulate, and evaluate. In contrast, unconscious thoughts occur automatically and may not be as available to introspection, critical evaluation, or deliberate suppression. Thus, unconscious thoughts may exist and influence us implicitly; that is, they exist and may affect us even if we are not aware of them. Greenwald and Banaji stated that the "signature of implicit cognition is that traces of past experience affect some performance, even though earlier experience is not remembered . . . it is unavailable to self-report or introspection" (pp. 4–5). Thus, because of our oppressive environment, our experiences in our society may lead to the development of unconscious—or implicit—thoughts or attitudes that are biased toward certain social groups. These **implicit prejudices** "are manifest as actions or judgments that are under the control of automatically activated evaluation, without the performer's awareness . . ." (Greenwald, McGhee, & Schwartz, 1998, p. 1464). Thus, many people may not identify that they hold negative attitudes or thoughts (stereotypes and prejudices) toward other people, which may influence their behaviors in subtle ways (Banaji & Greenwald, 1994)—behaviors that may be seen as examples of subtle or aversive oppression.

The existence and seeming growth of subtle forms of oppression are a clear indication that oppression is still around, despite (or perhaps because of) the social unacceptability of oppression. Even further, the fact that many people still end up behaving in oppressive ways—or still find ways to behave in oppressive ways despite social pressures not to—suggests that many people may still hold oppressive attitudes and beliefs within them. Whether we know it or not, or whether we acknowledge it or not, Banaji and Greenwald (2016) explain that all people have "blindspots," which are the implicit biases hidden in our unconscious but nevertheless influence our behaviors. These blindspots influence our behaviors toward things, people, situations, and social groups, but we are often oblivious to that influence (Banaji & Greenwald, 2016). Using methods such as the **implicit association test** (Greenwald et al., 1998) and **lexical decision priming tasks** (for a review, see Fazio, 2001), both of which capture how quickly people react to certain stimuli (e.g., the words "ugly" or "beautiful") in association with certain social groups (e.g., faces of Black people or White people), research suggests that many of the decisions we make on a daily basis about people are influenced by automatically activated biased attitudes. Thus, *although people may in fact genuinely believe that they are well-intentioned and good people, oppressive attitudes about certain social groups may still exist within them* outside of their awareness, intention, and control.

■ MICROAGGRESSIONS

Back in the 1970s, professor and psychiatrist Chester M. Pierce (1974) used the term "microaggressions" to describe

> . . . assaults to Black dignity and Black home (that) are incessant and cumulative. . . . In fact, the major vehicle for racism in this country is offenses done to Blacks by Whites in this sort of gratuitous, never-ending way. These offenses are microaggressions. Almost all Black–White racial interactions are characterized by White put-downs, done in automatic, pre-conscious, or unconscious fashion. These mini-disasters accumulate. It is the sum total of multiple microaggressions by Whites to Blacks that has pervasive effect to the stability and peace of this world. (p. 515)

Building on Pierce's description, Sue and colleagues (2007) synthesized the literature on modern oppression (McConahay, 1986), symbolic oppression (Sears, 1988), subtle oppression (Dovidio, Gaertner, Kawakami, & Hodson, 2002), and implicit bias (Greenwald & Banaji, 1995) and developed an integrated conceptualization of nonblatant forms of oppression. In their highly influential work, Sue and colleagues defined **microaggressions** as "brief and commonplace daily verbal, behavioral, and environmental indignities, whether intentional or unintentional, that communicate hostile, derogatory or negative racial slights and insults to the target person or group" (p. 273).

Sue and colleagues' (2007) theoretical framework included a delineation of three types of microaggressions: (a) microassaults, (b) microinsults, and (c) microinvalidations. Out of the three, **microassaults** most closely

OVERT

resemble the more traditional, overt forms of discrimination in that they are characterized by openly hostile, insulting, and discriminatory behavior. Examples include the use of derogatory epithets, demeaning jokes, and preferential treatment for members of dominant groups. However, microassaults differ from more traditional, overt forms of discrimination in that microassault perpetrators often attempt to hide their behavior by, for example, telling demeaning jokes only around friends who share their perspectives in an attempt to avoid social judgment or retaliation. Microassaults are sometimes difficult to detect because of their clandestine nature, but they are perpetrated consciously and deliberately. In this way, microassaults are most similar to the concepts of covert and modern oppression.

COVERT

Microinsults are more difficult to detect and identify than microassaults, because they most often occur outside of the conscious awareness of the perpetrator, and many times even the recipient. Nevertheless, they still communicate demeaning messages of inferiority and undesirability to the recipient. In this way, microinsults are similar to the concept of subtle oppression. Examples of microinsults include ascription of less intelligence based on a person's social group membership (e.g., repeatedly failing to ask a person of color to be the lead on a project), treatment of a person as a second-class citizen (e.g., giving a person of color poor service at a restaurant), and pathologizing the culture of a social group (e.g., expressing disgust to certain food with which one may be unfamiliar but is considered a delicacy in another culture; Sue et al., 2007). Similarly, **microinvalidations** are unconscious messages that communicate invalidation, minimization, or negation of the reality of an individual's experiences as a member of a marginalized social group. Microinvalidations involve denying the reality that oppression still exists in society. Some examples include believing in the myth of meritocracy (i.e., systemic barriers based on group membership do not exist and everyone can succeed as long as they work hard enough) and subscribing to a **color-blind ideology** (e.g., "I don't see color" or "all people are the same"), which on the surface may look like a commitment to egalitarianism but in actuality operates to invalidate the uniqueness, distinctiveness, and diversity of people.

COVERT

Although the three types of microaggressions often occur during interpersonal interactions, microaggressions may also be encountered through various physical contexts we typically encounter (e.g., schools, workplaces, recreation facilities, hospitals, clinics, public spaces). One example of **environmental microaggressions** is a college or university that features mostly White, male students in their advertising (i.e., sending the message that if you are not White or male, you are not wanted here). Another example is a health clinic that stocks informational pamphlets related to safe sex only for monogamous, heterosexual couples (i.e., sending the message that only certain types of people should be having sex). Another example of environmental microaggressions is when a restaurant (or other public place) has diaper changing stations only in the women's restroom (i.e., sending the message that only women should be changing diapers). In addition to a setting's physical features, environmental microaggressions can also refer to discrimination and marginalization at the institutional level in the forms of policy, procedure, and law. Some examples include the denial of protection from discrimination for sexual- and gender-minority individuals, couples, and families; voter identification mandates that target primarily people of color and individuals of low socioeconomic status; and the lack of accessible public spaces for individuals with disabilities. Over the past decade, research seems to suggest that microaggressions are salient for various marginalized social groups such as African Americans (e.g., Sue et al., 2008), Asian Americans (e.g., Sue, Bucceri, Lin, Nadal, & Torino, 2009), indigenous peoples (e.g., Clark, Spanierman, Reed, Soble, & Cabana, 2011), lesbians, gay, and bisexual individuals (e.g., Nadal et al., 2011), transgender individuals (e.g., Nadal, Skolnik, & Wong, 2012), and women (e.g., Capodilupo et al., 2010; Derthick, 2015).

■ FROM BLATANT TO SUBTLE, AND BACK AGAIN?

As you can see, the nature and expression of social group oppression has changed over time: from overt, blatant, explicit, and easy-to-detect words and actions to more subtle, ambiguous, and difficult-to-detect communications of hostility, derogation, or exclusion. These more contemporary forms of oppression, which may be conceptualized under the microaggressions framework, have unique potential to have negative consequences for various marginalized social groups that experience them constantly (discussed in Chapter 6). It is important to understand that subtle forms of oppression can occur outside the conscious awareness of both perpetrators and targets, so the seemingly best way to fight these forms of oppression is to bring them into our personal and collective consciousness. We must include them in public discourse and formal education, so all of us who have these blindspots can be aware of their existence and impact, and collectively come up with ways to address them.

The seemingly growing awareness and emphasis on subtle forms of oppression today, however, should not be taken to mean that overt or blatant forms of oppression no longer take place in our contemporary society. In fact, as previously mentioned, there are some indications that social norms may be changing yet again toward a zeitgeist that is more "tolerant" of clear, unconcealed, and deliberate forms of oppression (e.g., see SPLC, 2016). For example, approximately 60 million American voters were able to look past Donald Trump's blatant and repeated displays of racism, xenophobia, sexism, and ableism and still elect him as president of the United States in the 2016 elections. Indeed, oppression—in all of its manifestations—continues to be alive and well in our modern-day world. In the next chapter, we discuss how widespread and embedded oppression is by exploring how it exists and operates at all levels of society—the interpersonal level, the institutional level, and the internalized level.

REFERENCES

Abeles, V., Allbright, T., Atlas, J., Brubaker, D., Thompkins-Buell, S., Costonazo, J., . . . Wilsey, D. (Producers), & Siebel-Newsome, J., & Acquaro, K. (Directors). (2011). *Miss representation* [Motion picture]. USA: Girls' Club Entertainment.

Alvarez, A. N., Juang, L., & Liang, C. T. H. (2006). Asian Americans and racism: When bad things happen to "model minorities." *Cultural Diversity and Ethnic Minority Psychology, 12*(3), 477–492.

Banaji, M. R., & Greenwald, A. G. (1994). Implicit stereotyping and unconscious prejudice. In M. P. Zanna & J. M. Olsen (Eds.), *The psychology of prejudice: The Ontario Symposium* (Vol. 7, pp. 55–76). Hillsdale, NJ: Erlbaum.

Banaji, M. R., & Greenwald, A. G. (2016). *Blindspots: Hidden biases of good people.* New York, NY: Bantam.

Banerjee, R., Reitz, J. G., & Oreopoulos, P. (2017). *Do large employers treat racial minorities more fairly? A new analysis of Canadian field experiment data.* Retrieved from http://www.hireimmigrants.ca/wp-content/uploads/Final-Report-Which-employers-discriminate-Banerjee-Reitz-Oreopoulos-January-25-2017.pdf

Benokraitis, N. V. (1997). *Subtle sexism: Current practice and prospects for change.* Thousand Oaks, CA: Sage.

Benokraitis, N. V., & Feagin, J. R. (1986). *Modern sexism: Blatant, subtle, and covert discrimination.* Englewood Cliffs, NJ: Prentice Hall.

Berterand, M., & Mullainathan, S. (2003). Are Emily and Greg more employable than Lakisha and Jamal?: A field experiment on labor market discrimination. *American Economic Review, 94*(4), 991–1013. doi:10.1257/0002828042002561

Buncombe, A. (2016). *Racism in the US: More than 200 incidents of harassment reported since Donald Trump won the presidency.* Retrieved from *Independent* website: http://www.independent.co.uk/news/world/americas/us-elections/racism-in-the-us-more-than-200-incidents-of-harassment-reported-since-donald-trump-won-presidency-a7413881.html

Butler, D., & Geis, F. L. (1990). Nonverbal affect responses to male and female leaders: Implications for leadership evaluations. *Journal of Personality and Social Psychology, 58*, 48–59. doi:10.1037/0022-3514.58.1.48

Capodilupo, C. C., Nadal, K. L., Corman, L., Hamit, S., Lyons, O. B., & Weinberg, A. (2010). The manifestation of gender microaggressions. In D. W. Sue (Ed.), *Microaggressions and marginality: Manifestation, dynamics, and impact* (pp. 193–216). Hoboken, NJ: Wiley.

Clark, D. A., Spanierman, L. B., Reed, T. D., Soble, J. R., & Cabana, S. (2011). Documenting weblog expressions of racial microaggressions that target American Indians. *Journal of Diversity in Higher Education, 4*(1), 39–50. doi:10.1037/a0021762

Crandall, C. S., Eshleman, A., & O'Brien, L. (2002). Social norms and the expression of prejudice: The struggle for internalization. *Journal of Personality and Social Psychology, 82*(3), 359–378. doi:10.1037/0022-3514.82.3.359

Derthick, A. O. (2015). *The Sexist MESS: Development and initial validation of the Sexist Microaggressions Experiences and Stress Scale and the relationship of sexist microaggressions and women's mental health* (Doctoral dissertation). Available from ProQuest Dissertations and Theses Global. (No. 3470179)

Dovidio, J. F., & Gaertner, S. L. (2000). Aversive racism and selective decisions: 1989–1999. *Psychological Science, 11*, 315–319.

Dovidio, J. F., & Gaertner, S. L. (2004). Aversive racism. *Advances in Experimental Social Psychology, 36*, 1–52.

Dovidio, J. F., Gaertner, S. L., Kawakami, K., & Hodson, G. (2002). Why can't we just get along? Interpersonal biases and interracial distrust. *Cultural Diversity and Ethnic Minority Psychology, 8*, 88–102.

Fazio, R. H. (2001). On the automatic activation of associated evaluations: An overview. *Cognition and Emotion, 15*(2), 115–141.

Greenwald, A. G., & Banaji, M. R. (1995). Implicit social cognition: Attitudes, self-esteem, and stereotypes. *Psychological Review, 102*, 4–27.

Greenwald, A. G., McGhee, D. E., & Schwartz, J. L. K. (1998). Measuring individual differences in implicit cognition: The Implicit Association Test. *Journal of Personality and Social Psychology, 74*, 1464–1480.

Kelly, C., Schneider, S. (Writers), King, D. R., & Briganti, P. (Directors). (2017). *Aziz Ansari/Big Sean* [Television series episode]. In Broadway Video & SNL Studios (Producers), *Saturday Night Live*. New York, NY: NBC.

Kinder, D. R., & Sears, D. O. (1981). Prejudice and politics: Symbolic racism versus racial threats to the good life. *Journal of Personality and Social Psychology, 40*(3), 414–431.

Klonoff, E. A., & Landrine, H. (1995). The Schedule of Sexist Events: A measure of lifetime and recent sexist discrimination in women's lives. *Psychology of Women Quarterly, 19*(4), 439–472.

Klonoff, E. A., & Landrine, H. (1999). Cross-validation of the Schedule of Racist Events. *Journal of Black Psychology, 25*, 231–255.

McConahay, J. B. (1986). Modern racism, ambivalence, and the Modern Racism Scale. In J. F. Dovidio & S. L. Gaertner (Eds.), *Prejudice, discrimination and racism* (pp. 91–126). Orlando, FL: Academic Press.

Moss-Racusin, C. A., Dovidio, J. F., Brescoll, V. L., Graham, M. J., & Handelsman, J. (2012). Science faculty's subtle gender biases favor male students. *Proceedings of the National Academy of Sciences, 109*(41), 16474–16479.

Nadal, K. L., Issa, M.-A., Leon, J., Meterko, V., Widerman, M., & Wong, Y. (2011). Sexual orientation microaggressions: "Death by a thousand cuts" for lesbian, gay, and bisexual youth. *Journal of LGBT Youth, 8*(3), 234–259.

Nadal, K. L., Skolnik, A., & Wong, Y. (2012). Interpersonal and systemic microaggressions toward transgender people: Implications for counseling. *Journal of LGBT Issues in Counseling, 6*(1), 55–82.

Nielsen, L. B. (2002). Subtle, pervasive, harmful: Racist and sexist remarks in public as hate speech. *Journal of Social Issues, 58,* 265–280. doi:10.1111/1540-4560.00260

Oreopoulos, P. (2011). Why do skilled immigrants struggle in the labor market? A field experiment with thirteen thousand resumes. *American Economic Journal: Economic Policy, 3*(4), 148–171.

Pierce, C. (1974). Psychiatric problems of the Black minority. In S. Arieti (Ed.), *American handbook of psychiatry* (pp. 512–523). New York, NY: Basic Books.

Sears, D. O. (1988). Symbolic racism. In P. Katz & D. Taylor (Eds.), *Eliminating racism: Profiles in controversy* (pp. 53–84). New York, NY: Plenum Press.

Southern Poverty Law Center Hatewatch. (2016, December 16). *Update: 1,094 bias-related incidents in the month following the election.* Retrieved from SPLC website: https://www.splcenter.org/hatewatch/2016/12/16/update-1094-bias-related-incidents-month-following-election

Steele, C. M. (1997). A threat in the air: How stereotypes shape intellectual identity and performance. *American Psychologist, 52,* 613–629.

Sue, D. W., Bucceri, J., Lin, A, I., Nadal, K. L., & Torino, G. C. (2009). Racial microaggressions and the Asian American experience. *Asian American Journal of Psychology, S*(1), 88–101. doi:10.1037/1948-1985.S.1.88

Sue, D. W., Capodilupo, C. M., Torino, G. C., Bucceri, J. M., Holder, A. M. B., Nadal, K., & Esquilin, M. (2007). Racial microaggressions in everyday life: Implications for clinical practice. *American Psychologist, 62*(4), 271–286. doi:10.1037/0003-066X.62.4.271

Sue, D. W., Nadal, K. L., Capodilupo, C. M., Lin, A. I., Torino, G. C., & Rivera, D. P. (2008). Racial microaggressions against Black Americans: Implications for counseling. *Journal of Counseling & Development, 86*(3), 330–338. doi:10.1002/j.1556-6678.2008.tb00517.x

Sue, D. W., & Sue, D. (2007). *Counseling the culturally diverse: Theory and practice* (5th ed.). Hoboken, NJ: Wiley.

Swim, J. K., & Cohen, L. L. (1997). Overt, covert, and subtle sexism: A comparison between the Attitudes toward Women and Modern Sexism Scales. *Psychology of Women Quarterly, 21*, 103–118. doi:10.1111/j.1471-6402.1997.tb00103.x

Watkins, M. B., Kaplan, S., Brief, A. P., Shull, A., Dietz, J., Mansfield, M.-T., & Cohen, R. (2006). Does it pay to be sexist?: The relationship between modern sexism and career outcomes. *Journal of Vocational Behavior, 69*, 524–537. doi:10.1016/j.jvb.2006.07.004

Wong, G., Derthick, A. O., David, E. J. R., Saw, A., & Okazaki, S. (2013). The what, the why, and the how: A critical review of racial microaggressions research. *Race and Social Problems, 6*(2), 181–200.

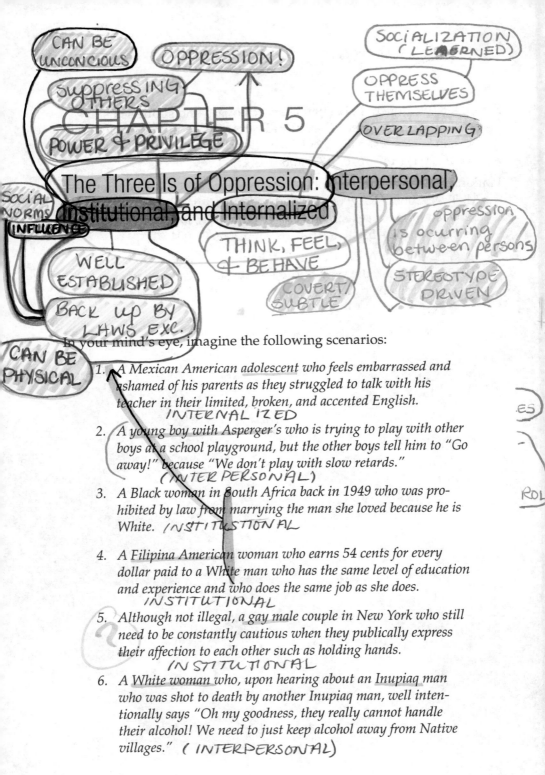

CAN BE UNCONCIOUS

OPPRESSION!

SOCIALIZATION (LEARNED)

SUPPRESSING OTHERS

OPPRESS THEMSELVES

POWER & PRIVILEGE

OVERLAPPING

SOCIAL NORMS

INFLUENCE

The Three Is of Oppression: Interpersonal, Institutional, and Internalized

oppression is ocurring between persons

THINK, FEEL, & BEHAVE

STEREOTYPE DRIVEN

WELL ESTABLISHED

COVERT/ SUBTLE

BACK UP BY LAWS EXC.

CAN BE PHYSICAL

In your mind's eye, imagine the following scenarios:

1. A Mexican American adolescent who feels embarrassed and ashamed of his parents as they struggled to talk with his teacher in their limited, broken, and accented English.
   INTERNALIZED

2. A young boy with Asperger's who is trying to play with other boys at a school playground, but the other boys tell him to "Go away!" because "We don't play with slow retards."
   (INTERPERSONAL)

3. A Black woman in South Africa back in 1949 who was pro- hibited by law from marrying the man she loved because he is White. INSTITUTIONAL

4. A Filipina American woman who earns 54 cents for every dollar paid to a White man who has the same level of education and experience and who does the same job as she does.
   INSTITUTIONAL

5. Although not illegal, a gay male couple in New York who still need to be constantly cautious when they publically express their affection to each other such as holding hands.
   INSTITUTIONAL

6. A White woman who, upon hearing about an Inupiaq man who was shot to death by another Inupiaq man, well inten- tionally says "Oh my goodness, they really cannot handle their alcohol! We need to just keep alcohol away from Native villages." (INTERPERSONAL)

WHAT LEVEL OF OPPRESSION ?!

7. *A man in India spending his hard-earned money to pay for treatments in a local skin-whitening clinic.*
   INTERNALIZED

8. *A mother in Canada who, while playing catch with her daughter, coaches her to "don't throw like a girl."*
   INTERNALIZED.

Although the scenarios above seem very wide-ranging, all of them actually have one thing in common: They are all examples of oppression. As we have learned so far, oppression of various groups (Chapter 2) has been happening all over the world throughout human history (Chapter 3). We have also learned that oppression can exist and operate subtly or blatantly (Chapter 4). Now, as suggested by the scenarios provided above, we are adding yet another dimension to the construct of oppression: *Oppression can exist and operate at the interpersonal level, the institutional level, and the internalized level.* In the given scenarios, you can probably now identify which ones are examples of subtle oppression and which ones are examples of blatant oppression. But can you identify which are examples of what level of oppression? If you considered numbers 2 and 6 as interpersonal; numbers 3, 4, and 5 as institutional; and numbers 1, 7, and 8 as internalized, then you are correct! If you got a few or all of them wrong, however, do not fret; the three levels of oppression are complicated, interrelated, sometimes overlapping, and can be very perplexing. For example, if you considered scenarios 1 and 8 as interpersonal, then you are also correct! Confused? Well, hopefully this chapter will clarify the three levels of oppression a little bit better. Let us begin our exploration with interpersonal oppression.

WHAT IS INTERPERSONAL OPPRESSION?

When we think of racism, sexism, heterosexism, classism, and other forms of oppression, it is easier to think of interpersonal examples. We might think of a teacher who more closely monitors the behaviors of her Black, Latino, and Native students because she assumes they are more likely to misbehave. We might think of a man who feels disgust upon seeing two gay men kissing each other. We might think of an adolescent boy saying something very offensive and hurtful to an adolescent girl about her weight and how she looks. We might think of anti-Islam demonstrators denigrating Islam and its prophet Mohammed outside mosques. We might think of a wealthy, highly educated couple who refuse to allow their daughter to marry a man from a poor family, referring to him as "trailer trash." These are all examples of oppression operating on the interpersonal level because it involves relatively more powerful and privileged individuals (or persons) engaging in biased thoughts, attitudes, and behaviors toward other individuals. That is, the oppression is occurring between persons, hence the term "interpersonal."

As you might recall from Chapter 1, interpersonal oppression is driven by and expressed as stereotypes (biased thoughts or *Cognitions*), prejudices (biased attitudes or *Affect*), and discrimination (biased actions or *Behaviors*). Remember *Biased CAB!* You may also notice that stereotypes, prejudices, and discriminatory behaviors are factors that are "within," "of," or "by" an individual. That is, all three exist and operate on the individual level, something that an individual can possess, have, believe, feel, do, or enact. Historically, psychology has focused on studying phenomena on the individual level, and this individualistic tendency has extended to how the field approaches the constructs of stereotypes, prejudices, and discrimination. In fact, the field has been a leader in studying these constructs on the individual level as we now have developed countless tools to capture and quantify them (for a review, see Fiske & North, 2015). As a result, many studies in psychology utilize tools that simply ask participants what they think (stereotypes) and feel (prejudices) about, and how they behave (discrimination) toward, certain groups of people. For example, the Quick Discrimination Index (Ponteroto et al., 1995)—one of the more popular measures of people's beliefs and attitudes about race and gender—asks participants to indicate their level of agreement to statements such as "I would enjoy living in a neighborhood consisting of a racially diverse population (Asian, blacks, Latinos, whites)," "I would feel OK about my son or daughter dating someone from a different race," "I do think it is more appropriate for the mother of a newborn baby, rather than the father, to stay home with the baby (not work) during the first year," and "Generally speaking, men work harder than women."

As you may infer from the example items above, self-report measures of stereotypes, prejudices, and discrimination require a good amount of self-awareness, introspection, and honesty. It is important to point out, however, that the existence and operation of biased thoughts, attitudes, and behaviors may also be unintentional, subtle, and unconscious. Indeed, many people may not be aware that they hold stereotypes and prejudices against some groups; they may not know that their thoughts and attitudes are biased; or they can easily not admit or even lie about the extent to which they engage in stereotypical thoughts, prejudiced attitudes, and discriminatory behaviors. In such cases, psychology has developed ways that go "beyond questionnaires" (Okazaki, 2002) in order to capture subtle,

"LIKELY TO BE THE CASE THAT ALL OF US HOLD—INACCURATE GENERALIZATIONS + BIASED ATTITUDES THAT MAY LEAD US TO BEHAVE UNFAIRLY."

automatic, and possibly unconscious biases. Two popular examples of these methods are the Implicit Association Test (Greenwald, McGhee, & Schwartz, 1998) and the Subliminal Priming Tasks (Fazio, Jackson, Dunton, & Williams, 1995; described in Chapter 4). In addition to priming and implicit association studies providing evidence that biased thoughts and attitudes can exist and operate outside one's intention, awareness, or control—and how such biased thoughts and attitudes may lead to biased behaviors—these studies also suggest that such *biases can exist and automatically operate in all of us!* Because our learning and socialization experiences are probably incomplete, distorted, or inaccurate in some way, it is likely to be the case that all of us hold inaccurate generalizations (stereotypes) and biased attitudes (prejudices) that may lead us to behave unfairly (discrimination) toward certain groups of people!

VI

It is a normal function of our brain to organize our complex world into *mental schemas,* which is our general pattern of perceiving and making sense of the world. That is, as we grow and experience different people, feelings, events, places, and everything else in our world, our brains automatically organize them into categories and create or diminish links between such categories (Piaget, 1957). If our experiences of different people are limited, incomplete, or distorted, then our schemas—our learned automatic patterns of thoughts and attitudes—toward different groups of people are going to be biased in some way. In psychology and cognitive science, this is how stereotypes and prejudices may be formed (for a review, see Augoustinos & Walker, 1998). You may notice, however, that many of us do not have a lot of control over our socialization and learning experiences. For example, as children—which is when schemas begin to develop—where we live, the kinds of people to whom we are exposed, and the education we receive are largely if not completely determined by our parents. Even as adults, in many cases, where we end up living and the people to whom we become regularly exposed are largely determined by our jobs and where we can afford to live. What we are exposed to through various media is also not completely in our control. Thus, it is almost inevitable that all of us are going to have limited, incomplete, inaccurate, and distorted beliefs about some groups of people due to our learning experiences that were largely out of our control. Therefore, it seems to be the case that *all of us may hold some form of stereotypes and prejudices toward certain groups of people.*

SOME WHAT OUT OF CONTROL
* LIVED EXPERIENCES.

Although all of us may hold stereotypes and prejudices, research, however, suggests that such biases—as subtle, automatic, and seemingly unconscious as they may be—do not necessarily always result into

RESEARCH > SUCH BIAS THAT IS -SEEMINGLY
SUGGESTS DISTORTED FROM LIVED > UNCONSCIOUS/
EXP. OUT OF OUR CONTROL -SUBTLE + AUTOMATIC.

discriminatory behaviors (Gawronski & Bodenhausen, 2006). This is especially true if we are aware of the strong possibility that biases may exist and automatically operate within us, and we are cautious and careful not to have our behaviors be driven by such biases. In other words, biased thoughts and attitudes exist in all of us and such biases can lead us to behave in ways that are unfair, especially if we are not aware of our biases or if we deny their existence within us. Therefore, by becoming aware of our biases or at least by acknowledging the very strong possibility that we may have them, we are in a better position to keep such biases in check and make sure that our behaviors are not driven by biased thoughts and attitudes.

However, even if we are not able to keep our biases in check and they consequently result into discriminatory acts, it still does not necessarily equal oppression! In other words, although all of us may hold stereotypes and prejudices and engage in discriminatory behaviors, it does not automatically mean that all of us are oppressive of others. For instance, a Black person may disagree with the statement "I would feel OK about my son or daughter dating someone from a different race" and behave in biased ways against non-Black people, but this does not mean that the person is oppressing non-Black people. A White person who disagrees with such an item and acts on it, however, is participating in the oppression of peoples of color. Similarly, a woman might agree with the item "I do think it is more appropriate for the mother of a newborn baby, rather than the father, to stay home with the baby (not work) during the first year" and behave accordingly, suggesting that she holds stereotypical views of women and men, but it does not mean she is oppressing men. However, a man who agrees with the same statement and behaves accordingly is participating in the oppression of women. So now you might be asking yourself: How is this so? The answer to this question is: White people hold more power and privilege than peoples of color, and men hold more power and privileges than women.

As noted in Chapter 1, necessary components of oppression are *power* and *privilege*. Just because people may hold stereotypes and prejudices that may lead them to discriminate against some groups of people, their biased thoughts, attitudes, and actions are not oppression unless they are also members of the dominant group that holds power and privileges over the group against which they are biased. For example, a "middle class" person who thinks that all wealthy people are arrogant snobs, who feels disgusted about wealthy people because they are perceived as selfish, and who therefore chooses to avoid being around wealthy people

IMPORTANT !!!

is not oppressing (more specifically, not classist against) wealthy people because wealthy people hold more power and privileges than middle class people. Similarly, although a person with dwarfism may hold a stereotype about people without dwarfism (e.g., they are all ignorant) and consequently mistrust and avoid people without dwarfism, it does not mean that the little person is oppressing the rest of us because our society—our entire world—is dominated by and designed for people without dwarfism! Disliking or preferring persons because of their social group membership is rude, problematic, and can hurt people. However, thinking, feeling, and behaving in biased ways do not automatically mean oppression; the individual's biased opinions or behaviors must be backed up, legitimized, protected, and supported by institutions, policies, norms, standards, and assumptions—power and privilege—for the stereotypical beliefs, prejudiced attitudes, and discriminatory behaviors to become oppression. As we shared in Chapter 1, always remember that *Interpersonal Oppression = Biased CAB + PP, with PP representing power and privilege.*

This power and privilege inequality between groups of people is key especially when we are faced with claims such as **"reverse racism," "reverse sexism,"** and other forms of **"reverse oppression"** by people who hold more power and privileges (e.g., Christians claiming that their rights are being violated when LGBTQ people gain equal rights). For example, research suggests that about half of White Americans believe they are just as oppressed, perhaps even more oppressed, than peoples of color (Jones, Cox, Cooper, & Lienesch, 2015; Jones, Cox, & Navarro-Rivera, 2014). Similarly, many of us may have heard of men who complain about being victims of "reverse sexism," or who believe that women get more privileges than men. Such claims do not make sense, however, because the evidence is overwhelming that White people—especially White men— are provided with more power and privileges throughout the world (as discussed in detail in Chapter 2). Here is another example: Does it make sense for people with no mobility problems to accuse people with limited mobility (e.g., people who use wheelchairs) who fight for buildings to be constructed with wheelchair ramps and elevators as "ableist" or, more specifically, engaging in "reverse ableism"? It does not make sense to argue for "reverse ableism" because people without disabilities hold more power and privileges in our world. This logic is why *reverse oppression of any kind does not make sense and, therefore, does not exist.*

The power and privilege inequality is also key in understanding why even so-called **positive stereotypes** are problematic. Some examples include stereotyping Asian Americans as good at math, African

Americans as athletic, and Asian American women as submissive and obedient. With these stereotypes, an employer may be more likely to hire an Asian engineer; coaches may be more likely to seek out, train, and mentor Black athletes; and men may have a preference—an exoticizing and fetishizing one—for Asian women as romantic partners. As "positive" as these stereotypes may seem, however, the growing research on the concept of **stereotype threat** (Steele & Aronson, 1995) suggests that even positive stereotypes can lead to increased anxiety for people to either disconfirm or live up to the stereotype and, thus, lead to poorer performance (Cheryan & Bodenhausen, 2000). In addition, positive stereotypes are problematic because it is the powerful and privileged group that gets to define, categorize, and limit the humanity of other groups. The "good athlete" stereotype for African Americans, for instance, may limit their range of skills and, consequently, the range of their potential careers and lives. The "submissive and obedient" stereotype of Asian women has led to the creation of the "mail-order bride" industry that puts women at risk for exploitation, abuse, and violence. Thus, even with positive stereotypes, it is the powerful group that defines what another group is good at and should be and what their place in society is. All stereotypes, even positive ones, ignore the diversity and complexities of peoples, simplifying their experiences and humanity. In other words, *all stereotypes, even positive ones, are narrow, limited, and limiting, and therefore do not provide people the dignity of living the full range of possibilities human beings can be*—a range of possibilities that the dominant group is privileged to be afforded.

■ WHAT IS INSTITUTIONAL OPPRESSION?

As emphasized in the previous section, oppression would not exist if there were no imbalance of power and privilege between groups. This imbalance is depicted in Figure 5.1, where we see that the only—*but big*—difference between the agent and the target is that the agent has power and privilege to back up, support, and legitimize its biased thoughts, attitudes, and practices. That is, the only thing that makes the agent person or group more powerful and privileged are those dashed circles on its side! What, then, are those dashed circles? What provides some groups of people with more power and privileges than others? The answer is this: *Institutions.*

Briefly, **institutions** are well-established laws, practices, customs, beliefs, assumptions, patterns of behaviors, roles, and relationships that are automatically regarded as normal, expected, or fundamental parts

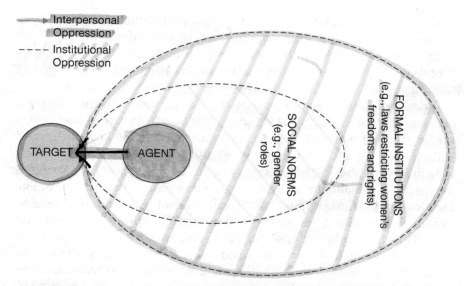

FIGURE 5.1   Power and privilege: The interactions between interpersonal and institutional oppression.

of a culture or society (Harvey, 1999; Young, 1990). Institutions can be physical "things" like organizations or governments and their policies and laws (e.g., using the "Robert's Rules of Order" for meetings and decision-making; a law preventing nonnative-born citizens from becoming president), and they can also be abstract constructs like traditions (e.g., giving gifts on Christmas), accepted attitudes and behaviors (e.g., marriage is between a man and a woman), or expected roles in society (e.g., women take care of children and manage the household; Asians cannot be professional athletes).

In the field of psychology, we refer to the informal or unwritten but widely accepted, expected, and normalized beliefs, attitudes, and behaviors of groups as **social norms** (Cialdini, 2007; Kahneman & Miller, 1986). Social norms determine, guide (sometimes even prescribe), control, and predict behaviors, rewarding those who follow the standards and punishing those who stray from them. Although most social norms are unwritten and informally enforced (e.g., giving a romantic partner a ring to signify engagement; regarding opposite-sex relationships or marriages as the "normal" type of relationship), social norms can also influence the creation of laws, policies, and reward-or-punishment structures. For example, the social norm that calls for separate restrooms for men and

SOCIAL NORMS > CAN INFLUENCE
        THE CREATION OF LAWS!

women has led to a law in North Carolina that requires individuals to use restrooms and changing facilities that correspond only to the sex on their birth certificates. In this and many other similar cases (e.g., laws prohibiting interracial marriages), we see that social norms can clearly become physical, concrete, and prescriptive formal institutions.

Institutions are created by people, and so people's values, worldviews, and standards are reflected by, drive, and influence the type of institutions that are created. For instance, if a group of people value knowledge and skills in farming, then they may create daily practices (e.g., bringing their kids to farms), physical institutions (e.g., a farming school), and policies (e.g., making it mandatory for kids to attend farming school) that promote farming and reward people who do well in farming. As you may now be thinking, what about people who do not value farming or people who would like to do other things? Indeed, people may have varying—many times even conflicting—values, worldviews, and standards. *So when the created institutions favor some people's values, worldviews, and standards more than others—sometimes even portraying some as legitimate, better, or superior while simultaneously denigrating others—then the created institutions are unfair because they provide some people with more power and privileges than others.* This is when institutions become oppressive. Figure 5.1 pictorially depicts how biased social norms and formalized institutions constitute institutional-level oppression.

As we shared in Chapter 1, *institutional oppression is when stereotypes, prejudices, and discrimination are expressed—whether intentionally or unintentionally, consciously or unconsciously, and overtly or covertly—through society's policies, laws, regulations, assumptions, standards, cultural norms, and practices.* An example of institutional oppression is how the U.S. educational system generally regards European history (e.g., the Renaissance period) and culture (e.g., Greek mythology, Shakespearean literature) as fundamental knowledge and whose inclusion in the curriculum is not faced by any resistance. In contrast, the inclusion of African history, Native ways of knowing, or any type of ethnic studies course into a school curriculum is met with extra scrutiny and regarded as "extra" or "supplemental." This imbalance between the value and legitimacy that is given to European history and culture versus how non-European history and culture is regarded privileges and benefits some people while simultaneously suppressing others; therefore, it is an example of institutional oppression.

It is important to note that oppression is not always consciously inflicted by ill-intentioned, evil, powerful, and privileged people and the institutions or policies they create. For instance, the extra scrutiny of and resistance against the inclusion of ethnic studies courses into a school curriculum is probably not consciously and deliberately driven by the individual-level desires of those in power to continue the subjugation of peoples of color. Some of the powerful decision-makers who are reluctant to include ethnic studies may even truly and genuinely sympathize with the importance of ethnic studies (some might even be peoples of color themselves!), but they can also simultaneously claim that there is nothing they can do because of reasons that are out of their control (e.g., limited budget). Nevertheless, in many cases—especially in our modern times—even well-intentioned people and the systems, institutions, and policies they develop and uphold may still inadvertently end up dehumanizing other people, limiting other people's access to resources, and constraining other people's freedoms. *Just like interpersonal oppression, institutional oppression can also exist and operate outside our awareness, intention, or control.* Because oppression may be very subtle and unnoticed, the various oppressive rules, standards, norms, habits, symbols, and assumptions that already permeate our society can eventually become widely accepted, unquestioned, or too daunting to even attempt to challenge and change, leading to the creation, maintenance, legitimization, or legalization of oppressive norms, organizations, and institutions (Young, 1990).

In addition to the fact that many people may be well intentioned, good-hearted, and may not even be aware—or may not be willing to admit—that they hold biases against some groups of people, it is also the case that many people do not engage in stereotypical, prejudiced, and unfair treatment of other people. Therefore, many people may find it difficult to see and appreciate one's privileges because they can point to the fact that they (or even their immediate ancestors) have never knowingly and intentionally participated in any behavior that has unfairly benefited them. In other words, they can truthfully claim that they have never personally oppressed anyone; that they are not guilty of interpersonal oppression! Nevertheless, *even if we take out interpersonal-level oppression, it does not necessarily mean that institutional-level oppression also goes away!* For instance, even if a man does not hold any stereotype or prejudice against women, and even if he's never ever behaved in an unfair manner toward any woman, it does not get rid of the fact that women still earn only 80 cents for every dollar that a man earns for doing the same job (Hegewisch & DuMonthier, 2016). In Figure 5.1, even if we erase the agent person circle and the arrow (interpersonal oppression) coming from it, the dashed circles (institutional oppression) still remain to oppress the target person circle!

Another example of how institutional oppression may still exist even in the absence of interpersonal oppression is the fact that many people today can point out that they (or their immediate ancestors) never owned slaves, never colonized a new territory and exploited indigenous peoples, never created a sexist policy, were never involved in the construction of a building that has no wheelchair access, were never part of a wealthy family, or never deported an immigrant and separated that person from his or her family. Thus, they can easily distance themselves from any biased and unfair practice, and convince themselves that they have never benefited from oppression that other people may have done. Although they may be factually correct, however, such reasoning fails to acknowledge how existing institutions have favored their identities, their worldviews, and their values, providing them with advantages that are denied to other people. For instance, the climate, methods of teaching, and standards of the U.S. educational institutions reflect and are more amenable to those students who are native English speakers and who hold Western, Christian, middle- to upper-class values. And even if students who fit such characteristics do not actively and directly engage in oppressive behavior, the fact that their worldview, values, and standards are considered the norm provides them with advantages that other students do not get. This is yet another reason why it is important to understand that oppression also exists and operates beyond the individual level; that there is also such a thing as institutional oppression. As noted sociologist Allan G. Johnson (2000) stated,

> (Institutional oppression) . . . should not be confused with the oppressive behavior of individuals. A white man may not himself actively participate in oppressive behavior directed at blacks or women, for example, but he nonetheless benefits from the general oppression of blacks and women simply because he is a white man . . . Social oppression becomes institutionalized when its enforcement is so of social life that it is not easily identified as oppression and does not require conscious prejudice or overt acts of discrimination.

Although it is important to recognize that interpersonal and institutional oppression are not the same, we also need to remember that they are linked and that they feed off each other. Individual-level stereotypes, prejudices, and discriminatory behaviors may lead to policies, procedures, and standards that in turn reflect, legitimize, and protect the stereotypes, prejudices, and discriminatory behaviors that created them. Eventually, people may no

A FULL CIRCLE OF OPPRESSION↑↑
DISCRIMINATION > POLICES > MORE OPPRESSION + DISCRIMINA

OVER TIME PeOPLE DON'T REALIZE THEIR ATTITUDE + PRACTICES ENCOURAGE OPPRESSION

longer notice that their climate and the beliefs, attitudes, and practices it encourages are oppressive—evaluating whether something is "right" or "just" by whether or not it is consistent with laws, regulations, or standard operating procedures—forgetting that such policies may have been driven by biases and, thus, are likely biased. In essence, individuals may use institutions to support and justify their worldviews and behaviors. We need to remember, however, that *just because something is "legal" or consistent with the law does not necessarily mean that it is right, fair, or just.*

An example of this feedback system between interpersonal and institutional oppression is how the United States has regarded homosexuality. Although there has been some progress, homosexuality is still strongly considered as nonnormal, deviant, or unacceptable—it still is outside the social norm! This is especially the case throughout U.S. history until the 1960s when such social norms were powerfully questioned by the gay rights movement. The antigay values and worldviews of people were backed up by social norms, and such norms were turned into formal institutions in various ways, such as criminalizing homosexuality through sodomy laws (which include sexual acts between persons of the same sex) that were in effect in many states until 2003 and pathologizing homosexuality by regarding it as a mental illness until 1987 (although the World Health Organization continued to consider homosexuality a mental illness until 1992). Such formal institutions legitimized many people's stereotypes, prejudices, and unfair behaviors toward homosexual people, creating a culture wherein it is legal, normative, and acceptable to hold certain oppressive beliefs (e.g., homosexuals are sexual perverts and pedophiles; there's something wrong with them) and behave in oppressive ways (e.g., not hiring gay people as teachers; using shock therapy or other treatment to "cure" gay people).

▪ WHAT IS INTERNALIZED OPPRESSION?

THINK / FEEL / BEHAVE → OPPRESS PEOPLE / OPPRESS THEMSELVE → SOCIALIZATION (LEARNED)

Now that we understand how oppression can exist and operate in our interpersonal interactions and in our social institutions, it is clear that oppression is all around us. But did you know that oppression can also exist and operate within us? As we introduced in Chapter 1, *internalized oppression is when the oppression that permeates the environment is able to seep into oppressed individuals who, in turn, begin to think, feel, and behave in biased ways toward themselves and their own group* (David, 2013, 2014). An example of this is when dark-skinned individuals learn to hate their skin tones because of the racism they have experienced or when they begin bleaching their skin and discriminating against other dark-skinned people. Essentially, internalized oppression is when oppressed individuals or groups come to oppress themselves because of the oppression they have experienced! As we proceed to discuss internalized oppression, we need to always remember that internalized oppression would not exist if oppression did not exist. This is important because it keeps us from blaming individuals for the oppression that they experience, and reminds us that the root of the problem does not reside internally within individuals. We need to always keep in mind the truth that the cause of internalized oppression is external or outside of individuals; the cause is oppression!

So how does something outside of individuals—like oppression— become internalized? In psychology, **socialization** is the process wherein we are taught, educated, or trained about the social norms (e.g., customs, traditions, values, ideologies, expected roles) in our society (Pinker, 2002). Socialization is one of the major ways in which we learn about ourselves and how we should, can, and cannot operate in the world. Essentially, we are socialized by our parents, teachers, peers, and everything else in our environment about the "dos" and "don'ts" of life. For instance, right from birth, many of us are already socialized by society about what boys and girls should wear, what color we should like, what toys we should play with, how we should act, what roles we can fulfill, and many others (Harter, 1999)! Similarly, we are also socialized about what society deems as appropriate or inappropriate, acceptable or unacceptable, and expected or unexpected of our other social identities as well (e.g., racial identity, national identity, religion, class) (e.g., Gutierrez, Goodwin, Kirkinis, & Mattis, 2014; Hughes et al., 2006).

As you may recall from the institutional oppression section earlier, the social norms and formal institutions we create can be biased, unfair, or oppressive. Even further, you may also recall that social norms and formal institutions can become widely accepted and regarded as "normal," "legal," and "right" as the biased ideologies and assumptions that shaped them become deeply embedded and hidden over time. Thus, people may eventually no longer see the social norms and formal institutions with which they grew up, became accustomed to, and habitually participated in as potentially oppressive. Therefore, many of our parents, teachers, peers, and other socializing influences may have been socialized to follow and accept oppressive norms and institutions that they, in turn, socialized us to also follow and accept. In other words, *right from very young ages, we were already being socialized to automatically believe the many potentially oppressive messages surrounding us, whether we were aware of them or not and whether we agreed with them or not.*

If the oppressive messages that we end up believing and accepting are about social identities that we hold—like our race, ethnicity, gender identity, sexual orientation, religion, and others—then from very young ages we were already vulnerable to internalizing the oppression directed at us. For instance, Kenneth and Mammie Clark's (1939) classic doll studies demonstrated that Black children as young as 3 years of age may have already internalized pervasive societal messages that attach negative traits to Black people and positive traits to White people. In their study, Clark and Clark found that Black children commonly identified White dolls as "nice" dolls and preferred playing with them, while identifying Black dolls as "bad" dolls that they also recognize as looking like them! In other words, they know they are Black; they know the negative messages society has attached to being Black; and they have begun to perceive being Black in the same oppressive way as society does! Consistent with these findings, recent research also shows that individuals who experience oppression more frequently and individuals who have seen, heard, or observed other people displaying internalized oppression (e.g., using skin-whitening products, hiding or denying one's identity) are more likely to have internalized oppression themselves (David & Okazaki, 2006). These findings suggest that *socialization and continued oppression can lead to internalized oppression.*

Now that we have a better understanding of how oppression can become internalized, you might be asking, what does internalized oppression look like? Well, *the expression or manifestation of internalized oppression varies considerably between groups and even among individual members of the same group.* For instance, internalized sexism, heterosexism, ableism, and racism are different from each other, and internalized racism may look different for African Americans, Asian Americans, Native Hawaiians, Pacific Islanders, Native Americans, Alaska Natives, Latinos/as, and multiracial people (see David, 2014). Even further, it is important to remember that not all oppressed individuals internalize the oppression they have experienced, and even people who have internalized oppression may also vary in terms of intensity and the extent to which it affects their lives and well-being. Nevertheless, although there are group and individual variations when it comes to the existence, manifestations, and implications of internalized oppression, recent research seems to suggest that there are some characteristics of internalized oppression that may be commonly experienced.

One of the seemingly consistent characteristics of *internalized oppression is that it can be manifested covertly or overtly* (e.g., for a review, see David, 2014). The more **covert, hidden, or not-easily-seen type of internalized oppression** is the attitudes and feelings persons may have about themselves, the group to which they belong, and other groups. For example, some folks may feel embarrassed, ashamed, inferior about their group characteristics (e.g., skin tone, language, cultural practices, being attracted to same-sex people), believe that their group should change to become better or "more civilized" (e.g., assimilationist attitudes), or perceive dominant groups as inherently better and dominated groups as inherently (or deservedly) inferior. Also, similar to stereotypes and prejudices, research suggests that these *covert manifestations of internalized oppression can exist and operate outside of awareness, intention, or control.* Indeed, using the Implicit Association Test (Greenwald et al., 1998) and the Subliminal Priming Tasks (Fazio et al., 1995) that are used to investigate implicit biases, a growing body of research has found that members of oppressed groups may have learned to automatically associate negative traits with their oppressed identity (e.g., Chae et al., 2014; David, 2010; David & Okazaki, 2010; Hatzenbuehler, 2009). The more **overt or easily seen type of internalized oppression** is the behaviors that express or are reflective of the oppressive attitudes and beliefs that people have already internalized. Some examples include folks who use bleach to whiten their skin, refuse to speak their heritage language because they think it is obsolete or a lower class language, and outwardly denigrate gay people to hide one's own gay sexual orientation. Among the scenarios presented in the beginning of this chapter, can you now identity which are examples of covert internalized oppression and which are examples of overt internalized oppression? If you identified scenario 1 as covert and scenarios 7 and 8 as overt, then you are correct!

Also, remember we stated in the beginning that scenarios 1 and 8 are also examples of interpersonal oppression. This speaks to how the three levels of oppression overlap and how *internalized oppression can exist and operate in the institutional and interpersonal levels.* How so? In case of scenarios 1 and 8, both are examples of how internalized oppression is expressed interpersonally; specifically, scenario 1 is covert internalized oppression and scenario 8 is overt internalized oppression that are both expressed in relation to another person. Hence, it is interpersonal oppression. Other examples of **interpersonal internalized oppression** are: immigrants denigrating other immigrants for being "backward" or not being assimilated enough; parents well-intentionally telling their children to stay away from the sun so they do not get too dark; and people advising others to use skin-whitening products. As for **institutional internalized oppression,** an example is the Philippines which is a country that has enacted laws to require their schools to use English as the primary language for books, exams, and instruction in the education of Filipino children instead of any of the local languages. Therefore, the institution is essentially propagating and reinforcing the oppressive message that indigenous languages are not as valuable, important, relevant, and necessary as the English language. In this case, we clearly see how internalized oppression can become so accepted and normative that it eventually becomes entrenched and institutionalized by society.

Finally, in cases wherein interpersonal or institutional internalized oppression is used against members of other oppressed groups or other members of one's own group, then lateral oppression may be operating. Briefly, **lateral oppression (or horizontal oppression)** is when members of oppressed groups use the oppressive views and/or institutions of the dominant society to oppress other groups or other people in their own group. Some examples provided earlier, such as dark-skinned people telling other dark-skinned people to use bleach or a gay person denigrating another person for being gay, are examples of *within-group lateral oppression.* Some examples of *between-groups lateral oppression* include Asian Americans who have come to believe society's negative view of African Americans and may unfairly discriminate against African Americans. Similarly, another example is an African American person who has come to believe society's stereotypical views of Asian Americans and who also unfairly discriminates against Asian Americans. Essentially, lateral oppression is when oppressed peoples are oppressing themselves and other oppressed groups. Thus, not only is lateral oppression damaging for an oppressed group because it keeps them subjugated, but lateral oppression also creates further divisions between different groups of people that prevent them from uniting in their similar struggles and fighting the actual problem which is oppression.

▪ THE SYSTEM OF OPPRESSION

As we can now see, the three levels of oppression—interpersonal, institutional, and internalized—are linked with each other and all three feed off of and reinforce each other. In other words, all three levels of oppression work together to maintain a state of oppression. For example, individual-level stereotypes and prejudices that some people may hold against Mexicans may come out in both blatant (e.g., "Build a wall!") and subtle ways (e.g., "I'm not against Mexicans, but we really ought to do something about the drug problem and I believe a lot of it comes from Mexico") (interpersonal). These attitudes and beliefs may become normalized, which may then lead to a formal policy or law against Mexican immigrants (e.g., more stringent immigration requirements for Mexican immigrants, a stronger focus on deporting Mexican immigrants) (institutional). Because of the negative connotations attached to being Mexican, some Mexican individuals may begin to perceive their Mexican heritage as a detriment, which may lead them to separate themselves from their Mexican heritage as much as possible or assimilate completely into mainstream America (internalized). People who assimilate are rewarded to some extent by society, relaying the message that for people to become accepted and do well, they will need to erase their Mexican heritage. People who hold on to their Mexican heritage, on the other hand, are blamed and punished for "choosing" to remain Mexican, which reinforces other people's stereotypes and prejudices against Mexicans. Essentially, the oppressed are blamed for their oppression. This vicious feedback loop between the different levels of oppression is what people call **"systemic oppression,"** as all three levels compose the seemingly inescapable system of oppression that has been destroying individuals, families, and communities for generations. In the next chapter, we discuss how oppression may affect the psychological experiences and mental health of oppressed groups.

REFERENCES

Augoustinos, M., & Walker, I. (1998). The construction of stereotypes within social psychology: From social cognition to ideology. *Theory & Psychology, 8*(5), 629–652.

Chae, D. H., Nuru-Jeter, A. M., Adler, N. E., Brody, G. H., Lin, J., Blackburn, E. H., & Epel, E. (2014). Discrimination, racial bias, and telomere length in African-American men. *American Journal of Preventive Medicine, 46*, 103–111.

Cheryan, S., & Bodenhausen, G. V. (2000). When positive stereotypes threaten intellectual performance: The psychological hazards of "model minority" status. *Psychological Science, 11*(5), 399–402.

Cialdini, R. (2007). Descriptive social norms as underappreciated sources of social control. *Psychometrika, 72*(2), 263–268.

Clark, K. B., & Clark, M. P. (1939). The development of consciousness of self and the emergence of racial identification in Negro pre-school children. *Journal of Social Psychology, 10,* 591–599.

David, E. J. R. (2010). Testing the validity of the Colonial Mentality Implicit Association Test (CMIAT) and the interactive effects of covert and overt colonial mentality on Filipino American mental health. *Asian American Journal of Psychology, 1,* 31–45.

David, E. J. R. (2013). *Brown skin, white minds: Filipino -/ American postcolonial psychology* (with commentaries). Charlotte, NC: Information Age Publishing.

David, E. J. R. (Ed.). (2014). *Internalized oppression: The psychology of marginalized groups.* New York, NY: Springer Publishing.

David, E. J. R., & Okazaki, S. (2006). The Colonial Mentality Scale (CMS) for Filipino Americans: Scale construction and psychological implications. *Journal of Counseling Psychology, 53,* 241–252.

David, E. J. R., & Okazaki, S. (2010). Activation and automaticity of colonial mentality. *Journal of Applied Social Psychology, 40,* 850–887.

Fazio, R. H., Jackson, J. R., Dunton, B. C., & Williams, C. J. (1995). Variability in automatic activation as an unobtrusive measure of racial attitudes: A bona fide pipeline? *Journal of Personality and Social Psychology, 69,* 1013–1027.

Fiske, S. T., & North, M. S. (2015). Measures of stereotyping and prejudice: Barometers of bias. In G. J. Boyle, D. H. Saklofske, & G. Matthews (Eds.), *Measures of personality and social psychological constructs* (pp. 684–718). London, England: Academic Press. doi:10.1016/B978-0-12-386915-9.00024-3

Gawronski, B., & Bodenhausen, G. V. (2006). Associative and propositional processes in evaluation: An integrative review of implicit and explicit attitude change. *Psychological Bulletin, 132,* 692–731.

Greenwald, A. G., McGhee, D. E., & Schwartz, J. L. K. (1998). Measuring individual differences in implicit cognition: The Implicit Association Test. *Journal of Personality and Social Psychology, 74,* 1464–1480.

Gutierrez, I. A., Goodwin, L. A., Kirkinis, K., & Mattis, J. S. (2014). Religious socialization in African American families: The relative influence of parents, grandparents, and siblings. *Journal of Family Psychology, 28*(6), 779–789. doi:10.1037/a0035732

Harter, S. (1999). *The construction of the self: A developmental perspective. Distinguished contributions in psychology.* New York, NY: Guilford Press.

Harvey, J. (1999). *Civilized oppression.* Lanham, MD: Rowman & Littlefield.

Hatzenbuehler, M. L. (2009). How does sexual minority stigma "get under the skin"? A psychological medication framework. *Psychological Bulletin, 145,* 707–730.

Hegewisch, A., & DuMonthier, A. (2016). *The gender wage gap: 2015.* Retrieved from http://www.iwpr.org/publications/pubs/ the-gender-wage-gap-2015-annual-earnings-differences-by -gender-race-and-ethnicity

Hughes, D., Rodriguez, J., Smith, E. P., Johnson, D. J., Stevenson, H. C., & Spicer, P. (2006). Parents' ethnic-racial socialization practices: A review of research and directions for future study. *Developmental Psychology, 42*(5), 747–770. doi:10.1037/0012-1649.42.5.747

Johnson, A. G. (2000). *The Blackwell dictionary of sociology: A user's guide to sociological language* (2nd ed.). Oxford, England: Blackwell.

Jones, R. P., Cox, D., Cooper, B., & Lienesch, R. (2015). *Anxiety, nostalgia, and mistrust: Findings from the 2015 American Values Survey.* Washington, DC: Public Religion Research Institute. Retrieved from http://www.prri.org/wp-content/uploads/2015/11/PRRI -AVS-2015-Web.pdf

Jones, R. P., Cox, D., & Navarro-Rivera, J. (2014). *Economic insecurity, rising inequality, and doubts about the future: Findings from the 2014 American Values Survey.* Washington, DC: Public Religion Research Institute. Retrieved from http://www.prri.org/ research/survey-economic-insecurity-rising-inequality-and -doubts-about-the-future-findings-from-the-2014-american -values-survey

Kahneman, D., & Miller, D. T. (1986). Norm theory: Comparing reality to its alternatives. *Psychological Review, 80,* 136–153.

Okazaki, S. (2002). Beyond questionnaires: Conceptual and methodological innovations for Asian American psychology. In G. C. Nagayama Hall & S. Okazaki (Eds.), *Asian American psychology:*

The science of lives in context (pp. 13–39). Washington, DC: American Psychological Association.

Piaget, J. (1957). *Construction of reality in the child.* London, England: Routledge & Kegan Paul.

Pinker, S. (2002). *The blank slate.* New York, NY: Penguin Books.

Ponterotto, J. G., Burkard, A., Rieger, B. P., Grieger, I., D'Onofrio, A., Dubuisson, A., . . . Sax, G. (1995). Development and initial validation of the Quick Discrimination Index (QDI). *Educational and Psychological Measurement, 55*(6), 1016–1031.

Steele, C., & Aronson, J. (1995). Stereotype threat and the intellectual test performance of African Americans. *Journal of Personality & Social Psychology, 69*(5), 797–811.

Young, M. I. (1990). *Justice and the politics of difference.* Princeton, NJ: Princeton University Press.

CHAPTER 6

So What? Psychological and Mental Health Implications of Oppression

On the eve of the year 2017, a woman in Las Vegas was caught on camera spewing hateful words toward her Filipino neighbor. "Orange motherf*cker! Go back to where you came from! We don't want you here!" she yelled. According to the woman, her Filipino neighbor is from "some piece of sh*t Manila-ass, f*cking ghetto, living-under-a-tarp piece of sh*t land." She further told him that Filipinos are "stupid, orange savages" who are "just one f*cking generation out of the jungle, like f*cking loin-cloth wearers!" She went on to shout that Filipina women are nothing but sex workers, that Filipinos do nothing but populate the world with "trashy people" who suck resources out of America, that Filipinos do not even know their own history, and that Filipinos should be thankful to America for saving, colonizing, and protecting the Philippines.

In previous chapters, we have discussed what oppression is, its evolution, its many dimensions and multilevel operations, and who experience it. We also now understand that oppression has been happening throughout history and that it is still widespread even to this day—in the year 2017! Therefore, in the case of the woman and her Filipino neighbor, we can see that it is an example of explicit racism (i.e., inferiorization of Filipino culture and people) that is rooted in both historical (i.e., colonialism) and contemporary (i.e., anti-immigrant sentiments; seeing Filipinos as draining the U.S. economy) oppression. We see this case as an example of interpersonal oppression that reflects institutional oppression (i.e., U.S. colonization and imperialist efforts in the Philippines; portrayal of the United States as Filipinos' liberating, civilizing saviors and protectors). We now—hopefully—have a basic understanding of the *what, who, how, where*, and *when* of oppression. But what about the *so what*? The first author, E. J., is a Filipino immigrant from the Philippines; how does the colonial history of Filipinos and their contemporary experiences of oppression—as exemplified by the case described in the beginning of this chapter—affect him? Does oppression—the fact that society perceives, regards, and treats Filipinos as inferior—matter to him, his family, and the larger Filipino community? The second author, Annie, is a lesbian woman; how does society's interpersonal (e.g., demeaning statements such as "That's so gay!" when referring to something dumb or stupid; catcalling women or treating them merely as sexual objects) and institutional (e.g., anti-LGBTQ laws such as prohibition to marry; unequal pay for women) devaluation of LGBTQ people and women affect her and her community? That is, so what if oppression happened and is still experienced by various groups in all aspects of their lives? In this chapter, we discuss the "so what" by providing an overview of the psychological and mental health implications of oppression.

■ OPPRESSION AND STRESS

As summarized in Table 6.1, which is by no means a comprehensive list, it is very well documented that marginalized groups face various health concerns. The increasing body of research on *racial health disparities*, for example, suggests that members of marginalized groups often face alarmingly higher risks for developing health concerns and face more barriers in the system that keeps them from getting quality health care than members of dominant or privileged groups. But does oppression play a role in the health issues facing marginalized communities? The answer to this question is a resounding *yes!*, and one way in which oppression affects the health of marginalized peoples is through stress. In general, **stress** is the process of adjusting to **stressors** (e.g., death of a loved one, facing a work deadline, moving to a new home), which are physical, social, environmental, mental, or emotional pressures, strains, weight, load, or tensions that force us to adapt or change (*Random House Webster's Dictionary*, 1992; Wheaton, 1999). Stress researchers have studied the full range of stressors we face: traumatic events (e.g., car accident), eventful life stressors (e.g., graduating from college; getting married), chronic stress (e.g., taking care of one's children), and daily hassles (e.g., facing heavy traffic every day to get to work and return home). Overall, the literature shows that we all face stressors and experience stress almost constantly (Dohrenwend, 1998). In other words, *stress is just a fact of life!*

TABLE 6.1 Some (of the Many!) Health Concerns Facing Marginalized Communities

- In general, a higher percentage of Native Americans and Alaska Natives, African Americans, Latinos/as, Asian Americans, and Pacific Islanders are in "poor mental health" than Whites (Kaiser Family Foundation, 2013)

- Native Americans and Alaska Natives, African Americans, Latinos/as, Asian Americans, and Pacific Islanders have higher depression rates than Whites (Centers for Disease Control and Prevention, 2013, as cited by He, 2015)

- Lesbian, gay, and bisexual individuals tend to be more hopeless and have lower self-esteem and weaker social support than heterosexual individuals (Plöderl & Fartacek, 2005; Wichstrom & Hegna, 2003)

- People with disabilities are more likely to be victims of a violent crime than people without disabilities (Krahn, Walker, & Correa-De-Araujo, 2015)

- An alarming 41% of transgender and gender nonconforming people have attempted suicide, compared to the national average of 4.6% (James et al., 2016)

- Females have higher lifetime prevalence rates of anxiety (e.g., generalized anxiety, posttraumatic stress) and mood disorders (e.g., depression, dysthymia) than males (Hong, Walton, Tamaki, & Sabin, 2014)

- African Americans have high incidences of stress-related diseases such as hypertension, cardiovascular disease, and coronary heart disease (Agency for Healthcare Research and Quality, 2009; U.S. Department of Health and Human Services, 2003)

- Asian Americans have higher prevalence rates of any mood, anxiety, and substance use disorder compared to the rates for the general population. Southeast Asians have higher rates of disorders compared to other Asian Americans (Lee, Martins, & Lee, 2014)

- Native Americans, African Americans, and Latinos/as have high rates of diabetes, and Native American elders die of diabetes at a rate that is two times higher than Whites (U.S. Department of Health and Human Services, 2003)

- Higher rates of anxiety, mood, and substance use disorders have been associated with being an immigrant man (Hong et al., 2014)

- Lesbian, gay, and bisexual individuals are socialized to use more alcohol and other substances than heterosexual individuals (Austin et al., 2004; Hatzenbuehler, Corbin, & Fromme, 2008)

- Native Americans and Alaska Natives have very high rates of substance use, alcohol dependence, and need for illicit-drug-abuse treatment (Substance Abuse & Mental Health Services Administration [SAMHSA], 2003)

- People with disabilities are more likely to have cardiovascular (heart) disease, be obese, and be a current smoker than people without disabilities (Krahn et al., 2015)

- Native Americans, Alaska Natives, Native Hawaiians/Pacific Islanders, and multiracial people have higher rates of illicit drug use and substance abuse than Whites (SAMHSA, 2014)

(continued)

TABLE 6.1   Some (of the Many!) Health Concerns Facing Marginalized Communities (*continued*)

- Latinos/as have higher lifetime prevalence rates of impulse control disorders and substance use disorders than Whites (Breslau, et al., 2006)

- Sexual minorities have higher levels of psychological risk factors for psychopathology than heterosexuals (Hatzenbuehler, McLaughlin, & Nolen-Hoeksema, 2008; Plöderl & Fartacek, 2005; Safren & Heimberg, 1999)

- African Americans get more sick and die more often from preventable and treatable illnesses than any other racial group (Edwards & Erwin-Johnson, 2003)

- People with disabilities are more likely to not receive medical care that they need because of financial costs than people without disabilities (Walker & Correa-De-Araujo, 2015)

- Suicide rates are troublingly high for transgender people of color, particularly those who are multiracial (54%) or American Indian or Alaska Native (56%) (James et al., 2016)

However, although all of us experience stress, this is yet another area in which we see imbalance or inequality between different social groups. This is because *members of oppressed groups face additional stressors that members of dominant or agent groups do not face.* For example, racism is one chronic stressor that leads to countless daily hassles (e.g., being pulled over by police; being constantly suspected of wrong-doing) and even many traumatic events (e.g., being physically harmed or threatened) that peoples of color face in the United States and to which White people are not subjected. Similarly, women, LGBTQ persons, and Muslims face the additional stressor of having to constantly worry about their physical safety—which may lead them to alter their behaviors in significant ways (e.g., avoid going to certain restaurants, bars, or clubs; limit the amount of time they spend in public; move to another house in a different neighborhood or city)—and with which men, non-LGBTQ, and Christian people are not burdened. In the case of the Filipino person who experienced blatant racism from his neighbor, he shared that he feared for the safety of his family—especially of his children—because he saw first-hand how "evil and hate can overpower a person" who is literally next door to his family. For him and his family, this is yet another chronic stressor—potentially even a traumatic one—with which they have to deal in addition to the general stressors (e.g., work, school, bills) that they already face.

According to the *Minority Stress Model* (Meyer, 2003) and the *Integrative General and Group-Specific Psychological Mediation Framework* (Hatzenbuehler, 2009), members of oppressed groups are burdened with having to allocate physical, mental, and emotional resources on the myriad of oppressions they face as they constantly think through, regulate their feelings, and respond to pervasive oppressive encounters and conditions. For example, a lesbian woman may have to face the daily stress of having to work for a company that does not recognize and value her marriage. Thus, she has to put in effort to regulate her frustrations and make behavioral adjustments while at work to cope with the belittling she faces there. Not only does she face stressors to which others are not subjected, but the fact that she must devote physical, mental, and emotional energy to cope with the stressor of oppression makes her more vulnerable to various harmful outcomes (e.g., frustration and anger that may lead to irritability and poor job performance; isolation from her coworkers; depression; anxiety; maladaptive coping such as alcohol and drug use). Indeed, research suggests that these *additional sources of stress for oppressed peoples may put them at higher risk for various mental and physical health concerns* (Allison, 1998; Clark, Anderson, Clark, & Williams, 1999; Hatzenbuehler, 2009; Meyer, 2003; Pearlin, 1999). For instance, experiences of discrimination have been linked to lower heart rate variability (HRV) (Hill et al., 2017), which suggests that the sympathetic nervous system—the part that is activated when we face stressors (i.e., the *fight or flight response*)—is dominant or always active. An overactive sympathetic nervous system is associated with inflammation of organs and weakening of the body (because it uses up our body's resources to "fight"); thus, low HRV is related to poorer health. Research (Ong, Williams, Nwizu, & Gruenewald, 2017) also suggests that facing the chronic stressor of discrimination is related to higher **allostatic load**—physiological dysregulations such as high blood pressure, high cortisol levels, and increased heart rate that are linked to various mental (e.g., depression, anxiety) and physical (e.g., hypertension, diabetes, heart disease) health issues.

Furthermore, as discussed in Chapter 4, oppression has evolved in such a way that it is often expressed today subtly as microaggressions. Such modern forms of oppression are much more confusing and potentially more mentally, emotionally, or psychologically taxing. Indeed, members of oppressed groups who encounter subtle forms of oppression often go through a chain of internal dilemmas because of such microaggressions. According to Sue's (2010) Microaggression Process Model, the fact that modern forms of oppression are often subtle, unclear, and confusing makes them more difficult for people to determine if what they experienced was indeed oppression (i.e., *attributional ambiguity*). The lack of clarity necessarily calls for more mental, physical, and emotional resources to be devoted to and used up on processing the encounter in order to better understand it and respond to it emotionally and behaviorally—if such cognitive, emotional, and behavioral clarities even arrive at all. Indeed, many times, microaggression experiences are left unresolved, continuing to linger in people's minds and hearts for long periods of time and, hence, continuing to use up people's physical, mental, and emotional resources. These experiences may lead members of oppressed groups to become hypervigilant, angry, mistrusting, fearful, fatigued, and hopeless. Such constantly heightened stress levels are associated with adverse health outcomes such as depression, anxiety, acute stress disorder, and post-traumatic stress disorder (Sue, 2010).

Another potential negative effect of microaggressions is that its subtlety and ambiguity puts members of oppressed groups at risk for questioning, disregarding, and minimizing their experiences of oppression. Even worse, as alluded to in Chapter 1, people may even end up blaming themselves for the oppression they faced, thinking along the lines of "Oh, it's my fault, I'm just being too paranoid and oversensitive." Even further, when people cannot identify and confront the source of their oppression that created the cognitive, emotional, and behavioral dilemmas, then their frustrations and anger may be directed inwardly toward themselves. In such cases, oppressed individuals become vulnerable to developing *internalized oppression* (as discussed in Chapter 5), which is a condition that has been linked to various mental health concerns such as low self-esteem, depression, anxiety, and low life satisfaction (David, 2014). Recent research has even linked internalized oppression to shorter telomeres, which are protein "caps" in our chromosomes associated with the age of our bodies and, thus, life expectancy (Chae et al., 2014). When it comes to telomere length, the longer the better, and the fact that internalized oppression is linked to shorter telomeres suggests that *oppression—especially when it is internalized—is literally shortening the lives of oppressed individuals. Oppression—internalized oppression particularly—is literally killing oppressed peoples.*

▪ OPPRESSION AND SELF-CONCEPT

Another way in which oppression is linked to mental health is through **self-concept**, which is our perception of the traits or characteristics that we have as a person. The extent to which we positively or negatively evaluate our traits or characteristics is what is popularly known as **self-esteem.** For instance, think of some of the traits or characteristics that you have.

Perhaps you are tall? Good at basketball? Not so great in math? Maybe you have brown hair? Perhaps you can type really fast? Or you might have a passion for social justice? Let us use this last one as an example; if being passionate about social justice is one trait or characteristic that you believe defines you as a person and if you see this as a good trait to have, then that is great for your self-esteem. However, if you regard such a trait as not so good, then your self-esteem may suffer. Now, then, you might be asking yourself: What helps us determine if the traits we have are "good" or "bad"? This is where social psychology comes in.

You may recall from your introductory psychology class that the subfield of social psychology seeks "to understand and explain how the thoughts, feelings and behaviors of individuals are influenced by the actual, imagined, or implied presence of other human beings" (Allport, 1985). In this definition, the "actual, imagined, or implied presence of other human beings" are important influential factors on our psychological experiences because we as people create expectations, assumptions, and standards for ourselves. These cultural norms that society has created help us determine if the traits or characteristics that define us—our self-concept—are "good" or "bad." In other words, *our social world—our cultural norms, expectations, assumptions, and standards—plays a large part in the extent to which we evaluate our traits or characteristics positively—our self-esteem.* Thus, if society regards a trait or characteristic that you have as desirable or "good"—such as being an amazing basketball player—then your evaluation of this trait will be positive and it will boost your self-esteem. However, if society regards a trait or characteristic that you have as undesirable or "bad"—such as not being able to read or write—then your evaluation of this trait will be negative and it will damage your self-esteem.

As we mentioned in Chapter 1, however, our self-concept and self-esteem are composed not just of the traits that we have as individuals such as being tall or short, having black hair, being athletic, or being a good video game player. Instead, we also have traits and characteristics that are associated with or linked to the social groups to which we belong. For instance, many people have darker skin complexions and such a trait is linked to their racial or ethnic group. Many people may speak a language other than English, or speak English with an accent, which is a characteristic that is linked to their cultural group. Another example is that many people may have worldviews, traditions, values, and beliefs due primarily to their spirituality or religion. Thus, in addition to **personal self-esteem**, we also have **collective self-esteem**—the extent to which we evaluate the traits or characteristics of the groups to which we belong positively. And according to *Social Identity Theory* (Tajfel & Turner, 1979, 1986), collective self-esteem is just as important for psychological well-being and mental health as personal self-esteem. Indeed, research has shown that *both personal self-esteem and collective self-esteem are linked to various health outcomes* such as life satisfaction, depression, anxiety, suicide ideation, general distress, poor school performance, and alcohol use (e.g., Bizman, Yinon, & Krotman, 2001; Booth & Gerard, 2011; Crocker, Luhtanen, Blaine, & Broadnax, 1994; Gupta, Rogers-Sirn, Okazaki, Ryce, & Sirin, 2014; Katz, Joiner, & Kwon, 2002; Pedersen, Hsu, Neighbors, Lee, & Larimer, 2013; Sharma & Agarwalaa, 2013; Wilburn & Smith, 2005; Woods, Zuniga, & David, 2012).

Just as personal self-esteem is largely influenced by our social world, our cultural norms, expectations, assumptions, and standards also play a large part in the extent to which we positively or negatively evaluate the traits or characteristics of our social groups. As discussed in Chapter 5, however, cultural norms, expectations, assumptions, and standards that become institutionalized or become unquestionably regarded as "normal" can privilege or benefit some groups of people while disadvantaging others; this is oppression. Thus, many of these that our society may have come to regard as "normal" or "abnormal," desirable or undesirable, "good" or "bad," and acceptable or unacceptable may lead individuals who are members of oppressed groups to negatively evaluate the traits and characteristics of their social group. For example, if a person lives in a context wherein one's indigenous traditions or rituals are seen as the "uncivilized" ways of "primitive savages," then one might cease to practice such traditions or rituals and regard them negatively, or practice them reluctantly or discretely due to shame, embarrassment, or fear of being ridiculed. In other words, *society's oppressive regard and treatment of marginalized groups can damage how members of such groups see themselves and their group characteristics* (e.g., language, traditions, values); oppression can damage their collective self-esteem.

We can easily see society's oppressive regard and treatment of various social groups through the existing stereotypes about such groups. For instance, many folks may stereotypically regard LGBTQ persons as morally corrupt sexual deviants, Black and Brown people as criminals, Native Americans and Alaska Natives as alcoholics, people with disabilities as unintelligent and helpless, and women as physically and emotionally weak. The case of the Filipino man and his neighbor that was presented in the beginning of this chapter suggests that Filipinos may be stereotypically seen as uncivilized savages who move to the United States and drain the country's resources. These stereotypes may influence members of marginalized groups to think, feel, and act in a variety of ways. If they come to believe or accept the inferiorizing views that the dominant society has about their social group characteristics (e.g., regard darker skin as less attractive, use skin-whitening products to whiten one's skin), then it becomes *internalized oppression—which is associated with lower collective self-esteem and various negative health outcomes* (David, 2013). But we need to also realize that even when people do not internalize or believe the stereotypes about their groups, or even when they do not perceive their groups to be lesser or inferior, just being aware of and conscious of the fact that inferiorizing stereotypes exist may still lead people to succumb to the stereotype! Indeed, the literature on **stereotype threat**—when an individual becomes vulnerable to being perceived, judged, and treated in ways that are consistent with the stereotypes about one's group— suggests that believing or internalizing stereotypes are not necessary for such stereotypes to have a mental, emotional, or behavioral toll on people that, in turn, may lead them to fulfill, "live up to," or behave according to the stereotypes about their group (Steele & Aronson, 1995). In other words, the mere fact that oppressive stereotypes exist and permeate our consciousness can already damage our well-being!

Another way in which oppressive stereotypes may affect those who face them is that members of oppressed groups may actively resist the inferiorizing stereotypes about their social group. However, in the process of resisting, oppressed individuals not only end up devoting and using physical, mental, and emotional resources that others are not forced to do, but they may also end up overdoing or overshooting cultural norms in their efforts to be accepted (Triandis, Kashima, Shimada, & Villareal, 1986). This desire to prove stereotypes wrong and be accepted by others may include denying membership to one's social group, distancing one's self from one's social group, or ceasing to participate or be involved in the traditions and practices of one's social group (David, 2013; Ellemers, Spears, & Doosje, 2002; Schmitt & Branscombe, 2001). For example, Cheryan and Monin (2005) found that Asian Americans who were subjected to the **perpetual foreigner stereotype**—when Asian Americans are regarded as less American than others or even non-American—end up putting more effort into proving their American identity by demonstrating knowledge of American TV shows and reporting higher levels of involvement in American sports, listening to American music, and having American friends than Asian Americans whose American identity was not challenged.

In another study, Guendelman, Cheryan, and Monin (2011) found that Asian Americans who were subjected to the perpetual foreigner stereotype were more likely to choose and consume prototypically American food (e.g., pizza, McDonald's Big Mac, prime rib, steak) than prototypically Asian food (e.g., stir-fried noodles, rice) than Asian Americans who did not experience the stereotype, suggesting the possibility that *Asian Americans may distance themselves from their heritage culture in their effort to resist stereotypes.* And as we have previously discussed, distancing one's self from one's social group—and for some even denying and rejecting one's social group—may lead to various psychosocial concerns such as loss of social support, lower self-esteem, lower life satisfaction, depression, and other health issues (e.g., David & Okazaki, 2006).

The effects of oppression on peoples' psychological experiences are not limited to their thoughts, feelings, and behaviors toward themselves. In other words, oppression does not affect just how one perceives (self-concept) and feels (self-esteem) about one's self. Instead, oppression also influences how people perceive, regard, and behave toward others who share the same or similar characteristics that they do, and others who do not share the same characteristics that they do. That is, *oppression may also influence people's thoughts, attitudes, and behaviors toward other members of their social group, other oppressed groups, and the dominant group.* In psychology, these topics are explored by identity development theories and there exists a wide variety of such models for different social groups (for a review, see Mio, Barker, & Domenech Rodriguez, 2016). For instance, there are several racial or ethnic identity development theories (including a White identity and a multiracial identity models), there is a gay/lesbian identity development model, and there is even a heterosexual identity development model. In all such models, *having a positive regard for one's social group, participating in the activities of one's social group, having pride in one's social group, having a good understanding of the history and contemporary reality of one's social group, and having a strong support network from one's social group are generally associated with better well-being.* Also in all of these models, society's messages about the traits and characteristics of social groups—many of which are driven by stereotypes that maintain oppressive conditions and processes—influence all phases or stages of identity development. Thus, according to these models, oppressive messages and conditions in society can negatively affect peoples' social identity development and well-being, and empirical research seems to support this (e.g., David, 2008; David & Okazaki, 2006; Rowley, Sellers, Chavous, & Smith, 1998; Sellers, Smith, Shelton, Rowley, & Chavous, 1998).

■ OPPRESSION ACROSS GENERATIONS

In addition to potentially leading to depression, psychological distress, and overall well-being issues, marginalized peoples' struggles with self-concept, collective self-esteem, and identity development due to the damages of oppression can also put them at higher risks for a range of other problems such as alcohol and drug use, suicide, poor school or job performance, gang involvement, crime, and various risky behaviors (e.g., unprotected sex that may lead to unintended pregnancies, sexually transmitted diseases). Therefore, it should be clear at this point that oppression is an important factor to consider when we think about the many health issues facing marginalized groups. However, we need to emphasize that we are not talking just about modern-day oppression here; *we must also understand that even oppression that happened a long time ago can still have effects on marginalized groups today!*

As discussed in Chapter 3, marginalized groups have experienced various forms of oppression throughout history. For instance, many peoples of color have experienced (and are still experiencing) colonialism wherein Western countries exploited their lands, inferiorized their bodies, and destroyed their cultures. Filipino peoples' colonial experience—as touched on the by the example given in the beginning of the chapter—is an example of this. Another instance of historical oppression is when Africans were taken from their homelands in the 1500s and enslaved for centuries. During World War II, the Aleut people of Alaska and Japanese Americans were forcibly relocated from their homes and placed in concentration camps by the U.S. government. Another example from World War II is when Jewish people faced genocide in Nazi Germany. Similarly, Native Americans faced (and are still facing) the brutal extermination of their culture by European settlers since the late 1400s. More recently, Vietnamese, Lao, and Cambodian people experienced mass death, destruction, and forced removal from their homelands during the Vietnam War from 1955 to 1975. In all of these examples, we are now finding out that the oppression directly experienced by peoples of earlier generations not only affected them, but seems to have also affected their descendants. Indeed, we are now learning that the disturbing psychological and mental health effects of oppression—as we discussed in the previous sections—are not due just to oppression that was directly or more proximally experienced by people. Instead, new research is showing that the oppression experienced by people from previous generations—the ancestors or previous in-group members of marginalized peoples today—may also significantly contribute to the psychological, behavioral, and mental health issues that their descendants are facing today.

According to scholars (e.g., Brave Heart, 2003; DeGruy; 2005; Duran & Duran, 1995; Nagata, Cheng, & Nguyen, 2012; Napoleon, 1996; White, 2012; Yehuda, 1999), the collective experience of oppression to which certain groups of people were subjected in the past may be conceptualized as **historical trauma**, which is the "cumulative emotional and psychological wounding over the lifespan and across generations, emanating from massive group trauma experiences" (Brave Heart, 2003, p. 7). In general, **trauma** is a deeply distressing experience that threatens one's life or safety (e.g., any form of violence, robbery, rape, accident, forced relocation and detention, or witnessing others experience such events) that elicits strong psychological responses. Extremely stressful experiences that make people feel less secure, more vulnerable, or in danger of being hurt physically, mentally, and emotionally can be considered traumatic. As mentioned earlier, many social groups have collectively experienced oppression throughout history, and such experiences may lead those who directly experienced the trauma to develop **historical trauma responses**, which are the mental, emotional, and behavioral consequences of the experienced trauma. According to Maria Yellow Horse Brave Heart (2003), a leading scholar in this area, historical trauma responses may be expressed as low self-esteem, depression, suicidal ideation and attempts, anxiety, anger, violence, and substance abuse.

The thoughts, emotions, and behaviors because of trauma—many of which are maladaptive and unhealthy (e.g., depression, anger, violence, substance abuse, suicide)—are witnessed and experienced by succeeding generations who, in turn, may also become traumatized by such experiences. These traumatic experiences from their ancestors, combined with continued experiences of contemporary oppression that mirrors the oppression of the past, can facilitate the intergenerational transmission of historical trauma responses. In other words, people today may be affected by historical trauma through its effects on their ancestors (e.g., the U.S. government's failure to honor the 1851 Treaty of Fort Laramie led to the loss of land, culture, and traditions for the Sioux people, traumatizing to many in the group) and may also be directly traumatized by contemporary forms of oppression that are similar to the historical oppression that their group faced (e.g., Western corporations and local police are intruding into Sioux territory today in Standing Rock, traumatizing people who are protecting the lands). Experiences of modern-day oppression may further complicate and exacerbate risk factors brought on by historical trauma (Brave Heart, 2003; Duran & Duran, 1995), further burdening the lives of marginalized peoples. This is why scholars (e.g., Kellermann, 2001; Myhra, 2011; Nagata, Kim, & Nguyen, 2015) have used the term **intergenerational trauma** to refer to the various manifestations of historical trauma faced by marginalized groups today as reflected by high rates of substance abuse, depression, suicide, domestic violence, and others.

More recently, an emerging body of research on **epigenetics** seems to suggest that the wounding that was caused by oppression that happened in the past extends beyond emotional and psychological damages. Instead, new research findings (Kellermann, 2013; Yehuda et al., 2016) seem to provide support to the notion that historical oppression may also influence our biology—our genes more specifically—and that these genetic level changes due to historical oppression may put later generations at higher risk for various health concerns. One mechanism through which historical oppression may be passed genetically is through methyl groups. Essentially, we have methyl groups in our system, and the amount of methyl groups we have in our bodies is influenced by factors in our environment and our life experiences. Thus, the amount, intensity, and chronicity of the stressors we face can influence the abundance of methyl groups we have. These methyl groups can attach to our DNA and, when the DNA has been methylated, alter the expression of the genes involved. If the altered genes are the ones associated with the trait of anger, for example, and if the *methylation altered the genes* in a way that expresses them as opposed to suppressing them, then the person becomes vulnerable to anger and other associated behaviors (e.g., violence). These altered genes—or genes that are either "turned on" or "turned off"—can be transmitted across generations.

One fascinating example of epigenetic changes through methylation is a study conducted by Yehuda and colleagues (2016) with people who were exposed and not exposed to the holocaust, along with their respective children. This study found that holocaust survivors had higher methylation levels of the *FKB5* gene—a stress-related gene associated with posttraumatic stress disorder and major depression—than people who did not experience the holocaust. Even further, the methylation levels of this gene between holocaust survivors and their children were correlated, leading the authors to conclude that "an intergenerational epigenetic priming of the physiological response to stress in offspring of highly traumatized individuals" may have taken place, and that such genetic "changes may contribute to the increased risk for psychopathology" for the descendants of traumatized individuals (p. 379). This study and the growing body of research on behavioral epigenetics (for a review, see Kellermann, 2013) are important because they suggest not only that oppression damages our biology (e.g., genes) in addition to damaging our psychology (thoughts, emotions, and actions), but also that the mental, emotional, and behavioral consequences of historical trauma (e.g., low self-esteem, depression, substance use, anger) may be passed on to later generations genetically in addition to passing them along through social-ization, parenting, or other direct first-hand experiences. Furthermore, these findings suggest that marginalized groups not only have to face the extra stressors brought on by modern-day oppression, but are also burdened and still have to cope with and overcome the stressors brought on by the historical oppression faced by their ancestors.

■ THE PSYCHOLOGICAL EFFECTS OF HISTORICAL AND CONTEMPORARY OPPRESSION

So to put it all together, *all types (e.g., racial, gender) and forms (e.g., subtle, blatant) of oppression at all levels (i.e., interpersonal, institutional, internalized)—whether they happened a long time ago (historical) or they were directly experienced in modern times (contemporary)—can negatively affect the psychological experiences and health of marginalized peoples.* As we present in Figure 6.1, we build on Hatzenbuehler's (2009) Integrative Mediation Framework of Group-Specific and General Psychological Processes to create a modified model that summarizes the potential consequences of historical and contemporary oppression on marginalized peoples' health and well-being. The variables in dashed-line rectangles represent the general stressors and stress responses that all people typically face; again, stress and our responses to them are just facts of life! Even further, we see that how we respond to the stressors we face can influence our health and well-being. However, as represented by the solid-line brown rectangles, individuals who are members of marginalized groups also face additional stressors to which they are forced to devote mental, emotional, and behavioral resources. Thus, there are stress responses that margin-alized peoples must also negotiate that are brought on by the stress of oppression. How marginalized peoples respond to the oppression that they face, in turn, may influence their health and well-being.

In addition to modern-day and more direct experiences of oppres-sion having an impact on marginalized peoples' health, we also see in Figure 6.1 that historical oppression through the intergenerational

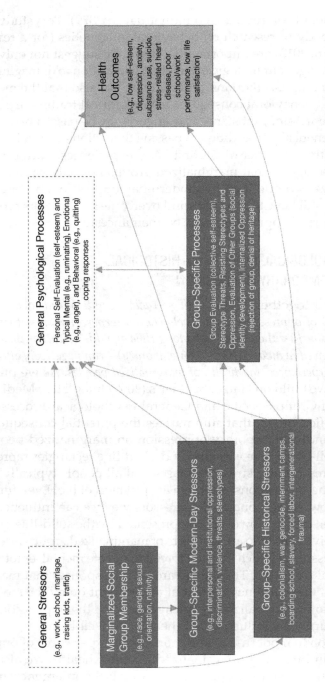

FIGURE 6.1 The potential consequences of historical and contemporary oppression on marginalized peoples' health and well-being.

transmission of historical trauma responses may continually affect marginalized peoples today. Also, the knowledge that one's social group has been experiencing oppression for generations may have a compounding effect on one's direct experiences of oppression. People, for example, may feel defeated, hopeless, angry, frustrated, or desperate to realize that their group has been fighting oppression for generations with very little—if any—success. Such a case may be what the Filipino man, described in the beginning of this chapter, may be feeling after his neighbor brought up—during the eve of the year 2017—blatantly racist views that started when the Philippines were colonized by the United States back in 1898! Thus, historical and contemporary oppression might interact with each other to affect peoples' psychological experiences and mental health. Even further, we are now learning that the intergenerational transmission of the effects of historical oppression on marginalized peoples' health does not just happen through socialization; instead, new evidence is emerging to suggest that the effects of oppression can be transmitted to later generations through epigenetic changes. Therefore, we see in the model that marginalized peoples not only have to face the extra stressors presented by modern-day oppression in addition to general stressors but are also burdened with the oppression experienced by their ancestors.

Finally, research has consistently found that *members of marginalized groups tend to underutilize mental health services*. Ethnic minorities, for example, are less likely to seek professional mental health treatment than Whites (e.g., Abe-Kim et al., 2007; Zhang, Snowden, & Sue, 1998). In addition to the stigma attached to psychological issues, historical and contemporary oppression may influence help-seeking attitudes and behaviors. Indeed, research suggests that marginalized peoples may learn to mistrust peoples and institutions because of oppression (e.g., Boyd-Franklin, 2003; David, 2010; Duran, 2006; Trimble & Gonzalez, 2008; Whaley, 2001), and so they choose not to seek services from people and institutions who they may perceive as representing or reflective of such oppression. Even further, other barriers that may be seen as instances of institutional oppression, such as lack of providers who are fluent in non-English languages, the insistence of agencies to adhere to culturally insensitive or inappropriate services, and the resistance to integrate other ways of healing (e.g., sweats) and value them, also contribute to why members of marginalized groups do not seek professional psychological help (Sue & Sue, 2013). Thus, combining the high rates of distress found among marginalized groups (as summarized in Table 6.1) and the fact that they face an overabundance of stressors brought on by historical and contemporary oppression (as summarized in Figure 6.1) with their low rates of service utilization, it is very likely that *many members of marginalized groups are not receiving the services they may need.* To this end, not only does oppression play a role in marginalized peoples' health, but it also influences marginalized peoples' access and utilization of health services that they may need—perhaps especially need—because of the damages brought onto them by oppression.

REFERENCES

Abe-Kim, J., Takeuchi, D. T., Hong, S., Zane, N., Sue, S., Spencer, M. S., . . . Alegría, M. (2007). Use of mental health-related services among immigrant and US-born Asian Americans: Results from the National Latino and Asian American Study. *American Journal of Public Health, 97*(1), 91–98.

Agency for Healthcare Research and Quality. (2009). *AHRQ activities to reduce racial and ethnic disparities in health care.* Retrieved from https://www.ahrq.gov/sites/default/files/publications/files/disparities.pdf

Allison, K. W. (1998). Stress and oppressed social category membership. In J. K. Swim & C. Stangor (Eds.), *Prejudice: The target's perspective* (pp. 145–170). San Diego, CA: Academic Press.

Allport, G. W. (1985). The historical background of social psychology. In L. Gardner & A. Elliot (Eds.), *The handbook of social psychology* (Vol. 1, pp. 1–46). Hillsdale, NJ: Lawrence Erlbaum.

Austin, S. B., Ziyadeh, N., Fisher, L. B., Kahn, J. A., Colditz, G. A., & Frazier, A. L. (2004). Sexual orientation and tobacco use in a cohort study of US adolescent girls and boys. *Archives of Pediatric and Adolescent Medicine, 158,* 317–322.

Bizman, A., Yinon, Y., & Krotman, S. (2001). Group-based emotional distress: An extension of self-discrepancy theory. *Personality and Social Psychology Bulletin, 27,* 1291–1300. doi:10.1177/01461672012710005

Booth, M. Z., & Gerard, J. (2011). Self-esteem and academic achievement: A comparative study of adolescents in British and American schools. *Compare, 41*(5), 629–648.

Boyd-Franklin, N. (2003). *Black families in therapy.* New York, NY: Guilford Press.

Brave Heart, M. Y. (2003). The historical trauma response among natives and its relationship with substance abuse: A Lakota illustration. *Journal of Psychoactive Drugs, 35*(1), 7–13.

Breslau, J., Aguilar-Gaxiola, S., Kendler, K. S., Su, M., Williams, D., & Kessler, R. C. (2006). Specifying race-ethnic differences in risk for psychiatric disorder in a U.S. national sample. *Psychological Medicine, 36*, 57–68.

Centers for Disease Control and Prevention. (2013). *Depression*. Retrieved from http://www.cdc.gov/mentalhealth/data_stats/depression.htm

Chae, D. H., Nuru-Jeter, A. M., Adler, N. E., Brody, G. H., Lin, J., Blackburn, E. H., & Epel, E. (2014). Discrimination, racial bias, and telomere length in African-American Men. *American Journal of Preventive Medicine, 46*, 103–111.

Cheryan, S., & Monin, B. (2005). "Where are you really from?": Asian Americans and identity denial. *Journal of Personality and Social Psychology, 89*(5), 717–730.

Clark, R., Anderson, N. B., Clark, V. R., & Williams, D. R. (1999). Racism as a stressor for African Americans. A biopsychosocial model. *American Psychologist, 54*(10), 805–816.

Crocker, J., Luhtanen, R., Blaine, B., & Broadnax, S. (1994). Collective self-esteem and psychological well-being among White, Black, and Asian college students. *Personality and Social Psychology Bulletin, 20*, 503–513.

David, E. J. R. (2008). A colonial mentality model of depression for Filipino Americans. *Cultural Diversity and Ethnic Minority Psychology, 14*, 118–127.

David, E. J. R. (2010). Cultural mistrust and mental health help-seeking attitudes among Filipino Americans. *Asian American Journal of Psychology, 1*, 57–66.

David, E. J. R. (2013). *Brown skin, white minds: Filipino -/ American postcolonial psychology* (with commentaries). Charlotte, NC: Information Age Publishing.

David, E. J. R. (Ed.). (2014). *Internalized oppression: The psychology of marginalized groups*. New York, NY: Springer Publishing.

David, E. J. R., & Okazaki, S. (2006). The Colonial Mentality Scale (CMS) for Filipino Americans: Scale construction and psychological implications. *Journal of Counseling Psychology, 53*, 241–252.

DeGruy, J. (2005). *Post-traumatic slave syndrome. America's legacy of enduring injury and healing.* Portland, OR: Uptone Press.

Dohrenwend, B. P. (Ed.). (1998). *Adversity, stress, and psychopathology.* New York: Oxford University Press.

Duran, E. (2006). *Healing the soul wound: Counseling with American Indians and other native peoples.* New York, NY: Teachers College Press.

Duran, E., & Duran, B. (1995). *Native American postcolonial psychology.* Albany: State University of New York Press.

Edwards, W. V., & Erwin-Johnson, C. (2003). NAACP to focus on minority health disparities. *Crisis (The New), 110,* 54–56.

Ellemers, N., Spears, R., & Doosje, B. (2002). Self and social identity. *Annual Review of Psychology, 53,* 161–186.

Guendelman, M. D., Cheryan, S., & Monin, B. (2011). Fitting in but getting fat: Identity threat and dietary choices among U.S. immigrant groups. *Psychological Science, 22*(7), 959–967.

Gupta, T., Rogers-Sirn, L., Okazaki, S., Ryce, P., & Sirin, S. R. (2014). The role of collective self esteem on anxious-depressed symptoms over time among Asian and Latino immigrant youth. *Cultural Diversity and Ethnic Minority Psychology, 20*(2), 220–230.

Hatzenbuehler, M. L. (2009). How does sexual minority stigma get "under the skin": A psychological mediation framework. *Psychological Bulletin, 135*(5), 707–730.

Hatzenbuehler, M. L., Corbin, W. R., & Fromme, K. (2008). Trajectories and determinants of alcohol use among sexual minority young adults and their heterosexual peers: Results from a prospective study. *Developmental Psychology, 44,* 81–90.

Hatzenbuehler, M. L., McLaughlin, K. A., & Nolen-Hoeksema, S. (2008). Emotion regulation and the development of internalizing symptoms in a longitudinal study of LGB adolescents and their heterosexual peers. *Journal of Child Psychology and Psychiatry, 49,* 1270–1278.

He, S. (2015, March). *Asian American mental health disparities and cultural psychiatry.* Presentation at George Washington University, Washington, DC. Retrieved from https://smhs.gwu.edu/psychiatry/sites/psychiatry/files/Sally%20He.pdf

Hill, L. K., Hoggard, L. S., Richmond, A., Gray, D. L., Williams, D. P., & Thayer, J. F. (2017). Examining the association between perceived discrimination and heart rate variability in African Americans. *Cultural Diversity & Ethnic Minority Psychology, 23*, 5–14.

Hong, S., Walton, E., Tamaki, E., & Sabin, J. (2014). Lifetime prevalence of mental disorders among Asian Americans: Nativity, gender, and sociodemographic correlates. *Asian American Journal of Psychology, 5*(4), 353–363.

James, S. E., Herman, J. L., Rankin, S., Keisling, M., Mottet, L., & Anafi, M. (2016). *Executive summary of the report of the 2015 U.S. transgender survey.* Washington, DC: National Center for Transgender Equality.

Kaiser Family Foundation. (2013). *Health coverage by race and ethnicity: The potential impact of the Affordable Care Act.* Menlo Park, CA: Kaiser Family Foundation. Retrieved from http://kff.org/disparities-policy/issue-brief/health-coverage-by-race-and-ethnicity-the-potential-impact-of-the-affordable-care-act

Katz, J., Joiner, T. E., & Kwon, P. (2002). Membership in a devalued social group and emotional well-being: Developing a model of personal self-esteem, collective self-esteem, and group socialization. *Sex Roles, 47*(9), 419–431.

Kellermann, N. P. F. (2001). Perceived parental rearing behavior in children of Holocaust survivors. *Israel Journal of Psychiatry, 38*, 58–68.

Kellermann, N. P. F. (2013). Epigenetic transmission of holocaust trauma: Can nightmares be inherited? *The Israel Journal of Psychiatry and Related Sciences, 50*(1), 30–39.

Krahn, G. L., Walker, D. K., & Correa-De-Araujo, R. (2015). Persons with disabilities as an unrecognized health disparity population. *American Journal of Public Health, 105*, 198–206. doi:10.2105/AJPH.2014.302182

Lee, S., Martins, S., & Lee, H. (2014). Mental disorders and mental health service use across Asian American subethnic groups in the United States. *Community Mental Health Journal, 51*(2), 153–160.

Meyer, I. H. (2003). Prejudice, social stress, and mental health in lesbian, gay, and bisexual populations: Conceptual issues and research evidence. *Psychological Bulletin, 129*, 674–697.

Mio, J. S., Barker, L. A., & Domenech Rodriguez, M. M. (2016). *Multicultural psychology: Understanding our diverse communities.* New York, NY: Oxford University Press.

Myhra, L. L. (2011). "It runs in the family": Intergenerational transmission of historical trauma among urban American Indians and Alaska Natives in culturally specific sobriety maintenance programs. *Journal of American Indian and Alaska Native Mental Health Research, 18*(2), 17–40.

Nagata, D. K., Cheng, W. J. Y., & Nguyen, T. U. (2012). Recollections of historical injustice: A qualitative investigation of emotions in Japanese American incarceration memories. In D. K. Nagata, L. Kohn-Wood, & L. A. Suzuki (Eds.), *Qualitative strategies for ethnocultural research* (pp. 103–118). Washington, DC: American Psychological Association.

Nagata, D. K., Kim, J. H. J., & Nguyen, T. (2015). Processing cultural trauma: Intergenerational effects of the Japanese American incarceration. *Journal of Social Issues, 71*(2), 356–370.

Napoleon, H. (1996). *Yuuyaraq: The way of the human being.* Fairbanks: University of Alaska Press.

Ong, A. D., Williams, D. R., Nwizu, U., & Gruenewald, T. L. (2017). Everyday unfair treatment and multisystem biological dysregulation in African-American Adults. *Cultural Diversity & Ethnic Minority Psychology, 23,* 27–35.

Pearlin, L. I. (1999). The stress process revisited: Reflections on concepts and their interrelationships. In C. S. Aneshensel & J. C. Phelan (Eds.), *Handbook of the sociology of mental health* (pp. 395–415). New York, NY: Springer.

Pedersen, E. R., Hsu, S. H., Neighbors, C., Lee, C. M., & Larimer, M.E. (2013). The relationship between collective self-esteem, acculturation, and alcohol-related consequences among Asian American young adults. *Journal of Ethnicity and Substance Abuse, 12*(1), 51–67. doi:10.1080/15332640.2013.759769

Plöderl, M., & Fartacek, R. (2005). Suicidality and associated risk factors among lesbian, gay, and bisexual compared to heterosexual Austrian adults. *Suicide and Life Threatening Behavior, 35,* 661–670.

Random House Webster's Dictionary. (1992). New York, NY: Random House.

Rowley, S. J., Sellers, R. M., Chavous, T. M., & Smith, M. A. (1998). The relationship between racial identity and self-esteem in African American college and high school students. *Journal of Personality and Social Psychology, 74,* 715–724.

Safren, S. A., & Heimberg, R. G. (1999). Depression, hopelessness, suicidality, and related factors in sexual minority and heterosexual adolescents. *Journal of Consulting and Clinical Psychology, 67,* 859–866.

Schmitt, M. T., & Branscombe, N. R. (2001). The good, the bad, and the manly: Threats to one's prototypicality and evaluations of fellow in-group members. *Journal of Experimental Social Psychology, 37*(6), 510–517.

Sellers, R. M., Smith, M. A., Shelton, J. N., Rowley, S. A. J., & Chavous, T. M. (1998). The multidimensional model of racial identity: A reconceptualization of African American racial identity. *Personality and Social Psychology Review, 2,* 18–39.

Sharma, S., & Agarwalaa, S. (2013). Contribution of self-esteem and collective self-esteem in predicting depression. *Psychological Thought, 6*(1), 117–123.

Steele, C., & Aronson, J. (1995). Stereotype threat and the intellectual test performance of African Americans. *Journal of Personality & Social Psychology, 69*(5), 797–811.

Substance Abuse & Mental Health Services Administration. (2003). *State estimates of substance use from the 2001 National Household Survey on Drug Abuse: Vol. II.* Individual state tables and technical appendices. Retrieved from http://oas.samhsa.gov/NHSDA/2k1State/pdf/2k1SAEv/pdf

Substance Abuse & Mental Health Services Administration. (2014). *Results from the 2012 National Survey on Drug Use and Health: Summary of National Findings.* NSDUH Series H-46, HHS Publication No. (SMA) 13-4795. Rockville, MD: Author.

Sue, D. W. (2010). *Microaggressions in everyday life: Race, gender, and sexual orientation.* Hoboken, NJ: Wiley.

Sue, D. W., & Sue, D. (2013). *Counseling the culturally diverse: Theory and practice.* New York, NY: Wiley.

Tajfel, H., & Turner, J. C. (1979). An integrative theory of intergroup conflict. In W. G. Austin & S. Worchel (Eds.), *The social psychology of intergroup relations* (pp. 33–47). Monterey, CA: Brooks/Cole.

Tajfel, H., & Turner, J. C. (1986). The social identity theory of intergroup behaviour. In S. Worchel & W. G. Austin (Eds.), *Psychology of intergroup relations* (pp. 7–24). Chicago, IL: Nelson-Hall.

Triandis, H. C., Kashima, Y., Shimada, E., & Villareal, M. (1986). Acculturation indices as a means of confirming cultural differences. *International Journal of Psychology, 21,* 43–70.

Trimble, J. E., & Gonzalez, J. (2008). Cultural considerations and perspectives for providing psychological counseling for Native American Indians. In P. B. Pedersen, J. G. Draguns, W. J. Lonner, & J. E. Trimble (Eds.), *Counseling across cultures* (pp. 93–111). Thousand Oaks, CA: Sage.

U.S. Department of Health and Human Services. (2003). *National Healthcare Disparities Report: Executive summary.* Washington, DC: Author. Retrieved from https://archive.ahrq.gov/qual/nhdr03/nhdrsum03.htm

Whaley, A. L. (2001). Cultural mistrust and the clinical diagnosis of paranoid schizophrenia in African American patients. *Journal of Psychopathology and Behavioral Assessment, 23*(2), 93–100. doi:10.1023/A:1010911608102

Wheaton, B. (1999). The nature of stressors. In A. F. Horwitz & T. L. Scheid (Eds.), *A handbook for the study of mental health: Social contexts, theories, and systems* (pp. 176–197). Cambridge, England: Cambridge University Press.

White, V. (2012). Historical, generational trauma haunt Vietnamese seniors in U.S. *New America Media.* Retrieved from http://newamericamedia .org/2012/01/historical-generational-trauma-haunt-vietnamese -seniors-in-us-editors-note-the-vietnam-war-continues.php

Wichstrom, L., & Hegna, K. (2003). Sexual orientation and suicide attempt: A longitudinal sample of the general Norwegian sample. *Journal of Abnormal Psychology, 112,* 144–151.

Wilburn, V. R., & Smith, D. E. (2005). Stress, self-esteem, and suicidal ideation in late adolescents. *Adolescence, 40*(157), 33–45.

Woods, T. M., Zuniga, R., & David, E. J. R. (2012). A preliminary report on the relationships between historical trauma, collective self-esteem, and mental health among Alaska Native peoples. *Journal of Indigenous Research, 1*(2), Article 1. Retrieved from http:// digitalcommons.usu.edu/kicjir/vol1/iss2/1

Yehuda, R. (1999). *Risk factors for posttraumatic stress disorder.* Washington, DC: American Psychiatric Press.

Yehuda, R., Daskalakis, N. P., Bierer, L. M., Bader, H. N., Klengel, T., Halsboer, F., & Binder, E. B. (2016). Holocaust exposure induced intergenerational effects on FKBP5 methylation. *Biological Psychiatry, 1*(80), 372–380.

Zhang, A. Y., Snowden, L. R., & Sue, S. (1998). Differences between Asian and White Americans' help seeking and utilization patterns in the Los Angeles area. *Journal of Community Psychology, 26*(4), 317–326.

CHAPTER 7

Why Is There Oppression?
Social Psychological Theories on the
Existence and Persistence of Oppression

Now that we know what oppression is, who has experienced oppression historically and contemporarily, how it may manifest and operate, how it has evolved over time, and that oppression has serious negative consequences, you may be thinking: *Well, what should we do to stop it*? Later in Chapters 8 and 9, we discuss some clinical and community efforts that may help us address oppression and its many consequences. Before we do that, however, we need to continue to better understand oppression by exploring its potential origins so that—hopefully—we can address it more completely and effectively. In other words, now that we have a basic understanding of the *what, who, when, how*, and *so what* of oppression, let us move on to the *why*: *Why does oppression exist and continue to persist*?

This chapter focuses on social psychological theories because, as we discussed in Chapter 6, social psychology is the study of how our thoughts, feelings, and behaviors are influenced by other people and the cultural norms, expectations, assumptions, and standards by which we live. And as we discussed in Chapter 5, cultural norms, expectations, assumptions, and standards that become institutionalized or become unquestionably regarded as "normal" can privilege or benefit some groups of people while disadvantaging others; *this is oppression!* This is why it is not surprising that many of the central topics examined in the subfield of social psychology—such as stereotypes, prejudices, discrimination, interpersonal processes, aggression, social group identity, and intergroup processes and dynamics—are related to oppression in very important ways. Thus, the subfield of social psychology has contributed significantly to

TABLE 7.1   Some Social Psychological Theories for Why Oppression Exists

Theory	Core Belief	What Motivates Oppression?	Perception of Out-Group
Social Identity Theory	People seek to have positive social identity	Protect or enhance self-esteem	Relatively "not-as-good" as in-group
Social Dominance Theory	Inevitable social group hierarchy	Competition for limited resources; maintenance of power	Competitors; enemies
Terror Management Theory	Mortality threatens erasure of worldview	Own worldviews must be preserved to transcend death	Foreigners imposing their worldviews
Right-Wing Authoritarianism	The world is dangerous	Protection of conventional values	Morally corrupt; deviants
System Justification Theory	The system is fair, legitimate, and just; people get what they deserve	Keep society stable and familiar	Resistors; anarchists
Colonial Theory	Perceived superiority of one's group	Manifest destiny; civilization	Inferior; unenlightened; undeveloped

our understanding of social group oppression, including why it happens. To this end, this chapter provides an overview of some leading theories in social psychology (listed and briefly described in Table 7.1) that may explain why oppression exists and has persisted throughout history. This way, we will better understand not only what oppression is, how it operates, whom it affects, and how it affects people, but also what might be causing and perpetuating it. Let us start with social identity theory (SIT).

■ SOCIAL IDENTITY THEORY

As discussed in Chapter 6, an important part of our self-concept, in addition to our personal or individual self, is our **collective self**—the part of our identity that is linked to the social groups to which we belong. This is why the way in which we feel about the characteristics of our social groups—our *collective self-esteem*—is as important to our well-being as how we feel about our personal or individual characteristics—our *personal self-esteem.* This notion that although we are all unique individuals, we are all still parts of social groups, and that our social group membership is an important component of our self-concept, is based on **social identity theory** (Tajfel & Turner, 1979). According to SIT, we have a need to positively regard our social identity—to protect or enhance our collective self-esteem—so we have a tendency to more positively regard the characteristics of the groups to which we belong (our *in-group*) compared to the characteristics of groups to which we do not belong (our *out-group*; Tajfel, 1981). Thus, based on SIT, *people favor their in-group and discriminate against out-groups in order to make themselves feel better about the in-group.* In this sense, all of us—including members of marginalized groups—may emphasize traits or characteristics of our in-group as better, more desirable, or advantageous than traits or characteristics of other groups in order to make us feel better about ourselves.

The existence of **in-group favoritism**—our tendency to favor the social groups to which we belong—is normal (Brewer, 1999). E.J.R. David, whose social identity includes being a Seahawks fan, tends to favor the Seattle Seahawks and put down Annie Derthick's hometown football team—the Atlanta Falcons. Such an example is common among sports fans whose self-concept includes being part of their team's "fanbase" (e.g., "The Cameron Crazies" of Duke University Basketball, the "Cheeseheads" of the Green Bay Packers). *The fact that we all have a tendency for in-group favoritism, however, does not automatically mean that we are all oppressive.* Just because E. J. as a Seahawks fan may "talk smack" about the Falcons and hurt Annie's feelings does not mean that E. J. is oppressing them because E. J. and the Seahawks do not have more power and privilege over the Falcons, Annie, and other Falcons fans. One example of a power and privilege imbalance, for instance, would be if the Seahawks get seven tries to get 10 yards while the Falcons get only five attempts. Fortunately, the National Football League (NFL) does not have rules that favor and advantage the Seahawks over the Falcons. Thus, there are no power and privilege imbalances between the Seahawks, the Falcons, or any other NFL team.

Beyond sports, however, our tendency to favor our in-group and devalue out-groups may become dangerous. This is because our preferences, favoritism, or discrimination based on social group membership are not all equally backed up, supported, or protected by institutionalized norms, expectations, assumptions, rules, and standards. In other words, there are existing imbalances in terms of power and privilege between different social groups (as discussed in Chapter 2). Thus, *this tendency to favor our in-group and discriminate against the out-group in order to protect or enhance our self-esteem becomes dangerous when it is done by social groups that are already powerful and privileged.* For example, LGBTQ people may regard heterosexist people as untrustworthy and choose not to invest in businesses owned by heterosexist people, but such a belief and resulting action does not take away from the power and privileges that heterosexual people have. On the other hand, if heterosexual people regard LGBTQ people as morally corrupt and choose not to serve, hire, or interact in any way with LGBTQ people, then LGBTQ people become even more powerless and vulnerable. This is because heterosexual people hold more power and privileges in our society than LGBTQ people. Always remember that *oppression has two Ps!* Therefore, more dominant, powerful, or privileged social groups that automatically regard the characteristics of their group as better or superior compared to the characteristics of other social groups—a strong tendency that we all have according to SIT—are engaging in the process of oppression and maintaining the state of oppression.

■ SOCIAL DOMINANCE THEORY

The existing power and privilege imbalance between social groups—*social hierarchies*—are inevitable and even normal, according to **social dominance theory** (SDT) (Sidanius & Pratto, 1999). SDT views social groups as competitors for limited resources, and the groups that are able to "win" and get more resources than others are deservedly on top of the social hierarchy whereas social groups who "lose" are rightfully at the bottom. In other words, SDT views the world as a competition, a "dog-eat-dog" world, if you may (Duckitt, 2001). Thus, according to SDT, *some social groups end up with more power and privilege than other groups, and end up working to maintain such a state of oppression, because of competition for limited resources.* For instance, SDT would explain that the dominance of White people, U.S. citizens, males, heterosexual folks, and nondisabled people in our current society is because such groups are "winning" the competition for the limited resources we have in our world.

Also in this perspective, societies, social groups, and individuals differ on the extent to which they believe in the inevitability, necessity, and even adaptability of a world arranged by social hierarchies—a construct called **social dominance orientation** (SDO). In other words, *SDT posits that people fall on a continuum in terms of how much they believe that social hierarchies—a state of oppression—are inevitable and necessary, from people who believe in equality between groups (low SDO) to those who believe* *that some groups should be more dominant and powerful than others (high SDO).* There are existing measures that attempt to capture and quantify the SDO construct, asking individuals to rate their level of agreement to items such as "Some groups of people are simply inferior to other groups," "Group equality should not be our primary goal," and "Some groups of people must be kept in their place." Higher scores on *SDO scales* indicate stronger belief in the inherent dominance of some groups and antiegalitarianism (Ho et al., 2015). Research has shown that people with higher SDO tend to also have higher levels of racism, cultural elitism, anti-Arab attitudes, sexism, and other biases, as well as lower levels of empathy, tolerance, communality, altruism, and openness to new experiences (Pratto, Sidanius, Stallworth, & Malle, 1994; Sidanius, Pratto, & Bobo, 1996).

In addition to providing an explanation for why people oppress (i.e., competition for limited resources), SDT is also a theory that attempts to explain how oppression is maintained. *In SDT, people oppress others to maintain their power and dominance.* Indeed, research suggests that people with more power and privilege are more likely to hold attitudes consistent with SDO, which in turn increases prejudice and in-group favoritism (Guimond, Dambrun, Michinov, & Duarte, 2003; Levin, Federico, Sidanius, & Rabinowitz, 2002). According to SDT, people high on SDO are more likely to create and believe in legitimizing myths (e.g., stereotypes) about different social groups that keep social groups in their respective places in society and, thus, maintain the existing hierarchy. **Legitimizing myths** are beliefs that justify the dominance of some social groups or the inferiority of other social groups (Sidanius & Pratto, 1999). For example, the notion of Manifest Destiny was used to justify U.S. imperialism and colonization of other peoples (e.g., Alaska Natives, Filipinos, Native Hawaiians, Chamorros, Puerto Ricans), riding the self-serving (and self-esteem enhancing) myth that it is the "White Man's Burden" to benevolently teach and civilize the unenlightened savages of the world (Kipling, 1899). More contemporarily, the widespread belief of many Americans on *meritocracy*—that all that is needed for one to succeed is hard work and ability—legitimizes the power and privileges that some social groups have because it is assumed that such dominance is well deserved due to such groups' skill, hard work, and effort. At the same time, the myth of meritocracy insinuates that those who are not successful—social groups that remain struggling at the bottom of the social hierarchy—are there simply because they are not competent, not capable, or not trying hard enough.

■ TERROR MANAGEMENT THEORY

Another theory that may explain why social group oppression exists is **terror management theory (TMT)** (Solomon, Greenberg, & Pyszczynski, 1991). According to TMT, people eventually realize that they are going to die at some point—a concept called *mortality salience* (Solomon, Greenberg, & Pyszczynski, 1991). This threat of inevitable death, but being uncertain about when it will happen and what comes next, creates *terror* and so people try to *manage* this terror by seeking ways to transcend death (Castano & Dechesne, 2005). One way through which people transcend death, per TMT, is by having worldviews—including a belief about the afterlife—that allow them to "survive" (albeit symbolically) even after death (Jonas & Fischer, 2006). Oftentimes, worldviews about larger issues such as the afterlife—and how one should live in order to get a good afterlife (e.g., heaven instead of hell, karma)—is strongly tied to people's religion or spirituality. For example, some people may manage their terror of death by believing in heaven, reincarnation, or resurrection after they die, all of which provide people with some idea (if not certainty) of what might happen after death.

In addition to influencing beliefs about the afterlife, *people's attempts to manage the terror of their mortality and transcend death by symbolically surviving also extend to their views on other large issues.* Similar to how one may view the afterlife, people's views on other large issues (e.g., what "American values" should be, equality for all of humanity, abortion, sexuality) are also often influenced by, if not tied to, their religion or spirituality. For instance, adhering to the Catholic religion and its teachings may lead a person to believe in the existence of heaven and hell, and hold the belief that living virtuously and without sin—which includes abortion and homosexuality, for example—determines whether one's soul goes to heaven or hell after death. Thus, people who adhere to Catholicism might also strongly oppose other large issues such as abortion rights and homosexuality, instilling such beliefs in their children and working to have such beliefs be institutionalized by the larger society (e.g., supporting antiabortion laws, not supporting gay marriage laws). Indeed, people tend to live their lives according to what their worldviews dictate as making a "good person" or defining a "good life," as this allows people to ease their anxieties about what will happen to them in the afterlife and their fears about potentially wasting their lives. In fact, TMT posits that people's evaluations of themselves—their self-esteem—is dependent on the extent to which they live their lives according to the worldviews to which they subscribe (Solomon et al., 1991).

Holding a particular view on large issues that will still be around and ongoing even after death gives people the sense that they belong to (e.g., national identity, cultural group, the ones who are "saved")—and are contributing to (e.g., preservation of culture, betterment of humanity)—something greater that will outlive them. Thus, people make sure that the worldviews to which they subscribe remain even after they die. To preserve their worldviews, people work to strengthen those who share the same worldviews as themselves—their in-group—which they see as outliving them and, thus, will continue to symbolically represent them even after death. It is logical, then, to see other groups that hold different worldviews as threats and to work toward eliminating such threats, or at least protecting one's in-group from the imposition of such threats. Thus, *in TMT, oppression happens because social groups are trying to protect their worldviews—worldviews that symbolically allow them to transcend death—from being erased and replaced by other worldviews that are held by other social groups.* Research seems to support this, as people whose mortality was made salient tend to preserve views that are familiar to them and react harshly to out-groups (Burke, Martens, & Faucher, 2010; Castano, 2004; Greenberg et al., 1990).

■ RIGHT-WING AUTHORITARIANISM

Similar to TMT, the literature on **right-wing authoritarianism (RWA)** also suggests that people cherish the values they hold and they also attempt to protect such values from being erased or replaced. However, TMT speaks to all social groups and how they all attempt to protect their value systems or worldviews, whereas RWA is a specific value dimension that only some people hold. In other words, TMT is a theory about how all social groups attempt to keep their respective worldviews, whereas the literature on RWA may be conceptualized as a theory about a specific worldview that some people hold and how they attempt to protect this worldview. Also unlike TMT, there is no focus in RWA on managing one's anxieties about one's impending death and to symbolically survive after death. Instead, *according to RWA, what people attempt to manage are their fears about living in a world they perceive as dangerous* (Duckitt, 2001).

So what is the RWA value dimension? *RWA is a tendency (a) to believe that authorities are legitimate; (b) to follow or obey authorities and not criticize them; (c) to be intolerant of others who hold different moral, racial, and political differences; (d) to adhere to societal conventions and norms, and value uniformity; and (e) to agree to hostile and punitive treatments (e.g., coercion, oppression) of people who do not follow authorities or adhere to social norms, rules, or expectations*

(Altemeyer, 1981; Mavor, Louis, & Sibley, 2010; Stenner, 2009). This strong belief in the importance of group cohesion, law and order, strict adherence to laws and policies, and conformity to cultural norms is rooted in the belief that the world is dangerous (Duckitt, 2001). RWA posits that people may regulate the threats of a dangerous world by preferring an orderly, well-regulated society that adheres to traditional or conventional values. Thus, worldviews and ways of living that challenge conventions are seen as threats to the social order that is believed to be necessary in a dangerous world. When conventional values are threatened by other values held by other social groups, then resistance happens. *This resistance against changing cultural norms, expectations, assumptions, and standards—conventions that are perceived to be necessary to protect against the dangers of the world—may be the occasion when social group oppression may happen.* In societies in which people who hold RWA beliefs and attitudes are in power, social group oppression may happen as people who adhere to RWA attempt to protect their worldviews, because—as research suggests—people who subscribe to the RWA worldview have a tendency to derogate out-groups and use coercion, force, intimidation, aggression, and punishment against those who are perceived as deviant out-groups (e.g., Altemeyer, 1981; Duckitt, 1993; Jost, Glaser, Kruglanski, & Sulloway, 2003; Stenner, 2009).

People vary on where they fall on the RWA dimension. By using the RWA scale (Altemeyer, 1981)—which asks people how much they agree with statements such as "The established authorities generally turn out to be right about things, while the radicals and protestors are usually just 'loud mouths' showing off their ignorance," "This country would work a lot better if certain groups of troublemakers would just shut up and accept their group's traditional place in society," and "There are many radical, immoral people in our country today, who are trying to ruin it for their own godless purposes, whom the authorities should put out of action"—researchers have learned that people high on RWA tend to hold prejudiced beliefs against women, feminists, gays, lesbians, and racial and ethnic minorities (Altemeyer, 2007; Duckitt, 1992; Duckitt & Farre, 1994; Goodman & Moradi, 2008; Haddock & Zanna, 1994; Haddock, Zanna, & Esses, 1993; Heaven & St. Quintin, 2003). Empirical research also suggests that people who strongly adhere to RWA worldviews are more likely to oppose abortion, support capital punishment, oppose gun control laws, not value social equality, accept covert governmental activities such as illegal wiretaps, deny that the Jewish Holocaust happened, and even support the repeal of the Bill of Rights (Altemeyer, 1996, 2007; Yelland & Stone, 1996).

■ SYSTEM JUSTIFICATION THEORY

Consistent with the arguments presented by the literature on RWA, **system justification theory (SJT)** also posits that some people are resistant to losing their values. SJT goes beyond values, however, to a stronger focus on the systems and institutions that implement, uphold, protect, and strengthen such values. Also, SJT does not apply to just the people who happen to adhere to one specific value system—which is what RWA is; instead, SJT applies generally to people who believe in the importance of preserving value systems that they may not even necessarily adhere to. In other words, *SJT is a theory about how people resist changes to the existing systems and institutions, regardless of whether such systems and institutions reflect or not reflect their values or worldviews, because existing systems and institutions are believed to be fair, legitimate, and just.* Even further, unlike SIT, SDT, TMT, and RWA—all of which argue that social group oppression happens because of self- or in-group-protecting or enhancing motivations—*SJT argues that oppression may also happen as social groups engage in a "process by which existing social arrangements are legitimized, even at the expense of personal and group interest"* (Jost & Banaji, 1994, p. 2). Indeed, according to Jost, Banaji, and Nosek (2004), the dominant view espoused by SIT, SDT, TMT, and RWA that "Ingroup favoritism and outgroup derogation may be relatively common" may be true, "but they are by no means the only reactions that people have to social groups, especially when status and power differences (between social groups) are involved" (p. 884). Thus, while SIT, SDT, TMT, and RWA focus on protecting, maintaining, and even strengthening one's self and one's in-group, *SJT focuses on protecting, maintaining, and even strengthening the systems that are in place.*

So how does SJT operate to ensure that the status quo remains unchanged? According to SJT, some people believe in the **just-world hypothesis** (or sometimes called the *just-world fallacy*; Furnham, 2003), a worldview that the world is just, which means that some people believe that people get what they deserve. For example, they may see poor people as deserving of their condition due to their own faults like laziness, unwillingness to work, lack of initiative, or lack of ability. Simultaneously, they may believe that all one must do in order to become successful in this world is to work hard, put in effort, have motivation, and be strongly determined. As you may notice, *this kind of thinking totally ignores the influence that existing systems and institutions may have on people— influences that favor or privilege some people while disadvantaging others (as discussed in Chapters 1 and 5)—and puts the responsibility entirely on people.* Thus, this often leads to a phenomenon called **victim-blaming**, wherein people are blamed and seen as deserving of undesirable life conditions or experiences. For example, women who are victims of sexual violence are often subjected to questions such as what were they wearing, what were they drinking, why were they at a particular place at a particular time of night, why were they alone, or why were they hanging out with certain people as if looking for a reason to blame the woman for being victimized and rationalize (if not justify) the violence they experienced. In the process, systems and institutions that normalize, protect, and even encourage the sexual objectification of women and the view of women as unequal to men remain unchallenged and, thus, unchanged—justifying and preserving the system.

Holding the belief that people get what they deserve may lead to the perception of those in power as completely and solely responsible for their success. That is, people see those in power as successful due only to their hard work, hustle, grit, effort, determination, and resilience—failing to recognize how existing systems and institutions may have favored such people and, thus, helped bring such people to power—further justifying existing systems and institutions and providing further "proof" that the status quo is legitimate and fair. When people in power believe they are solely responsible for their success, and that others are less privileged due solely to their own faults, then it is what scholars call **false consciousness.** When people who are marginalized believe that those who are in power got there solely because of their own doing and that existing systems and institutions did not benefit or advantage them in any way, and that marginalized groups are such only because of their own faults (e.g., laziness, unwillingness to work hard), then it is what scholars call **out-group favoritism** (Jost & Hunyady, 2002)—a manifestation of internalized oppression. *Thus, in SJT, we see how institutional oppression may lead to internalized oppression which, in turn, operates to justify institutional oppression.*

■ COLONIAL THEORY

Speaking of people who come to adhere to and protect the systems that oppress them, the literature on colonial theory also provides important insight into why oppression—including the internalization of oppression—happens. According to **colonial theory** (Fanon, 1965), *some groups of people exploit other lands and the peoples of such lands because of a belief that it is their destiny or right to do, which is based on their perceived inherent superiority over other people.* Unlike SIT, SDT, RWA, TMT, and SJT, all of which attempt to protect something that is perceived to be threatened (e.g., self-esteem, worldviews, stability of system), colonial theory is about passing on or propagating what one believes are superior, better, or more civilized ways of believing and doing things (e.g., Christianity, capitalism, Western culture and norms). Thus, colonizing groups may believe that their intention is benevolent as they forcefully civilize, enlighten, or develop the lives of who they perceive as uncivilized, unenlightened, or undeveloped people. In the process, *anything that is of the colonizing group is associated with superiority or desirability whereas anything that is of the "other" is associated with inferiority and undesirability.* Eventually, the institutions that are developed in the colony are designed to benefit the colonizers and people who have assimilated or adopted the colonizers' characteristics, worldviews, standards, culture, and norms. An example of this is how the United States forcefully took lands from Native Americans to exploit the resources, forced Native Americans to attend boarding schools, violently erased indigenous languages, worldviews, and ways of living by associating them with inferiority, and forcefully replaced them with what the colonizers portrayed as superior or more civilized ways (e.g., the English language, Christianity). Native Americans who assimilate and forget their indigenous ways (a manifestation of internalized oppression) are rewarded by the colonial society, whereas Native Americans who hold on to their indigenous ways are continued to be regarded as backward, primitive savages.

It is important to note that although Fanon's (1965) classic theory was based on and for the experiences of oppression by colonized racial or ethnic groups, *this colonial framework may also be applied to the experiences of other oppressed groups* such as women (e.g., Comas-Diaz, 2010), sexual minorities (e.g., Hawley, 2001), and people with disabilities (e.g., Kumari-Campbell, 2008). For example, our contemporary understanding of **gender**—the societal creation and implementation of what roles and behaviors are appropriate for men and women, as well as the limited conceptualization of gender in binary terms of masculinity and femininity—was instituted by colonialism and has been protected, legitimized, and strengthened over time through the systems, institutions, and social norms that were established in colonized societies (Crouch & David, 2017). Colonialized gender norms were rooted in **patriarchy**, the male domination of all aspects of society with women being "othered" or being regarded as less than, similar to how colonized groups are regarded as being inferior to colonizing groups. In a patriarchal world, men have privileges and advantages (e.g., voting, allowed to run for governmental office, allowed to attend school, play certain sports, get paid more) that women do not and being a woman is associated with being physically, emotionally, and intellectually weak.

It is also important to point out that colonial theory is applicable not just to the past "colonial times." In other words, colonial theory is not obsolete or irrelevant today. This is because *there are still colonies to this day* (e.g., Puerto Rico, Guam, American Samoa) wherein the colonized lands and peoples continue to be exploited and oppressed by colonizers who continue to benefit and profit from them, and wherein the colonized are still regarded as less than the colonizer (e.g., colonized people are not regarded as citizens and, thus, they do not hold rights that citizens do). Further, although some places and peoples may no longer be officially colonized (e.g., the Philippines), the systems and institutions that exist in such places today continue to operate in the same colonized manner—a condition scholars call **neocolonialism**—that continue to benefit the former colonizers and subjugate the former colonized (e.g., educational system in the Philippines still operates to serve Western nations, primarily the United States). Also, scholars (e.g., Rimonte, 1997) have argued that many of the experiences of racial minority groups today in various countries (e.g., the United States, Canada, the United Kingdom, Australia, New Zealand) mirror a colonial state even though there might be no recent forceful colonization—what such scholars call **internal colonialism**. Even further, the legacy of colonialism affects not only land, economy, and sovereignty but also extends to the mind and "leaves behind germs of rot which we must clinically detect and remove" (Fanon, 1965). This germ of rot is **colonial mentality** (David, 2013), or more generally, internalized oppression—oppression's third "I"—which we now have learned to be a consequence of oppression that has also become an important construct that allows oppression to exist and persist across generations and through time (as discussed in Chapter 4).

▪ SUMMARY OF THE POTENTIAL "WHYs"

As you may have noticed, the social psychological theories we reviewed in this chapter have several overlaps. One of the more important similarities between most of them, as summarized in Table 7.1, is the notion of a "threat." For instance, SDO, TMT, and RWA posit that social group oppression happens because there are threats to a social group's self-regard, resources, worldviews, values, or stability. Another similar theme among the theories is that of resisting change. For instance, SDO, TMT, RWA, and SJT all speak to believing in the importance of keeping the status quo, regarding existing institutions as legitimate and fair and viewing those who threaten to change the existing system in derogatory ways. You may have also noticed overlaps between SDO, SJT, and the colonial theory in terms of the mechanisms that operate to legitimize and maintain existing systems of oppression (e.g., just-world hypothesis, legitimizing myths, victim-blaming).

Speaking of mechanisms that perpetuate oppression and allow it to exist and persist across generations and through time, you may have also noticed that internalized oppression is implicated in several theories as an important factor to consider when thinking about the psychological experiences of marginalized social groups. This, in turn, may remind you of Chapter 6 wherein we discussed how internalized oppression is one pathway through which oppression can negatively affect the mental health and well-being of historically and contemporarily oppressed groups. It must be emphasized, however, that there would be no internalized oppression if oppression did not exist. In other words, we must always remember that although there is such a thing as internalized oppression, there are also oppressors and oppressive systems that are the root causes of many negative consequences—which included internalized oppression. Thus, in order to address oppression, we cannot focus just on changing the oppressed—that would be victim-blaming and an act of oppression as well! Instead, to truly address and eliminate the consequences of oppression, we need to address oppression. To this end, in the next two chapters, we discuss some clinical and community efforts that may help us address oppression at all levels along with its many negative consequences.

REFERENCES

Altemeyer, B. (1981). *Right-wing authoritarianism.* Winnipeg, Canada: University of Manitoba Press.

Altemeyer, B. (1996). *The authoritarian specter.* Cambridge, MA: Harvard University Press.

Altemeyer, B. (2007). *The authoritarians.* Winnipeg, Canada: University of Manitoba.

Brewer, M. B. (1999). The psychology of prejudice: Ingroup love or outgroup hate? *Journal of Social Issues, 55,* 429–444.

Burke, B. L., Martens, A., & Faucher, E. H. (2010). Two decades of terror management theory: A meta-analysis of mortality salience research. *Personality & Social Psychology Review, 14,* 155–195. doi:10.1177/1088868309352321

Castano, E. (2004). In case of death, cling to the ingroup. *European Journal of Social Psychology, 34,* 375–384.

Castano, E., & Dechesne, M. (2005). On defeating death. Group reification and social identification as immortality strategies. In W. Strobe & M. Hewstone (Eds.), *European review of social psychology* (Vol. 16, pp. 221–256). New York, NY: Psychology Press.

Comas-Diaz, L. (2010). LatiNegra: Mental health issues of African Latinas. *Journal of Feminist Family Therapy, 5,* 35–74. doi:10.1300/J086v05n03_03

Crouch, M., & David, E. J. R. (2017). Colonialism and gender. In K. L. Nadal (Ed.), *SAGE encyclopedia of psychology and gender* (pp. 348–352). Thousand Oaks, CA: Sage.

David, E. J. R. (2013). *Brown skin, white minds: Filipino -/American postcolonial psychology* (with commentaries). Charlotte, NC: Information Age Publishing.

Duckitt, J. (1992). *The social psychology of prejudice.* New York, NY: Praeger.

Duckitt, J. (1993). Right-wing authoritarianism among white South African students: Its measurement and its correlates. *Journal of Social Psychology, 133*(4), 553–574.

Duckitt, J. (2001). A dual-process cognitive-motivational theory of ideology and prejudice. In M. P. Zanna (Ed.), *Advances in experimental social psychology* (Vol. 33, pp. 41–113). New York, NY: Academic Press.

Duckitt, J., & Farre, B. (1994). Right-wing authoritarianism and political intolerance among Whites in the future majority-rule South Africa. *Journal of Social Psychology, 134,* 735–741. doi:10.1080/00224545.1994.9923008

Fanon, F. (1965). *The wretched of the earth.* New York, NY: Grove.

Furnham, A. (2003). Belief in a just world: Research progress over the past decade. *Personality and Individual Differences, 34,* 795–817.

Goodman, M. B., & Moradi, B. (2008). Attitudes and behaviors toward lesbian and gay persons: Critical correlates and mediated relations. *Journal of Counseling Psychology, 55,* 371–384. doi:10.1037/0022-0167.55.3.371

Greenberg, J., Pyszczynski, T., Solomon, S., Rosenblatt, A., Veeder, M., Kirkland, S., & Lyon, D. (1990). Evidence for terror management II: The effects of mortality salience on reactions to those who threaten or bolster the cultural worldview. *Journal of Personality and Social Psychology, 58,* 308–318. doi:10.1037/0022-3514.58.2.308

Guimond, S., Dambrun, M., Michinov, N., & Duarte, S. (2003). Does social dominance generate prejudice? Integrating individual and contextual determinants of intergroup cognitions. *Journal of Personality and Social Psychology, 84*(4), 697–721. doi:10.1037/0022-3514.84.4.697

Haddock, G., & Zanna, M. P. (1994). Preferring "housewives" to "feminists": Categorization and the favorability of attitudes toward women. *Psychology of Women Quarterly, 18*(1), 25–52.

Haddock, G., Zanna, M. P., & Esses, V. M. (1993). Assessing the structure of prejudicial attitudes: The case of attitudes toward homosexuals. *Journal of Personality and Social Psychology, 65*(6), 1105–1118.

Hawley, J. C. (2001). *Postcolonial, queer: Theoretical intersections.* Albany: State University of New York Press.

Heaven, P. C. L., & St. Quintin, D. (2003). Personality factors predict racial prejudice. *Personality & Individual Differences, 34,* 625–634.

Ho, A. K., Sidanius, J., Kteily, N., Sheehy-Skeffington, J., Pratto, F., Henkel, K. E., . . . Stewart, A. L. (2015). The nature of social dominance orientation: Theorizing and measuring preferences for intergroup inequality using the new SDO7 scale. *Journal of Personality and Social Psychology, 109*(6), 1003–1028.

Jonas, E., & Fischer, P. (2006). Terror management and religion: Evidence that intrinsic religiousness mitigates worldview defense following mortality salience. *Journal of Personality and Social Psychology, 91*(3), 553–567. doi:10.1037/0022-3514.91.3.553

Jost, J. T., & Banaji, M. R. (1994). The role of stereotyping in system-justification and the production of false consciousness. *British Journal of Social Psychology, 33,* 1–27.

Jost, J. T., Banaji, M. R., & Nosek, B. A. (2004). A decade of system justification theory: Accumulated evidence of conscious and unconscious bolstering of the status quo. *Political Psychology, 25*(6), 881–919.

Jost, J. T., Glaser, J., Kruglanski, A. W., & Sulloway, F. J. (2003). Political conservatism as motivated social cognition. *Psychological Bulletin, 129*(3), 339–375.

Jost, J. T., & Hunyady, O. (2002). The psychology of system justification and the palliative function of ideology. *European Review of Social Psychology, 13,* 111–153. doi:10.1080/10463280240000046

Kipling, R. (1899). The White man's burden: The United States and the Philippine Islands. *The New York Sun.* Retrieved from http://historymatters.gmu.edu/d/5478

Kumari-Campbell, F. (2008). Exploring internalized ableism using critical race theory. *Disability and Society, 23*(2), 151–162.

Levin, S., Federico, C., Sidanius, J., & Rabinowitz, J. (2002). Social dominance orientation and intergroup bias: The legitimation of favoritism for high-status groups. *Personality and Social Psychology Bulletin, 28,* 144–157.

Mavor, K. I., Louis, W. R., & Sibley, C. G. (2010). A bias-corrected exploratory and confirmatory factor analysis of right-wing authoritarianism: Support for a three-factor structure. *Personality and Individual Differences, 48*(1), 28–33. doi:10.1016/j.paid.2009.08.006

Pratto, F., Sidanius, J., Stallworth, L. M., & Malle, B. F. (1994). Social dominance orientation: A personality variable predicting social and political attitudes. *Journal of Personality and Social Psychology, 67*(4), 741–763.

Rimonte, N. (1997). Colonialism's legacy: The inferiorizing of the Filipino. In M. P. P. Root (Ed.), *Filipino Americans: Transformation and identity.* Thousand Oaks, CA: Sage.

Sidanius, J., & Pratto, F. (1999). *Social dominance: An intergroup theory of social hierarchy and oppression.* New York, NY: Cambridge University Press.

Sidanius, J., Pratto, F., & Bobo, L. (1996). Racism, conservatism, affirmative action, and intellectual sophistication: A matter of principled conservatism or group dominance? *Journal of Personality and Social Psychology, 70,* 476–490.

Solomon, S., Greenberg, J., & Pyszczynski, T. (1991). A terror management theory of social behavior: The psychological functions of self-esteem and cultural worldviews. *Advances in Experimental Social Psychology, 24*(C), 93–159.

Stenner, K. (2009). Three kinds of conservatism. *Psychological Inquiry, 20*, 142–159. doi:10.1080/10478400903028615

Tajfel, H. (1981). *Human groups and social categories.* New York, NY: Cambridge University Press.

Tajfel, H., & Turner, J. C. (1979). An integrative theory of intergroup conflict. In W. G. Austin & S. Worchel (Eds.), *The social psychology of intergroup relations* (pp. 33–47). Monterey, CA: Brooks/Cole.

Yelland, L. M., & Stone, W. F. (1996). Belief in the Holocaust: Effects of personality and propaganda. *Political Psychology, 17*, 551–562.

CHAPTER 8

Adopting a Social Justice Orientation: Addressing Oppression in the Clinical Context

> *It is no measure of health to be well-adjusted to a profoundly sick society.*
>
> —*Jiddu Krishnamurti*

The literature is clear: The various forms of oppression are connected to poorer mental health (e.g., Kessler, Mickelson, & Williams, 1999). As we reviewed in Chapter 6, the link between oppression and health has consistently been demonstrated for various socially oppressed groups such as racial and ethnic minorities (e.g., Landrine & Klonoff, 1996), immigrants (e.g., Gee, Ryan, Laflamme, & Holt, 2006; Noh, Kaspar, & Wickrama, 2007), women (e.g., Derthick, 2015), lesbian, gay, bisexual, and transgender individuals (e.g., Burgess, Lee, Tran, & van Ryn, 2008; Mays & Cochran, 2001), and people with disabilities (e.g., Krahn, Walker, & Correa-De-Araujo, 2015). Not only are oppressed individuals more likely to experience mental, emotional, or behavioral disorders— what the field calls "**psychopathology**"—they are also less likely to seek treatment for such concerns (e.g., Burgess et al., 2008; Nickerson, Helms, & Terrell, 1994), particularly from service providers and service settings that represent oppressor groups. Therefore, the clinical implications of social group oppression are twofold: (a) recognizing and treating the psychological impact of oppression on marginalized groups and (b) recognizing and addressing the barriers to care that are in place for oppressed peoples.

To this end, this chapter provides an overview of both of these clinical implications for oppressed peoples. We begin with a description of traditional theoretical frameworks that the field of psychology utilizes to help people with their psychological well-being and mental health, followed by a discussion of how such frameworks may be limited in their ability to incorporate oppression as a major psychological well-being and mental health issue for marginalized social groups. The chapter then goes on to provide a discussion of social justice frameworks for addressing oppression and how such frameworks may be integrated with clinical psychology practice to help us better serve clients who are members of marginalized groups.

■ TRADITIONAL THEORETICAL FRAMEWORKS

Over the years, our society has increasingly emphasized the use of **evidence-based practices** (EBPs) in healthcare, and this emphasis has extended to mental health services (Norcross, Beutler, & Levant, 2006). The American Psychological Association's Society of Clinical Psychology (Division 12), the largest and most influential organization of clinical psychologists in the country, even established a task force to identify and disseminate a list of **empirically supported treatments** (ESTs; e.g., Chambless & Hollon, 1998; Chambless et al., 1996). Despite significant progress over the past couple of decades, there remain many limitations and controversies regarding EBPs in mental health (Norcross et al., 2006)—especially regarding their applicability and validity for various oppressed groups. For example, the effectiveness of these practices and treatments for non-White or non-Western individuals remains unclear (e.g., Sue & Zane, 2006). Indeed, *various researchers have even commented that there is not one EST for ethnic minority groups* (Bernal & Scharron-del-Rio, 2001; Chambless et al., 1996; Sue & Zane, 2006; Zane, Hall, Sue, Young, & Nunez, 2003).

Consequently, there has been a recent push toward making psychological treatments more culturally appropriate and, thus, more effective for members of oppressed social groups (e.g., Sue & Zane, 1987). According to Hall (2001), **culturally sensitive therapies** (CSTs) are interventions that incorporate clients' cultural or sociopolitical contexts, and CSTs have become more widely used in the treatment of individuals who are members of various oppressed groups (Flaskerud, 1986; LaFromboise &

Howard-Pitney, 1995; Lau & Zane, 2000; Malgady, Rogler, & Costantino, 1990; Zane, Hatanaka, Park, & Akutsu, 1994). One notable example of such an effort is Hays's and Iwamasa's (2006) edited text *Culturally Responsive Cognitive-Behavioral Therapy: Assessment, Practice, and Supervision*. Although it is a worthy effort to make existing services more appropriate, sensitive, and effective for individuals who are members of oppressed social groups, such treatments are still fundamentally rooted in the field's traditional theoretical orientations that may be inherently limited in their ability to consider and address oppression.

Traditional psychological conceptualizations of human behavior are **reductionistic,** a tendency to attribute the causes of phenomena to factors that reside within the person. Indeed, all five of the major theories of psychotherapy—the Medical Model, Psychodynamic approaches, Behaviorism, Cognitive Theories, and Humanistic or Client-Centered Therapy—all explain pathology and change at the individual level. This tendency can be easily seen with the **Medical Model,** which assumes that pathology is the result of malfunctioning physiology (e.g., disproportionate neurotransmitter activity); therefore, the intervention occurs at the cellular level (e.g., medication). However, the other theoretical foundations are equally reductionistic, even if they do not appear to be so on the surface. For instance, although **Psychodynamic theories** vary, all of their variations still relate pathology to unresolved conflicts embedded deep within an individual's unconscious. Similarly, **Behaviorism** explains pathology as maladaptive stimulus–response pairings (i.e., an individual has *learned* to be unwell) that seem to exist in an individual's brain or mind. Speaking of brain or mind, **Cognitive theories** emphasize, as the name implies, the role of thinking patterns in the development and resolution of pathology, which is also conceptualized as residing in the brain. **Humanistic approaches** might seem to break free from the patterns of reductionism outlined by its predecessors by emphasizing the role of potential, autonomy, and choice among human beings. However, under closer examination, these explanations are also rooted deep within an individual. Potential, for example, is the bedrock that Rogerian Humanism argues to guide human behavior, and a failure to meet one's potential leads to distress. Where exactly, then, does this potential reside? Within the individual. And whose fault is it if one fails to meet his or her potential? It appears to be the individual.

As briefly reviewed in the previous paragraph, the premise of all the traditional (and most known, taught, and utilized) psychological approaches to help people is that something has gone awry at the individual level.

Therefore, the onus of responsibility for "fixing" the "problem" lies on the individual, who must (a) summon enough energy and motivation to seek out counseling services; (b) find the time to attend counseling sessions; (c) apply the effort to make use of counseling resources; and perhaps most burdensome, (d) pay for the services, which are increasingly expensive. With such a perspective, the problem is seen simply as a unique individual problem instead of a problem that may be affecting plenty of people, and the individual is perceived as the only one who needs to change instead of environmental or sociocultural contexts also needing change. Indeed, as you have already learned in the preceding chapters, these *traditional approaches to understanding psychopathology neglect, in varying degrees, to account for what is outside the individual factors such as oppression on the mental health and well-being of all people,* and particularly of oppressed people, who are most likely to experience oppression and who are more likely to experience barriers to accessing resources.

■ LIMITATIONS OF TRADITIONAL FRAMEWORKS: A CASE STUDY

As an example of how conventional clinical psychology frameworks may be limited in terms of addressing oppression, allow us to share a story about Annie when she first began clinical psychology work several years ago. One of Annie's first clinical clients was a young transgender woman, who was already in the process of transition from male to female. The client reported feeling depressed. She said she had little energy most days, and she hardly ever felt motivated to go to work. She reported thoughts of hopelessness and helplessness, and she believed she was always making mistakes, for which she always felt guilty, even when other people were actually to blame. She described having very poor self-esteem and a negative self-image. She reported lying in bed at night and thinking about how terrible a person she was, so much so that she was sleeping only a few hours a night, mostly tossing and turning. She said she had stopped spending time with friends, and that she avoided other people at work as much as she could.

As the client described her "symptoms," Annie found herself thinking that she did indeed sound very depressed. She thought about her clinical training, and remembered that **behavioral activation** was an evidence-based treatment for depression (Dimidijan, Martell, Addis, & Herman-Dunn, 2008). Therefore, Annie commenced in outlining a schedule of activities with the client for the client to complete, hopefully initiating the behavior–reward–behavior cycle that theoretically leads to improved mood by receiving positive re-enforcement (viz., good feelings from pro-social behavior). Well, week after week, the client failed to follow through with her planned activities, initially leading to thoughts about the client's lack of motivation to change, lack of personal responsibility, failure to adhere to treatment, and other "client-blaming" (or victim-blaming) explanations for why the client was not following treatment and, thus, not getting better. It was only after Annie and the client started discussing some of the barriers of the client's treatment plan that Annie came to realize that she was the one who was failing.

When Annie initially conceptualized her patient's "problem," she did so from the lens of Behaviorism, which, as outlined above, suggests that pathology (i.e., her client's depressed mood) is the result of maladaptive learning and, consequently, maladaptive patterns of behaviors. Therefore, the solution was to create new opportunities for learning by having her engage in pro-social behavior during which she would experience lots of good feelings, which would lead her to engage in more pro-social activities, which in turn would produce more good feelings, and so on and so forth until she was no longer depressed. This approach has been proven to be clinically efficacious, repeatedly. However, as the client told Annie more about her life, she shared that her family had rejected her because she is transgender. Additionally, she had lost a professional job she really loved and was now working as a day laborer, which would have been fine for her, except she did not feel accepted by anyone at her job. She said that her coworkers made comments under their breath about "trannies," and some even called her a "freak" to her face (*interpersonal oppression*). Further, she said she had found pornographic pictures on her locker, with the words "he–she" and "faggot" written on them. She explained that even when she went home at the end of the day, she did not experience any relief because she lived in constant fear that her landlord would discover that she was transgender and evict her due to the lack of antidiscrimination laws in the city to protect her (*institutional oppression*). In fact, while she was seeing Annie for treatment, there was an antidiscrimination ordinance that was introduced into the municipality in which she was living. She and Annie discussed the heightened emotions that surrounded this ballot measure, and Annie remembers her client coming in for session one day crying because of a television commercial she had seen that opposed the measure that would essentially protect her from discrimination. The commercial she saw dehumanized trans people by depicting them in a stereotypical and threatening way.

As the client told Annie more about the context in which she lived every day, Annie found herself thinking, "Well, no wonder she is depressed!" It has become clear that the client was the target of subtle and overt, interpersonal, environmental, and institutional oppression in all aspects of her life. So, it was no surprise that she did not want to go to work. It was no surprise that she felt hopeless and helpless about the future. It was no surprise that she had low self-esteem. It was no surprise that she believed she was depressed. Yet, it was important to also realize that she was not to blame! *The client's cognitive, emotional, and behavioral experiences were all logical and appropriate reactions to living in an oppressive environment.* She was having a *normal* reaction to oppression. Yet, she was the one who had to make time to come to therapy. She was the one who had to figure out how to pay for it. She was the one who was responsible for making herself feel better. She was the one who had to adapt, tolerate, and change even though she was not the problem and the problem does not reside within her (i.e., it was not her thoughts, emotions, or behaviors). The problem was outside of her. The problem was the system in which she lived, and by blindly following a "best practice" in conceptualizing the client's experiences and in treating the client's concerns, Annie felt complicit in the cover-up.

Annie eventually realized that by failing to consider the sociopolitical context in which her client lived, she had reduced the client's "symptoms" to a maladaptive learning pattern that the client herself was ultimately responsible for "fixing." Essentially, by focusing on the client's behavior and not addressing the context in which she lived, Annie was teaching the client how to simply tolerate oppression. By failing to address the root cause of her client's "symptoms," Annie was essentially teaching her client how to live in an oppressive context and not be negatively affected by it. Annie realized that she was teaching her client to be "well-adjusted to a profoundly sick society." This realization disturbed Annie, as this was not the kind of help she wanted to offer her client, and this was not the kind of clinician she wanted to be.

■ SOCIAL JUSTICE FRAMEWORKS

We recognize that the case example we have discussed in the previous section may be an overly simplistic representation of very complex and nuanced theoretical frameworks in psychology. Nevertheless, the assertion is true that traditional theories of psychotherapy are almost exclusively focused on identifying and changing individual-level variables that contribute to distress, and that such theories largely fail to account for the psychological impact of oppression (e.g., Greenleaf & Bryant, 2012). Therefore, we must turn elsewhere beyond the most popular, most taught, and most used psychological frameworks in our desire to incorporate a more complete sociopolitical understanding into our clinical work—to make our work "**oppression-informed**," if you may—and supplement our traditional clinical approaches in order to improve our services for individuals who are members of socially oppressed groups.

In this regard, **social justice approaches** to clinical work that acknowledge the role of systems of oppression in the development and maintenance of psychological distress (or psychopathology) may be useful (Ratts, 2009). These frameworks have developed largely in reaction to the perceived limitations of traditional theories, which fail to account for the sociopolitical contexts in which clients live (Prilleltensky, 1994). Further, social justice frameworks articulate that a theory of social justice in clinical work is important, because "it provides counselors with a theoretical framework for understanding the role oppression plays in shaping human behavior and the means to actualize advocacy in counseling" (Ratts, 2009, p. 161). As an example, Ratts's (2009) **Social Justice Counseling** model fills in the limitations of traditional theoretical models' descriptions of human behavior and counseling in three domains: (a) etiology of distress; (b) counselor role and identity; and (c) clinical skills.

First, Ratts (2009) explains that traditional models of psychotherapy have relied extensively on individual-level explanations of distress (e.g., unresolved conflict, distorted cognitions), but a social justice framework looks **beyond the individual for systemic causes of distress** (i.e., oppression). Ratts (2009) argues that helping clients to connect their distress to the distressing dynamics in their environment is empowering, particularly for historically (and contemporarily) oppressed groups of people. This concept is modeled on Paulo Freire's (1970) understanding of conscientization, or critical consciousness, and Ignacio Martín-Baró's (1996) work in **Liberation Psychology**. The process of **conscientization** involves an iterative process of reflection and action that leads to awareness of how one has responded, intrapsychically, to oppressive systems (Freire, 1970; Martín-Baró, 1996). In clinical work, this necessitates, on behalf of the therapist and in collaboration with the client, a dialogue about oppression.

This dialogue can be uncomfortable. This dialogue has the potential to manifest dynamics of power and privilege that can be challenging to confront, both for clients and for clinicians. In order, for example, to talk to clients about the oppression they experience in their lives, the clinicians must be able to acknowledge the ways in which they are aligned with the oppressor. In other words, *clinicians must understand in what ways they may hold or represent powerful and privileged positions in society.* For example, Annie encounters this frequently in her clinical work with underserved and historically marginalized clients. She has had clients who are people of color describe the effects of racism on their self-esteem, mood, and orientation to reality. As a White clinician, Annie must acknowledge and accept that she is a member of the oppressing group in these clients' stories. Although Annie tries very hard in her personal life to advocate for equality and promote racial healing, she is still White. Her membership in the oppressing group may not be a reflection of what is in her heart, but it is a reality that she must confront in order to initiate and sustain a conversation with her clients who are members of oppressed groups. This acknowledgment is difficult for many to bear; indeed, Annie continues to struggle with it, regardless of her training and experience. *Because it is difficult and perhaps perpetually ongoing, many people choose to deny or ignore their status of power and privilege for this very reason.* It is uncomfortable, and it is even painful. It is painful to reconcile our values as a person with the actions of the group to which we are a part, to own our own culpability in the perpetration of oppression by sheer group membership. Therefore, many of us protect ourselves from this pain by denying or ignoring the ways in which we benefit from the status quo. However, we need to realize that to recognize one's culpability for the oppression of others, regardless of individual values or behavior, will naturally lead to the acceptance of one's responsibility in healing the wounds of oppression. This must occur before one can be effective as a social justice counselor or therapist. This is a precondition. This acknowledgment must be a part of clinicians' professional identity, because we will not be able to support our clients in understanding the forces of oppression if we cannot see them for ourselves.

To develop your social justice-oriented professional (and personal) identity, and to begin to become comfortable understanding your own experiences of power and privilege, please consider some of the following questions in relation to Hays's (2003) ADDRESSING framework (discussed in Chapters 1 and 2): age, disabilities, religion, ethnicity, socioeconomic status, sexual orientation, indigenous heritage, national origin, and gender or sex.

1. What are my cultural identities?

2. What would someone who does not belong to my group(s) consider a privilege of belonging to my group(s)?

3. What role have members of my group(s) played in the oppression of others throughout history?

4. What do most people in my group(s) think about people in other groups?

5. What do people in my group(s) say about people in other groups when they are not around?

Reflect on where you are in the ADDRESSING dimensions from time to time as you work with different clients (or, if you are not a clinician or clinician-in-training, as you interact with people from other social groups). Reflect on how your answers to these questions might be influencing your work (or interactions with other people). Remember that this is an ongoing process, that *we are never "done" in our personal and professional conscientization journey.*

Awareness of one's positions in society's power hierarchy is directly related to developing a clear **professional (and personal) identity**, which is the second tenet of Social Justice Counseling. Ratts (2009) outlines two components of professional identity for the social justice counselor: (a) community-based work and (b) advocacy. He explains that in order to do social justice counseling, one must be flexible enough to envision clinical work as extending beyond the therapy room and to connect it to systems in which people actually live. Ratts (2009) stated that "this framework *requires* counselors to intervene in the social system when they recognize cultural or institutional barriers that might negatively impede client well-being" (p. 164, emphasis added). *To practice from a social justice perspective, clinicians must be willing to work toward systemic change when they recognize impediments to psychological health.* Indeed, Martín-Baró (1996) even said that *it is the duty of the social scientist to change the world*! These scholars argue that because we understand the connections between oppression and psychological health, it is our mandate to work toward social justice. Psychologists have for decades understood that racism, sexism, ableism, homophobia, and other forms of oppression are linked to poorer mental health outcomes, so social justice scholars argue that we have an obligation to use that knowledge—along with our positions of power—to address the oppressive systems directly. In other words, *to do social justice counseling means that we are doing clinical work even when we are not sitting across from our clients inside the therapy room!* Social justice counseling and therapy posit that we are doing clinical work when we vote, when we decide where to spend our money, even when we decide the kind of people with whom we want to associate. This is all clinical work, according to a social justice framework, because it all impacts the systems we share with our clients. The question we must ask ourselves is: What kind of system will we create, work toward, or maintain? A system that perpetuates the oppressive status quo or one that moves toward social justice?

Given that social group oppression has been happening throughout history (as discussed in Chapter 3) and our conventional clinical work has not seemed to be effective in addressing or eliminating oppression, psychology must now also address systemic injustices directly through community-based intervention and social justice advocacy. It is not enough to be a "good" person, but we must actively seek opportunities to change the system. Bailey, Getch, and Chen-Hayes (2007) argue that in order to work successfully with the most vulnerable in our communities, we must be willing to engage the community—perhaps even considering the community as our client (Ratts, 2009). What this means in practice will be different depending on our varying circumstances. For the authors of this book, it often means being involved in professional organizations and political movements, where we try to influence local and national policy. In the age of social media, this has also meant for both of us to have a presence in the popular dialogue, guide narrative to be more accurate and less oppressive, and connect political rhetoric to psychological principles and the dynamics of oppression. For example, in addition to taking part in and organizing **nonviolent direct actions** (what some folks refer to as "nonviolent resistance" or "civil resistance"), E. J. is also committed to **"giving psychology away"** by making psychological literature that is accessible to larger audiences beyond academia, contributing to popular media sources such as *The Huffington Post* and *Psychology Today* where he outlines complex psychological phenomena in accessible language.

These "beyond the therapy room" methods require Ratts's (2009) third tenet of Social Justice Counseling, which is the need for social justice clinicians to **learn community-level skills to do community-level work.** Traditional "micro-level" skills (e.g., reflective listening, unconditional positive regard, agenda-setting) do not necessarily prepare a clinician for social justice work. Rather, Ratts (2009) argues that clinicians need to be taught how to organize a rally or protest, collaborate with community leaders and lawmakers, lobby, write grants, and meet with politicians. These are the "meso- and macro-level" skills needed to work toward social justice; unfortunately, these skills are not regularly taught in graduate education for future clinicians. Social justice counselors might need to look beyond psychology and counseling programs to acquire these skills. Programs that train people in **Community Psychology**—the subfield of psychology that emphasizes sociopolitical context, diversity, and social change (discussed in more detail in Chapter 9)—and other fields such as social work or community organizing are more likely to offer students and future professionals opportunities to hone these "beyond the therapy room" skills.

■ INTEGRATING SOCIAL JUSTICE INTO AN EXISTING ORIENTATION

As Ratts (2009) outlines, there are some differing opinions about how to conceptualize social justice counseling; some describe it as a "fifth force" (e.g., Ratts, D'Andrea, & Arrendondo, 2009), a distinct theoretical orientation similar in nature to Psychodynamic, Behavioral, Cognitive, or Humanistic theories, while others argue that social justice is a "recurring wave" that has been present in clinical work from the beginning, taking different forms through the years (e.g., Ratts, 2009). Regardless of how one may conceptualize the social justice framework, it is clear that we definitely can use more of it in our work with clients who are members of historically and contemporarily oppressed groups.

It should be noted that we understand that most people reading this book will most likely have training in or previous exposure to more traditional models of human behavior. Utilizing social justice frameworks in our clinical work and becoming a social justice clinician, however, do not necessarily mean that we need to completely abandon our training, experience, and existing theoretical orientations. In fact, the most popular EST and most common approach to counseling and psychotherapy—Cognitive Behavioral Therapy (CBT) (Norcross, Hedges, & Prochaska, 2002)—fit nicely with the social justice framework described above (e.g., David, 2009; Hays & Iwamasa, 2006). For example, the process of critical consciousness can be framed as a form of **cognitive restructuring** (i.e., learning to think about psychological distress as a reasonable reaction to living under oppression, rather than an inherent flaw). To provide an example of how one might integrate a social justice perspective into a formally articulated theoretical orientation, here is how Annie describes her orientation with her clinical work:

> My fundamental approach to case conceptualization, intervention, and outcome assessment is guided by the principles of Cognitive Behavioral Therapy (CBT). I believe the way individuals think about, or interpret, the world around them influences emotional and behavioral responses to events and experiences. Therefore, if an individual presents to treatment with emotional distress or problematic behaviors, I work with the client to connect their emotions and behaviors to patterns of thinking and interpretation. Most importantly, one of my goals as a clinician is to teach clients how to critically evaluate their own thought patterns and related responses. This way, clients possess the skills necessary to continue monitoring the ways in which their interpretations of events influence the way they feel and behave in their worlds.
>
> However, clients do not develop patterns of cognition in a vacuum; rather, they do so in the context of a rich and dynamic sociopolitical-cultural-economic-historical context. Therefore, I incorporate concepts from Liberation Psychology into my clinical formulation as well. The fundamental assumption of liberation psychotherapy is that psychological distress is not caused by an individualized flaw per se; rather, psychological distress is conceptualized as the manifestation of experiences of systemic oppression, discrimination, marginalization, and disenfranchisement. Therefore, intervention includes consideration of systemic and environmental factors that contribute to these conditions. This is achieved in many ways, such as incorporating the notion of critical consciousness into therapy. This involves bringing to conscious awareness a critical understanding of systemic influences on psychological health. I blend this with a CBT perspective by examining the ways in which social, economic, political, historical, and cultural contexts shape individual interpretations of events.

Using this formulation to understand her clients, Annie often incorporates social justice action into her treatment plans. Remember, according to the work of Freire (1970) and Martín-Baró (1996), critical consciousness is an iterative process of reflection and action. The emphasis in both of their works is on the *action*. In other words, it is not enough to simply understand how systems work and function on oneself, it is also important to feel empowered to work toward changing those systems. For example, Annie has suggested that her clients attend rallies, work phone banks, write letters to politicians, organize groups, and attend assembly meetings as part of their treatment plans as they continue to develop critical consciousness about their contexts. It is not always appropriate or necessary for every client to become an activist, but according to theories of social justice counseling (Ratts, 2009), it is necessary for clients to identify ways that they can take action and break the cycle of oppression in their own lives.

Finally, all clinicians, regardless of orientation, training, or experience, can commit to being more aware of the sociopolitical contexts in which their clients live. Clinicians must continue to work toward becoming more engaged as citizens and becoming more critical as consumers of information. Social justice clinicians must strive to know what is happening in the world and challenge themselves to think about how sociopolitical events might be impacting their clients. We are living in a world where old threats to the psychological health and the well-being of marginalized communities continue to exist. Further, we also live in a world wherein new threats to oppressed peoples surface every single day. As liberation psychology founder Martín-Baró (1996) noted, we must not ignore the ongoing state and process of oppression that exists in our world because a failure to acknowledge and combat injustice is not unbiased objectivity—as conventional science and ways of helping might lead us to believe—rather, it is a tacit endorsement of the status quo that undoubtedly damages various groups of peoples. Therefore, as psychologists who serve diverse peoples and who are working toward the mental well-being of all, we must challenge oppressive systems and advocate for social justice.

■ SUMMARY

Traditional approaches to psychotherapy emphasize factors that exist and operate at the individual level and have the unfortunate consequence of placing the onus of responsibility for change entirely on the individual. However, individuals and the thoughts, beliefs, emotions, and behaviors they develop do not exist in a vacuum, wherein they spontaneously develop problems. Instead, we all live in a world where systemic oppression exists (as discussed in Chapters 2, 3, and 5) and has profound impacts on mental health (as discussed in Chapter 6). Increasing appreciation of the link between social group oppression and mental health has led influential organizations such as the American Counseling Association and the American Psychological Association to develop guidelines for clinicians to consider social justice issues and improve their cultural competency (American Psychological Association, 2002; Ratts et al., 2015). Utilizing a social justice framework will allow clinicians to incorporate an understanding of these dynamic and complex sociopolitical factors into their clinical work. At the same time, social justice frameworks encourage, and even challenge, clinicians to broaden their definition of clinical work, reconceptualize their professional identity, and accept as their mandate an obligation to fight for social justice in an oppressive world.

REFERENCES

Bailey, D. F., Getch, Y. Q., & Chen-Hayes, S. F. (2007). Achievement advocacy for all through transformative school counseling programs. In B. T. Erford (Ed.), *Transforming the school counseling profession* (2nd ed., pp. 98–120). Upper Saddle River, NJ: Pearson.

Bernal, G., & Scharron-del-Rio, M. R. (2001). Are empirically supported treatments valid for ethnic minorities? Toward an alternative approach for treatment research. *Cultural Diversity and Ethnic Minority Psychology, 7,* 328–342.

Burgess, D., Lee, R., Tran, A., & van Ryn, M. (2008). Effects of perceived discrimination on mental health and mental health services utilization among gay, lesbian, bisexual and transgender persons. *Journal of LGBT Health Research, 3*(4), 1–14. doi:10.1080/15574090802226626

Chambless, D. L., & Hollon, S. D. (1998). Defining empirically supported therapies. *Journal of Consulting and Clinical Psychology, 64,* 497–504.

Chambless, D. L., Sanderson, W. C., Shoham, V., Johnson, S. B., Pope, K. S., Crits-Christoph, P., . . . McCurry, S. (1996). An update on empirically validated therapies. *The Clinical Psychologist, 49,* 5–14.

David, E. J. R. (2009). Internalized oppression, psychopathology, and cognitive-behavioral therapy among historically oppressed groups. *Journal of Psychological Practice, 15,* 71–103.

Derthick, A. O. (2015). *The Sexist MESS: Development and initial validation of the Sexist Microaggressions Experiences and Stress Scale and the relationship of sexist microaggressions and women's mental health* (Doctoral dissertation). ProQuest Dissertations and Theses Global. (No. 3470179)

Dimidijan, S., Martell, C. R., Addis, M. E., & Herman-Dunn, R. (2008). Behavioral activation for depression. In D. H. Barlow (Ed.), *Clinical handbook of psychological disorders: A step-by-step treatment manual* (4th ed., pp. 328–364). New York, NY: Guilford Press.

Flaskerud, J. H. (1986). The effects of culture-compatible intervention on the utilization of mental health services by minority clients. *Community Mental Health Journal, 22*(2), 127–141.

Freire, P. (1970). *The pedagogy of the oppressed.* New York, NY: Continuum.

Gee, G., Ryan, A., Laflamme, D. J., & Holt, J. (2006). Self-reported discrimination and mental health status among African descendants, Mexican Americans, and other Latinos in the New Hampshire REACH 2010 initiative: The added dimension of immigration. *American Journal of Public Health, 96*(10), 1821–1828. doi:10.2105/AJPH.2005.080085

Greenleaf, A. T., & Bryant, R. M. (2012). Perpetuating oppression: Does the current counseling discourse neutralize social action? *Journal of Social Action in Counseling and Psychology, 4*(1), 18–29.

Hall, G. N. (2001). Psychotherapy research with ethnic minorities: Empirical, ethical, and conceptual issues. *Journal of Consulting and Clinical Psychology, 69,* 502–510.

Hays, P. A. (2003). *Addressing cultural complexities in practice: A framework for clinicians and counselors.* Washington, DC: American Psychological Association.

Hays, P. A., & Iwamasa, G. Y. (Eds.). (2006). *Culturally responsive cognitive-behavioral therapy: Assessment, practice, and supervision.* Washington, DC: American Psychological Association.

Kessler, R. C., Mickelson, K. D., & Williams, D. R. (1999). The prevalence, distribution, and mental health correlates of perceived discrimination in the United States. *American Sociological Association, 40*(3), 208–230.

Krahn, G. L., Walker, D. K., & Correa-De-Araujo, R. (2015). Persons with disabilities as an unrecognized health disparity population. *American Journal of Public Health, 105*, 198–206. doi:10.2105/AJPH.2014.302182

LaFromboise, T., & Howard-Pitney, B. (1995). The Zuni life skills development curriculum: Description and evaluation of a suicide prevention program. *Journal of Counseling Psychology, 42*(4), 479–486.

Landrine, H., & Klonoff, E. A. (1996). The Schedule of Racist Events: A measure of racial discrimination and a study of its negative physical and mental health consequences. *Journal of Black Psychology, 22*(2), 144–168.

Lau, A., & Zane, N. (2000). Examining the effects of ethnic specific services: An analysis of cost-utilization and treatment outcome for Asian American clients. *Journal of Community Psychology, 28*(1), 63–77.

Malgady, R. G., Rogler, L. H., & Costantino, G. (1990). Culturally sensitive psychotherapy for Puerto Rican children and adolescents: A program of treatment outcome research. *Journal of Consulting & Clinical Psychology, 58*(6), 704–712.

Martín-Baró, I. (1996). *Writings for a liberation psychology.* New York, NY: Harvard University Press.

Mays, V. M., & Cochran, S. D. (2001). Mental health correlates of perceived discrimination among lesbian, gay, and bisexual adults in the Unites States. *American Journal of Public Health, 91*(11), 1869–1876. doi:10.2105/AJPH.91.11.1865

Nickerson, K. J., Helms, J. E., & Terrell, F. (1994). Cultural mistrust, opinions about mental illness, and Black students' attitudes toward seeking psychological help from White counselors. *Journal of Counseling Psychology, 41*(3), 378–385. doi:10.1037/0022-0167.41.3.378

Noh, S., Kaspar, V., & Wickrama, K. A. S. (2007). Overt and subtle racial discrimination and mental health: Preliminary findings for Korean immigrants. *American Journal of Public Health, 97*(7), 1269–1274. doi:10.2105/AJPH.2005.085316

Norcross, J. C., Beutler, L. E., & Levant, R. F. (Eds.). (2006). *Evidence-based practices in mental health: Debate and dialogue on the fundamental questions.* Washington, DC: American Psychological Association.

Norcross, J. C., Hedges, M., & Prochaska, J. O. (2002). The face of 2010: A Delphi poll on the future of psychotherapy. *Professional Psychology: Research and Practice, 33*(3), 316–322.

Prilleltensky, I. (1994). *The morals and politics of psychology: Psychological discourse and the status quo.* Albany: State University of New York Press.

Ratts, M. J. (2009). Social justice counseling: Toward the development of a fifth force among counseling paradigms. *Journal of Humanistic Counseling, Education, and Development, 48,* 160–172.

Ratts, M. J., D'Andrea, M., & Arrendondo, P. (2004, July). Social justice counseling: 'Fifth force' in field. *Counseling Today, 47,* 28–30.

Sue, S., & Zane, N. (1987). The role of culture and cultural techniques in psychotherapy: A critique and reformulation. *American Psychologist, 42*(1), 37–45.

Sue, S., & Zane, N. (2006). Ethnic minority populations have been neglected by evidence-based practices. In J. C. Norcross, L. E. Beutler, & R. F. Levant (Eds.), *Evidence-based practices in mental health: Debate and dialogue on the fundamental questions* (pp. 329–337). Washington, DC: American Psychological Association.

Zane, N., Hall, G. N., Sue, S., Young, K., & Nunez, J. (2003). Research on psychotherapy with culturally diverse populations. In M. J. Lambert (Ed.), *Bergin and Garfield's handbook of psychotherapy and behavior change* (5th ed., pp. 767–804). New York, NY: Wiley.

Zane, N., Hatanaka, S., Park, S. S., & Akutsu, P. (1994). Ethnic-specific mental health services: Evaluation of the parallel approach for Asian-American clients. *Journal of Community Psychology, 22*(2), 68–81.

CHAPTER 9

Beyond Laboratories, Clinics, and Classrooms: Community Efforts to Address Oppression

> *On March 8, 2017, during Annie's cab ride home, the cab driver began to complain about refugees and immigrants in the United States. He blamed them for recent violent crimes in the country (although the crimes he was referencing had not been perpetrated by refugees or immigrants), and he demanded to know Annie's stance on the topic. When Annie replied that she would rather not engage in this conversation because she actually works with refugees and has a very different opinion, the cab driver began calling Annie a "jihadist-sympathizer and a traitor." He said, "You probably have a burka that you like to lounge around in at home, don't you?" Then he said, "Well, I'll give you a ride anyways." Annie suggested that no, he did not need to give her a ride, and asked him to pull over at a gas station. When he refused to stop and kept driving, Annie insisted that he stop and to redirect their route to drop her off at her wife's work instead, which was only one block away from where they were at that point. The cab driver proceeded to call Annie a "queer" and, as she was getting out of the cab, screamed at her that she needed to "read the constitution," because she was "aiding and assisting the enemy."*

Annie's experience reflects many of the layers and complexities of oppression that we have already discussed in this book. For instance, it shows that oppression is experienced by various social groups (e.g., lesbians, gays, queer people, Muslims, immigrants, refugees). It is also clear from Annie's experience that oppression continues to persist and exist today in both blatant and subtle forms (in this case, it is quite blatant), that it

155

operates on multiple levels (in this case, she experienced interpersonal oppression that is influenced by institutionalized negative sentiments toward Muslims, refugees, and immigrants), and that it has serious negative consequences on people's well-being (i.e., Annie felt very vulnerable and was distressed for days). At the very least—even if we are not able to identify the specific social groups that were implicated in Annie's experience, name whether the oppression Annie experienced was blatant or subtle, specify what levels of oppression were at work, or recognize in what ways it may have affected Annie's well-being—we should now be able to see from Annie's experience that oppression is a complicated construct that many people may find elusive, confusing, and even mystifying because of its many facets, manifestations, and implications.

Yes, there are many difficult things to know and understand about oppression and this may seem daunting. However, *if there is only one thing we need to always remember about oppression, we believe it should be the fact that it is an environmental construct that is external to people.* Indeed, even internalized oppression (discussed in Chapter 5) would not exist if oppression in our external world did not exist. That is, there would be nothing for individuals to internalize—or nothing would seep into individuals' minds—if external oppression was not around them. Therefore, we need to always remember that oppression exists and operates outside of individuals. And in order to most effectively address external factors like oppression, we need to change oppressive factors that are outside of individuals; we need to create social change.

In the field of psychology, it is the subfield of community psychology that is most dedicated to considering factors that are outside individuals and to promoting social change in order to help our communities. To this end, this chapter focuses on describing the subfield of community psychology along with some ways we can facilitate civil action or social change processes on a larger scale—beyond just individual-level therapeutic value (as described in Chapter 8)—as attempts to reclaim power and reappropriate the responsibility of addressing oppression from the oppressed to the systems of oppression. We begin the chapter with a discussion of community psychology, its guiding principles, and how such principles may be helpful in addressing oppression. We follow this with some recent and ongoing examples of how the field of psychology can go beyond our conventional roles as researchers, clinicians, and educators to help our society address oppression and become more just, fair, and healthy. Then, we end the chapter with some tips on how we can remain steadfast in our social change efforts.

■ COMMUNITY PSYCHOLOGY

The subfield of community psychology developed during the 1960s—largely influenced by the freedom movements of that era (e.g., civil rights movement, women's rights movement, community mental health movement)—out of the dissatisfaction of many psychologists (many of whom were clinical psychologists) with what they perceived as psychology's narrow conceptualizations of phenomena and limited ways of helping. During a 1965 meeting in Boston—a meeting that will eventually become known as the **Swampscott Conference**—these psychologists called for a "novel approach to mental health that emphasized prevention over treatment, targeted social systems in which individuals lived, and participated in social change efforts" (Rudkin, 2003, p. 12). Out of the Swampscott Conference came **community psychology**, a subfield that attempts to "find other alternatives for dealing with deviance from societal-based norms . . . and support every person's right to be different without risk of suffering material and psychological sanctions" (Rappaport, 1977, p. 1), an approach that calls for a "shift from an emphasis on intrapsychic factors to understanding and changing larger social contexts" that consequently "require new conceptualizations and tactics (Sarason, 1974, p. 155).

Based on these stated goals from its founders, Rudkin (2003) conceptualized community psychology work as being driven by **five guiding principles** (summarized in Table 9.1). The first principle is **context**—community psychology acknowledges that individuals and communities are influenced by the social contexts, both historically and contemporarily, within which they live. This principle reminds us to look

TABLE 9.1   Rudkin's Five Guiding Principles of Community Psychology

---

Context. Individuals and communities are influenced by the social contexts, both historically and contemporarily, within which they live

Appreciating Diversity. There are different perspectives, worldviews, ways of doing things, and cultures that must be heard, considered, valued, and honored

Values. Everything we do—in our research, teaching, and helping work—all develop within and are influenced by values (oftentimes the dominant values in our society)

Embracing Social Change. Improving people's lives through the creation of a more just, fair, and healthy society often requires changing factors that are external to people

Strengths-Based Perspective. We need to consider the strengths and resiliencies of communities instead of simply looking for their deficiencies, difficulties, or issues

---

Source: Adapted from Rudkin (2003).

beyond the individual for factors that may influence, explain, or cause phenomena. The second principle is **appreciating diversity**—community psychology acknowledges and values the perspectives, worldviews, ways of doing things, and cultures of the various social groups in our world. This principle makes sure that we do not further propagate the oppression of historically and contemporarily marginalized peoples. The third principle is **values**—community psychology recognizes the fact that everything we do—in our research, teaching, and helping work—all develop within and are influenced by values. This principle acknowledges that dominant values seep into everything we do, and we cannot pretend that they do not. Failing to see this or pretending that we are "value-free" or objective may lead our assumptions and values (e.g., the tendency to emphasize biological, genetic, or other within-the-individual factors to explain phenomena) to further oppress people (e.g., simply attributing poverty to people being lazy instead of also considering external factors like low wages). The fourth principle is **embracing social change**—community psychology believes that improving people's lives often requires changing factors that are external to people. This principle allows us to put the onus to change on the systems of oppression instead of on the oppressed, liberating or freeing oppressed social groups from the burden of having to tolerate, adjust, and adapt to an oppressive environment. Lastly, the fifth principle is **strengths-based perspective**—community psychology remembers to also consider the strengths of communities instead of simply looking for their deficiencies, difficulties, or issues. This principle reminds us of the resiliencies of marginalized peoples and keeps in check our tendency to pathologize marginalized groups' characteristics or to look for what we often assume to be inherently wrong in them.

The five guiding principles of community psychology can lead us to better understand what factors might protect people from the damages of oppression. The identification of such factors, in turn, may lead to the development of "new tactics" such as **prevention programs** that may keep people from suffering from the damages of oppression. For example, perhaps we can develop interventions that enhance **resiliency or protective factors** (e.g., understanding oppressive history, enculturation) to prevent the internalization of oppression (e.g., Lin & Israel, 2012). Perhaps we can develop interventions that enhance factors such as racial or ethnic identity and cultural connectedness (e.g., Goodkind, LaNoue, Lee, Freeland, & Freund, 2012; Halagao, 2004; Strobel, 2015), factors that seem to buffer people from the stress and consequences of oppression (for a review, see Neblett, Rivas-Drake, & Umaña-Taylor, 2012). These types of prevention efforts are sometimes called **secondary prevention** (G. Caplan, 1964) because, although the potential negative consequences of oppression are prevented or "nipped in the bud" (Rudkin, 2003, p. 247) by helping people resist and cope with oppression better, the occurrence of oppression is left unchanged and people are still exposed to oppression at the same rate.

Therefore, in addition to helping people be better protected from oppression, perhaps there are things we can do to reduce and eliminate oppression so that we prevent people from experiencing such stressors to begin with! To do this kind of prevention effort, what some scholars (e.g., Cowen, 1996, 1997) may consider as **primary prevention** because it aims to reduce the incidence of people who are exposed to oppression, we need to start thinking of ways to eliminate oppressive systems. That is, we need to change institutions and systems that are maintaining and inflicting injustice and unfairness. And to do so, we need communities to work together and we need to work with communities. Just like with individual-level stages of change model (Prochaska & DiClemente, 1992), an essential component in **community readiness to change** (Plested, Edwards, & Jumper-Thurman, 2006; Plested, Jumper Thurman, Edwards, & Oettling, 1998) is awareness of the problem. Thus, community psychologists can help communities with various "new tactics" such as awareness raising, town hall or small group discussions, media campaigns, or other educational outreach efforts—tactics and strategies that are beyond the conventional roles of many psychologists (e.g., therapist, researcher, professor).

Once a community becomes aware that a problem exists and that interventions, programs, or some form of action must be taken, then there are even more tactics and strategies (e.g., needs and assets assessment, skills training, workshops, social change movements, community organizing, direct actions) that community psychologists can help facilitate in collaboration with—perhaps even led by—the community itself. In essence, we can work in collaboration with communities toward developing **group empowerment** for them: (a) to know that they can change societal factors (e.g., they have the knowledge, skills, competence, and power); (b) to know how to change societal factors (e.g., influence policy decisions); and (c) to effectively mobilize and utilize their resources to obtain and sustain the change that they seek (for a review on various ways to conceptualize empowerment, please see Zimmerman, 1995, 2000). As we mentioned in Chapter 8, these "new tactics" (e.g., organizing a rally or protest, collaborating with community leaders and lawmakers, lobbying, writing grants with nonprofit agencies, meeting with politicians) are the "beyond the therapy room" or "beyond the clinic" methods of helping that the third tenet of Social Justice Counseling (Ratts, 2009) calls for in order to work effectively with communities in creating social change to dismantle systems of oppression.

■ BEYOND THE INDIVIDUAL: #SOCIAL CHANGE MOVEMENTS

Now that we have a basic understanding of community psychology, we see that this subfield calls for psychologists to *go beyond the walls of our research laboratories, clinics, hospitals, therapy rooms, offices, classrooms, and universities in order to be more useful to our society* (N. Caplan & Nelson, 1973). Also as previously discussed, community psychology posits that many of the issues (e.g., poverty, substance use, crime, poor mental health) that we see in our society are social problems that are created and maintained by social factors (e.g., unfair policies, biased assumptions, unequal access to power and resources), which necessarily call for social change (e.g., Albee, 1981). That is, the causes or roots of many social ills are factors that reside outside of people. Thus, we can no longer simply change people to solve such social problems; instead, we need to change society. To this end, let us now move on to a discussion of some modern-day examples of social change movements. As we go through these examples, perhaps you can think of ways through which psychologists can take part in such movements.

In our contemporary society, it is easy to identify examples of social change movements primarily because many of such movements have not just become more visible through social media, but may have even started on social media. The best recent example of this is the **#BlackLivesMatter** movement (as mentioned in Chapter 1), one of the most iconic social change movements of the last few years. The #BlackLivesMatter movement began as a social media campaign and exploded a few years ago after multiple reports came of unarmed Black men being murdered by police with seeming impunity, beginning with Trayvon Martin in 2012 (who was actually killed by a civilian, George Zimmerman, who was found not guilty), and followed by a deluge of other deaths including Deontre Hamilton (who was diagnosed with schizophrenia and was fatally shot 14 times by police in Milwaukee), Eric Garner (who was killed by police placing him in a chokehold while he cried, "I can't breathe"), and Michael Brown, Jr. (who was unarmed when killed by police in Missouri; for an exhaustive list, please see Quah & Davis, 2015). The #BlackLivesMatter movement has grown to become "a chapter-based national organization working for the validity of Black Life . . . working to (re)build the Black Liberation Movement" (Black Lives Matter, 2017). There is no official leader of the movement; rather, in communities across the globe and online, anyone can use the #BlackLivesMatter rallying cry and apply it to protests, rallies, conversations, and commentary. What appears to unify the movement is a shared awareness and understanding that Black people have been systematically targeted and oppressed by systems of power, and that the world is not just until this oppression is overturned.

Another example of a recent social change movement that has a strong social media presence is **#Resist**, which started in response to the election of Donald Trump as president of the United States. Immediately following the 2016 election, there was widespread outcry on social media calling for people to #Resist both (a) the discriminatory rhetoric that characterized Trump's campaign and (b) the many attempts to dismantle recent gains made for social justice (e.g., transgender rights, reproductive rights, and immigrant rights). In just 4 months following the election, #Resist appeared in more than 2.5 million tweets and "has come to symbolize the fight for all those most vulnerable under Trump—immigrants, Muslims, people of color, women, members of the LGBTQ community, and anyone else who feels targeted" (Wenzke, 2017). The impetus for the #Resist movement appears to be fear that oppressed people will lose the rights they have gained under previous administrations. For example, marriage equality was granted only in 2015 and Trump's vice president—Mike Pence— has actively worked to oppress LGBTQ rights over the years (Drabold, 2015). The #Resist movement also manifests "IRL" (in real life) through #ResistTrumpTuesdays, which involve physical protests, rallies, or direct actions around the world that challenge Trump's agenda (Wenzke, 2017).

Speaking of protests, rallies, or direct actions "in real life," perhaps the biggest recent example is the **#WomensMarch,** during which millions of people around the United States and in more than 600 different loca- tions around the world (even in Antarctica!) rallied to stand for women's rights (Kenneally, 2017). In Washington, DC alone, close to a half a million people showed up to resist Trump and advocate for women's rights. Primarily organized using social media, over 11.5 million social media posts with the hashtag #WomensMarch were made on that day! Another excellent example of sustained efforts to resist and eliminate oppression "in real life" is the **#StandingRock, #NoDAPL, #IAmStandingRock,** or **#WaterIsLife** movement. In 2016, the Dakota Access company was granted permission to build an oil pipeline that would run directly through the main water source of the Standing Rock Sioux Tribe in North Dakota (Meyer, 2016). Soon after, protestors from the community launched social media campaigns to #RespectOurWater because people #CantDrinkOil. As the protest in Standing Rock gained momentum, people from all over the world provided support to the #StandingRock message via social media, showing solidarity in Native Americans' continued fight against colonialism. Since then, several other marches, protests, and rallies have been organized throughout the United States and the world using social media, including actions in support of refugees and immigrants (e.g., **#NoBanNoWallNoRaids**) and evidence-based information (e.g., **#MarchForScience**).

■ BEYOND THE CLINIC: COMMUNITY ORGANIZING

As we now see, social media has definitely made it easier than ever for individuals and communities to organize around a common cause. The increased visibility that social media has provided to social change movements makes it clear how powerful a united (and nationwide!) voice can be in raising awareness (an important part of social change!), being heard, and sparking societal reform. There are many models of community organizing, and the use of social media is constantly changing the landscape of traditional organizing efforts. Nevertheless, traditional community organizing remains a very powerful "beyond the clinic" helping method—especially when it comes to local community issues—as it is a tactic that is rooted in creating, fostering, and building on real relationships that people have with one another.

One common example of traditional community organizing is efforts to facilitate **civic engagement** among community members. These efforts may take the form of mobilizing people to register voters, encouraging people to vote, actively campaigning to support candidates who may bring forward desired community changes, or even running for leadership or elected office. Addressing the problem of oppression can take many forms, from making a commitment to limit the ways one might perpetrate oppression in one's own life, to being involved in social change movements, to legislative advocacy. Whatever form a chosen solution may take, active civic engagement is an important component of exercising one's voice and working toward social change. As discussed throughout this book, oppression exists in interpersonal relationships, but it also operates and is maintained in social systems through unjust legislation and policies. Therefore, it is crucial that individuals and communities hold their local, state, and national representatives responsible for enacting legislation that promotes equality and justice for all people. One small step we can all take is learning who our representatives are and research where they stand on the issues we have discussed in this book. If we do not like their stance, we must let them know through letters or emails, phone calls, attending assembly meetings, and votes. Indeed, for those of us who are privileged to be allowed to vote, we must remember that our vote is one way through which we hold power over the decision-makers in our society.

Another example of a locally based, traditional community organizing is Annie's experiences with the Anchorage Faith and Action Congregations Together (AFACT), a group that uses a **faith-based community organizing model** to create social change in addressing their local communities' issues. One of the tenets of faith-based organizing is that relationships are powerful; in fact, Annie's supervisor at AFACT often said, "forming relationships are the most radical thing we do in organizing" (personal communication with Angela Liston, 2012). In a faith-based organizing model like AFACT, leaders—people who care about the community and who are willing to step up and have conversations about how the community could be better—are identified in congregations. The leaders receive training about community organizing, and then they go out into the congregation to develop and nurture relationships with other members. Leaders have one-to-one meetings with as many members as possible, who are asked to share what it is like to live in their community, what they love about their community, and what they wish was different. Then, the leaders bring these issues back to the local organizing committee (LOC)—the group of leaders in the congregation—and the LOC identifies a common concern of many members of the congregation. The "issue" can be large, like immigration reform, or small, like the need for an extra bus stop, but each issue is germane to that congregation and has come *from the people*, not from the leaders or the organizers. This process reflects the community psychology principles of *context* and *appreciating diversity*, in that the LOC looks to the diverse experiences, expectations, and needs of the community to guide and direct their course of action.

Once an issue is identified, the LOC conducts research on the issue to operationalize the problem, identify a solution, and, most importantly, identify a person (or people) who have the power to make a decision that may alleviate the problem. For example, if the issue is related to immigration reform, the target decision-maker might be a U.S. representative; if the issue is the need for an extra bus stop, it might be the local public transportation office. Research often involves meeting with many different people in different positions of power. The LOC conducts these meetings with the support of the organizers. The organizers do not speak for the LOC; they are present only for consultation if needed. Therefore, the LOC learns how to contact public servants (e.g., congressional representatives), request and schedule meetings, develop an agenda, and conduct the interviews. When the research is finalized, an **Action** is held in which the target decision-maker is invited to meet with the people who are affected by the problem. This action is chaired by a leader from the LOC. One of the most powerful parts of the Action is when members of the community are invited to give public testimony about how the problem has impacted their lives. One of the tenets of this model of community organizing is "bring the power and the pain in the same room." Imagine how empowering it must feel to be able to tell your story directly to the person who holds the power to make significant change. During this testimony, the decision-makers do not respond; they are asked only to listen. Annie has been to several Actions, the most recent of which was related to increasing the number of detox beds in the city. The state's Director of Behavioral Health Services was present, as well as the Municipal Assembly members for the city. One by one, members of the community stepped up and told a story about how their lives had been impacted by addiction and access (or lack thereof) to treatment. Actions such as this are very powerful—empowering—to community members.

At the conclusion of an Action, target decision-makers are asked to commit, in front all of the people whose stories they have just heard, to making a change that will alleviate the negative effects of the problem (e.g., supporting immigration reform, increasing the number of services). Of course, there is celebration when there is a favorable outcome, and the target decision-maker commits to the social action requested by the community, but regardless of whether the decision-maker commits or not, the real success is when members of a community walk away feeling empowered to tell their stories, to ask for social change, and to have a conversation with people who are often in positions of power. In this way, community organizing aligns with the community psychology principle of having a *strengths-based* approach to complex problems. No matter what the outcome of an Action is, the leaders and LOC walk away with skills necessary to tackle any subsequent problems that might arise in their communities. That is where the transformation lies. That is where the power begins to shift.

■ BEYOND THE LABORATORY: COMMUNITY-BASED RESEARCH

Another area wherein we need to shift power is in the research context. When conducting research, one way to shift power is to equalize the power inequality that is typically seen between the "expert" researcher and the research "subject." To do this, community psychologists who conduct research often utilize a process that is analogous to community organizing called **community-based participatory research** (CBPR)—sometimes also called Community-Based Participatory *Action* Research—which is a research approach that is guided by the needs, values, and wishes of the community. Topics and methods of inquiry are not conjured up in university laboratories by a "panel of experts"; rather, they are developed *in collaboration with the community to meet the needs of the community and to harness the inherent strengths of the community so that the intervention is sustainable in the community.* This kind of collaboration, much like relationship-building in community organizing, is often the most radical work a community researcher does because it requires a shift in perspective that not all are able to make.

To conduct research from a community-based, collaborative, and participatory framework means that researchers must be humble and open to learning from others, which can be difficult for some researchers who are used to being the "expert." It requires researchers to re-evaluate their "standard operating procedures" and keep their assumptions in check. CBPR also requires flexibility and patience, because to truly partner and collaborate with communities means listening and seeking feedback along the way, in each phase or step of the project, and incorporating such feedback into the project. In many ways, research is much easier when it is conducted in isolation from the community in the comforts of a laboratory; researchers can pretend they are in complete control of what happens. But the illusion of control (and objectivity) is certainly shattered when we truly embrace community partnership and collaboration. Like community organizing, CBPR is about working with community members to provide the training and support needed for the community to take ownership and control over the created interventions or projects. Community researchers are partners to the community, consultants in many ways. A community-based researcher's job is to listen, and with the community's permission, maybe speak as an **advocate** on behalf of, but never *for,* the community.

■ BEYOND THE CLASSROOM: COMMUNITY EDUCATION

In addition to going beyond psychologists' conventional roles as therapists and researchers, community psychology also encourages psychologists to expand the scope of their role as educators. Given how widespread oppression is and given its many serious effects on the lives of people—especially people who may not be privileged to be given the opportunity and space to learn about, read about, or talk about oppression—it is important to have ongoing conversations about these concepts and issues beyond classrooms and universities. Some of the ways we can do this is through social media or other formats (e.g., newspaper op-eds, blogs, podcasts) so that more people will have access to information and resources and, potentially, feel empowered with that knowledge to organize for changes in their lives and their communities. Consistent with this notion of making psychological knowledge more accessible to more people, widening psychology's impact, and making psychologists more useful to society beyond their conventional roles, many psychologists (e.g., Blakeslee, DiChristina, Raeburn, & Lambert, 2012; Klatzky, 2009; Miller, 1969) have advocated for various ways to **give psychology away**.

In their efforts to give psychology away, many psychologists have embraced **social media platforms** to teach the public about how psychological concepts manifest in their everyday lives. For example, Dr. Kevin Nadal hosts an online show in New York City called *Out Talk* where he holds conversations about "topics that we sometimes don't want to talk about" like microaggressions, mental health stigma, racial profiling, the Model Minority Myth, and intersectional identities (Nadal, 2017). Similarly, Dr. Ali Mattu, recognized for launching the viral #ThisPsychMajor campaign in response to Jeb Bush's claim during the 2016 presidential campaign that psychology majors are destined to work in fast food restaurants, hosts a YouTube channel called *The Psych Show* that profiles various psychological concepts to explain everyday experiences like dating, traveling, nature, and pop culture. Dr. Mattu, who was featured in an article by the American Psychological Association called "#GivingPsychologyAway" (Chamberlain, 2016), states that his goal is to help people use psychology to improve the lives of people—particularly young people (Mattu, 2017). Other psychologists have found other ways to make psychological knowledge more accessible, like Dr. Andrea Letamendi, who hosts podcasts on a variety of psychological topics including the psychology of superheroes and villains; and Dr. Josué Cordona, whose news website called "Geek therapy: How geek is saving the world" discusses mental health topics that are brought up by popular culture (Chamberlain, 2016).

Another common example of giving psychology away is by writing about psychological research, theories, and concepts in a jargon-free way to make it more accessible and readable to people outside of the field of psychology. For instance, E. J. frequently requires his students to practice this form of giving psychology away by writing about how psychological knowledge may inform current national and local events, not for peer-reviewed journals, but for the general public in **local newspapers and popular magazines** like *Psychology Today* and *The Huffington Post*. Beyond writing, another way to give psychology away is through community workshops and trainings. For instance, Annie is often involved in hosting **community workshops** on confronting and eliminating oppression such as how LGBTQ youth can talk to their friends and families about harmful microaggressions. Whatever form it may take, the point of giving psychology away is that *psychologists should not hoard information only for ourselves or those who are privileged to have access to universities, journal articles, textbooks, and professional conferences.* We need to stop talking just among ourselves (e.g., through journals, conferences); instead, we need to share knowledge in such a way so all people can start to think about concepts like oppression, microaggressions, colonization, and critical consciousness. These issues and concepts, and the conversations about them, should not exist solely in classrooms, universities, scientific journals, or textbooks; they should be discussed in public spheres to shine light on their existence and consequences, and to issue a rallying cry for social change.

Another way to extend our roles as educators is to **respond to oppression in everyday life** (for excellent tips on how to facilitate difficult but needed conversations that resist oppression, particularly racial oppression, please see Sue, 2015). In this sense, we are educating people who perhaps need it most—the perpetrators of oppression. One consistent message in "giving psychology away" efforts, like the ones described previously, is the power of using our voice. Our voice is powerful because it belongs to us. Our voice is imbued with the richness of our experiences, and it is the most powerful tool we have to challenge the oppression in our world. Thus, when we see oppression unfolding around us, we must say or do something. If we are feeling oppressed in a particular environment, we must say or do something. We do acknowledge, however, that it can be very scary to speak up or do something to resist oppression, especially since oppression is rooted in the very dynamics of power and privilege that silences voices of opposition. We understand that responding to oppression often involves making oneself vulnerable. We can appreciate this, and we recognize that above all, people must keep themselves safe.

But if we ever feel comfortable enough to take a risk and resist oppression, here are a few suggestions about how to frame our message:

1. **Rehearse**—As we stated above, standing up to oppression can make people feel vulnerable, and so it becomes important to empower yourself as much as possible. Rehearsing what you want to say can make you feel more confident.

2. **Anticipate defensiveness**—Most people react defensively when their oppressive words and behavior are questioned. Anticipate this reaction and try not to take it personally. That person is responsible for his or her own behavior, and it is not a reflection on you.

3. **Tell your story**—It is impossible (though some may try) to argue with your experience. That is why it is important for you to let perpetrators of oppression see you as a human being, one who is affected by words and actions. If you feel comfortable, share with them how their words and actions impact you personally. If you have to choose between sharing statistics and sharing your story, share your story. Your story is powerful.

4. **Enlist support**—Unfortunately, many people feel too threatened by these kinds of conversations to engage with you, no matter how you approach the conversation. So, it is important to talk to friends, peers, and mentors who understand what you might be experiencing and who can provide you with support to keep going.

■ PRAISING PARADOX

As you may have observed by now, community psychology work can get overwhelming and even depressing. The fact that social problems—in our case, oppression—are complicated, that they are ever-changing, that we need to consider multiple contributing factors, and that we need to think through multiple potential solutions while also taking into account the diverse values, perspectives, and cultures of the communities with which we work may lead many of us to a state of defeat and hopelessness. Even further, standing up against oppression requires that we take serious risks and make ourselves vulnerable. Thus, to help us deal with such seemingly inevitable desolation, discomfort, and pain, we end this chapter by sharing one of the best strengths of community psychologists: our inclination and capacity to **embrace paradox** (Rappaport, 1981). According to Rudkin

(2003), "When we recognize the simultaneous truth of two seemingly opposite poles of thought, we gain insight and direction" (p. 172). To this end, in the form of paradoxes, we now present some tips from Rudkin to help us remain strong and committed to creating social changes that are aimed toward dismantling systems of oppression.

First, we need to remember that **the situation is urgent, so we must take our time.** Always remember that there is an entire network of people who are resisting other forms of oppression or other social justice issues, so we should never feel like we have to do it all. We can focus on what we can do and do it as well as we can as much as we can, wherever and whenever we can. Second, as we now realize, **the problems are huge, so we must think small.** One way for us to do this is to reflect on where we might be able to make the greatest impact. Oftentimes, this means taking action at the local or state level. Yes, it would be great if we were able to get to Washington, DC, and march with hundreds of thousands of other people. But being on a national stage is not the only way to contribute. Perhaps we could make even more of an impact if we organized a march in our community. Perhaps we can donate what we are able to local social justice organizations, charities, or associations. Third, we now also know that **social change is complex, so we should keep it simple.** We need to do something, anything, just *DO*. Action is the antithesis of hopelessness. Once we identify a cause that is important to us, we must find one way that we can support it by actually getting up and doing something. That might mean volunteering hours, or stuffing envelopes, or working at a phone bank. Any action. There is plenty of work that needs to be done, and there is the added benefit that when we keep moving and keep doing, we start to feel more hopeful and optimistic about the future. So, it is a win–win!

The fourth Rudkin (2003) paradox we want to share is that **social change is serious business, so we must have fun.** We must find a community, or create a community, in order to connect with others. There is no *social* justice without relationships. We must find someone, or a group of people, whom we can talk to about these topics, move toward social action with, and depend on for mutual support. One of the most meaningful interactions we have had recently is when people have checked in with us with a simple text message, "these are crazy times, I just want you to know I'm on your team." It is important to know we are not alone, and part of that is reaching out to others who might also be grappling with these ideas. Finally, as we have learned, it takes a long time for social change to occur and there will be many barriers to social change. Thus, **social change requires staying on course, so we must relinquish control.** One way to do this is to think about what is most important to

TABLE 9.2   Rudkin's Paradoxes

Paradox	Meaning
The situation is urgent, so take your time	Combine a sense of urgency (because the work is important) with a long-term commitment (because the work is never-ending). Also remember that you are not alone in resisting oppression; you should not bear the burden of being solely responsible for social change.
The problems are huge, so think small	It is overwhelming to think about tackling problems like systemic injustice, so try and identify a few small contributions you can make. Solving problems of systemic injustice will require many people, each working on small parts of the problem.
Social change is complex, so keep it simple	It is easy to fall into the trap of philosophizing about problems of injustice; we can even *think* ourselves into a spiral of helplessness. So focus your attention on what you are able to *do*.
Social change is serious business, so have fun	It is easy to feel helpless and hopeless when thinking about systemic injustice, so remember to let yourself experience joy and happiness. Find ways to laugh at yourself, and make time to spend with others who nurture your spirit and help you feel optimistic about the future.
Social change requires staying on course, so relinquish control	Find ways to connect your work to a greater purpose (e.g., creating a better world for future generations) and use that to help you keep going despite the uncertainties, "unpredictabilities," and chaos.

Source: Adapted from Rudkin (2003).

us, reflect on where these issues touch our lives, and ask ourselves what is our inspiration for wanting to make changes on these issues. Then we can connect our plans for action to what is most important and essential to us (e.g., the future generations, our children, our belief in equality, our religion, our spiritual beliefs). We can focus on these "higher powers" to help us manage the inherent unpredictability and uncontrollability of the world and stay resolute in our social change efforts. These paradoxes are summarized in Table 9.2 so that we can easily refer to it as we forge ahead with our struggles.

REFERENCES

Albee, G. W. (1981). Politics, power, prevention, and social change. In J. M. Joffe & G. W. Albee (Eds.), *Prevention through political action and social change* (pp. 3–24). Hanover, NH: University Press of New England.

Black Lives Matter. (2017). Retrieved from http://blacklivesmatter.com

Blakeslee, S., DiChristina, M., Raeburn, P., & Lambert, K. (2012). Behavioral neuroscience and the media. *Physiology and Behavior, 107*(5), 617–622.

Caplan, G. (1964). *Principles of prevention psychiatry.* Oxford, England: Basic Books.

Caplan, N., & Nelson, S. D. (1973). On being useful: The nature and consequences of psychological research on social problems. *American Psychologist, 28*, 199–211.

Chamberlain, J. (2016). #givingpsychologyaway: Meet four mental health professionals using social media to share psychology. *Monitor on Psychology, 47*(1), 40.

Cowen, E. L. (1996). The ontogenesis of primary prevention: Lengthy strides and stubbed toes. *American Journal of Community Psychology, 24*, 235–249.

Cowen, E. L. (1997). On the semantics and operations of primary prevention and wellness enhancement (or will the real primary prevention please stand up?). *American Journal of Community Psychology, 25*, 245–255.

Drabold, W. (2015). Here's what Mike Pence said on LGBT issues over the years. *Time.* Retrieved from http://time.com/4406337/mike-pence-gay-rights-lgbt-religious-freedom

Goodkind, J., LaNoue, M., Lee, C., Freeland, L., & Freund, R. (2012). Feasibility, acceptability, and initial findings from a community-based cultural mental health intervention for American Indian youth and their families. *Journal of Community Psychology, 40*(4), 381–405. doi:10.1002/jcop.20517

Halagao, P. E. (2004). Holding up the mirror: The complexity of seeing your ethnic self in history. *Theory and Research in Social Education, 32*, 459–483.

Kenneally, M. (2017). More than 1 million rally at women's marches in US and around world. *ABC News.* Retrieved from http://

abcnews.go.com/Politics/womens-march-heads-washington-day
-trumps-inauguration/story?id=44936042

Klatzky, R. L. (2009). Giving psychological science away: The role
of applications courses. *Perspectives in Psychological Science,*
4(5), 522–530.

Lin, Y.-J., & Israel, T. (2012). A computer-based intervention to reduce
internalized heterosexism in men. *Journal of Counseling Psychology,*
59(3), 458–464.

Mattu, A. (2017). The psych show. *YouTube.* Retrieved from https://
www.youtube.com/user/thepsychshowdotcom

Meyer, R. (2016). The legal case for blocking the Dakota Access
Pipeline: Did the U.S. government help destroy a major Sioux
archeological site? *The Atlantic.* Retrieved from https://www
.theatlantic.com/technology/archive/2016/09/dapl-dakota
-sitting-rock-sioux/499178

Miller, G. (1969). Psychology as a means of promoting human welfare.
American Psychologist, 24, 1063–1075.

Nadal, K. (2017). *Out talk.* Retrieved from http://kevinnadal.com/
outtalk.php

Neblett, E. W., Rivas-Drake, D., & Umaña-Taylor, A. J. (2012). The
promise of racial and ethnic protective factors in promoting ethnic
minority youth development. *Child Development Perspectives, 6*(3),
295–303. doi:10.1111/j.1750-8606.2012.00239.x

Plested, B. A., Edwards, R. W., & Jumper-Thurman, P. (2006).
Community readiness: A handbook for successful change. Fort Collins,
CO: Tri-Ethnic Center for Prevention Research.

Plested, B. A., Jumper Thurman, P., Edwards, R. W., & Oettling,
E. R. (1998). Community readiness: A tool for community
empowerment. *Prevention Researcher, 5*(2), 5–7.

Prochaska, J. O., & DiClemente, C. C. (1992). Stages of change in the
modification of problem behaviors. In M. Hersen, R. M. Eisler, &
P. M. Miller (Eds.), *Progress in behavior modification* (pp. 184–218).
Sycamore, IL: Sycamore Press.

Quah, N., & Davis, L. E. (2015). Here's a timeline of unarmed Black
people killed by police over past year. *BuzzFeed News.* Retrieved
from https://www.buzzfeed.com/nicholasquah/heres-a-timeline

-of-unarmed-black-men-killed-by-police-over?utm_term=
.nrDk9g8q1#.sqArJ1B3q

Rappaport, J. (1977). *Community psychology: Values, research, and social action.* New York, NY: Holt, Rinehart, and Winston.

Rappaport, J. (1981). In praise of paradox: A social policy of empowerment over prevention. *American Journal of Community Psychology, 9,* 1–25.

Ratts, M. J. (2009). Social justice counseling: Toward the development of a fifth force among counseling paradigms. *Journal of Humanistic Counseling, Education, and Development, 48,* 160–172.

Rudkin, J. K. (2003). *Community psychology: Guiding principles and orienting concepts.* Upper Saddle River, NJ: Pearson.

Sarason, S. B. (1974). *The psychological sense of community: Prospects for a community psychology.* San Francisco, CA: Jossey-Bass.

Strobel, L. M. (2015). *Coming full circle: Narratives of decolonization among post-1965 Filipino Americans* (2nd ed.). Santa Rosa, CA: Center for Babaylan Studies.

Sue, D. W. (2015). *Race talk and the conspiracy of silence: Understanding and facilitating difficult dialogues on race.* Hoboken, NJ: Wiley.

Wenzke, M. (2017). *One hashtag is united Americans in the fight against Trump.* Retrieved from http://mashable.com/2017/02/02/resist-hashtag-trump-america/#yWAstL6kxqqD

Zimmerman, M. A. (1995). Psychological empowerment: Issues and illustrations. *American Journal of Community Psychology, 23,* 581–599.

Zimmerman, M. A. (2000). Empowerment theory. Psychological, organization, and community levels of analysis. In J. Rappaport & E. Seidman (Eds.), *Handbook of community psychology* (pp. 43–63). New York, NY: Kluwer Academic/Plenum.

CHAPTER 10

Future Directions: Some Suggestions for the Continued Growth of Psychological Work on Oppression

Whew! We have now made it to the final chapter and, along the way, we have covered plenty of material! We have gone through a basic but wide-ranging overview of oppression: what it is, what the different kinds of oppression are, how oppression may be manifested in a variety of ways, the different levels at which oppression exists and operates, why oppression exists and continues to exist, what oppression looked like in the past and what it looks like contemporarily, who experiences oppression and how their psychological experiences may be affected by it, and what we can do to address oppression and perhaps even eliminate it. We discussed many historical and contemporary examples of oppression, and even did some self-examinations of our social identities to see where we are in the social hierarchy of power. So yes, whew!!! And come to think of it, the material we discussed in the first nine chapters is not even exhaustive of all psychological work that is relevant to understanding and addressing oppression! That is, there is even more literature on and examples of oppression that we did not cover. So again, whew!!!

Although there seemingly is a lot of research, clinical efforts, and community work that have already been done on oppression, it does not mean that we now understand everything about it and that we know exactly how to best address it. Indeed, there are still plenty of gaps and holes in our understanding of oppression, and there is still plenty of work to do in the field of psychology to build on what we have now and continue to contribute to our society's collective efforts to eliminate oppression. In other words, *there are still plenty of ways for psychology to help address oppression and help create a more fair, just, and healthy society!* To this end, we close the book with some general suggestions for the continued growth of psychological work on oppression. Let us begin with recommendations for future research.

■ RECOMMENDATIONS FOR PSYCHOLOGICAL RESEARCH ON OPPRESSION

In terms of continuing to improve our understanding of the concept of oppression, *more research is needed on how the various oppressed groups experience and are affected by oppression.* Understandably, given their long and painful histories of oppression, a large proportion of what we currently know about oppression is based on literature about African Americans and women. For example, a search on PsycINFO with "women" and "oppression" as keywords produced 273 hits, while the keywords "Black" and "oppression" resulted in 111 hits (note: "African American" and "oppression" produced 76 hits). However, the amount of psychological literature on "oppression" and other marginalized groups as keywords such as "Latino/a" (19 hits), "Asian American" (10 hits), "Native American" (13 hits), "mixed race" (4 hits), "Hawaiian" or "Pacific Islander" (1 hit), "LGBT" (10 hits), "religion" (28 hits), "Muslim" (18 hits), "poor" (10 hits), "working class" (7 hits), and "disability" (56 hits) was significantly fewer (as of February 1, 2017). Thus, given the diversity of oppressive experiences between social groups, there seems to be plenty of much-needed research opportunities in this area.

One important example in which the various marginalized groups (Chapter 2) may differ in their experiences of oppression is with colonialism; that is, some groups experienced (or are still experiencing) colonization whereas other groups never did. For instance, the Filipino American and South Asian communities are often subsumed into the larger umbrella category of "Asian American" with other groups such as Chinese, Japanese, and Korean. Thus, Filipinos' (e.g., David, 2013) and South Asians' (e.g., Paranjpe, 2006) long histories of colonialism under Western nations (i.e., Spain, the United States, the United Kingdom) are often overlooked, if not altogether forgotten or disregarded, limiting our understanding of how historical oppression may continue to affect various aspects of peoples' psychological experiences. Indeed, the majority of research on oppression is focused on recent, contemporary, or directly experienced types of oppression, and *there is not as much psychological literature on historical, collective, or vicariously experienced oppression and their effects.* For instance, out of the approximately 1,900 PsycINFO hits for the keyword "oppression," only 36 hits were about "historical oppression."

One interesting concept regarding historical or vicariously experienced oppression is historical trauma (discussed in Chapters 2, 3, and 6) and how it and its effects are experienced across generations (leading some to refer to it as "intergenerational trauma"). Although there is growing research suggesting that historical trauma is a salient and common experience among groups of people who were subjected to historical oppression (e.g., Brave Heart, 2003; Duran, 2006; Duran & Duran, 1995; Evans-Campbell, 2008), some scholars remain critical of the construct and are calling for continued refinement of historical trauma theory and for more rigorous research on the specific mechanisms through which historical trauma is passed down intergenerationally and how it relates to current health outcomes (e.g., Gone, 2014; Kirmayer, Gone, & Moses, 2014). Indeed, it is important to consider historical context and how it may continue to influence oppressed peoples' contemporary experiences, and in this sense historical trauma is a promising construct that seems to be meaningful and relevant to many oppressed peoples. However, *continued research is needed to answer serious conceptual limitations about historical trauma for it to remain a viable and useful psychological construct* (Gone, 2014).

Our call for more psychological research on historical oppression should not be taken to mean that we should stop paying attention to oppression that is happening today. Certainly, *there is still plenty we need to learn about contemporary forms of oppression and how they influence peoples' psychological experiences, including their mental health.* For example, although there has been a rapid surge of psychological literature on the concept of microaggressions (discussed in Chapter 4), a type of social group discrimination that is more subtle, vague, and perhaps even unintentional (or even well intentioned in some cases, like when people ask Asian Americans "Where are you really from?" or tell African Americans "Wow, you are so articulate!" or when people compliment Latino/a Americans for speaking English well) that may be more common in our contemporary world (Sue et al., 2007), there are still some serious confusions about how microaggressions are defined and conceptualized (e.g., is microassault really a microaggression or is it an overt form of discrimination?), and there are still limitations on the methods (e.g., lack of studies with longitudinal and experimental designs) that have so far been used to study microaggressions (e.g., Lau & Williams, 2010; Wong, Derthick, David, Saw, & Okazaki, 2014).

Given that oppression may be more subtle and vague today, making it more difficult for people to definitively identify their experience as oppression and to clearly attribute oppression to someone (or something), then the internalization of oppression may become more common (as discussed in Chapter 5). That is, people who experience subtle forms of oppression may be more likely to internalize the confusions and emotions caused by oppression, attributing such negative consequences to one's self as one's own fault (e.g., "I'm just being too paranoid" or "I'm just being oversensitive"). Therefore, people may be prone to develop internalized oppression. However, although there has been a recent increase in the psychological literature on internalized oppression (for a review, see David, 2014) supporting the notion that internalized oppression is a salient construct for various social groups (e.g., Chae et al., 2014; David, 2010; Hatzenbuehler, 2009), research on this construct is still lagging compared to the literature on other "levels" of oppression. For instance, PsycINFO produced 125 hits for the keyword "interpersonal oppression," but produced only 55 hits for "internalized oppression." Thus, there are still plenty of unanswered questions (e.g., what are some protective or resiliency factors that may prevent the internalization of oppression?), and *more research on internalized oppression is needed.*

The existing psychological literature's heavy tilt toward interpersonal oppression is likely a reflection of the field's long-standing emphasis on individual-level factors (e.g., stereotypes, prejudices) and individual-level units of analyses (e.g., individual scores on Social Dominance Orientation, as discussed in Chapter 7). Indeed, psychology as a field—just like other scientific disciplines—has tended to focus on factors within the individual (e.g., biological factors like genes or psychological factors like attitudes and emotions) to study various phenomena. Unlike its long history and seeming expertise in capturing biases on the individual level, psychology has not really paid serious attention to factors beyond the individual such as social injustice, privilege, and power inequities. That is, the field of psychology's appreciation of how oppressive environments operate and influence our psychological experiences (thoughts, emotions, and behaviors) is not on par with its emphasis on individual-level factors. Thus, similar to how internalized oppression remains to be understudied, it is not surprising that psychological research on institutional oppression (PsycINFO produced only 13 hits) is also lagging behind psychological work on interpersonal oppression. *A more balanced research emphasis on all three levels of oppression (i.e., interpersonal, institutional, and internalized) is needed for us to move toward a more accurate and complete understanding of oppression.*

In addition to how psychological research needs to more accurately reflect the reality that oppression may exist and operate at multiple levels, psychological research also needs to reflect the reality that people simultaneously hold multiple identities and such identities may interact with each other to influence peoples' psychological experiences in very complex ways. Thus, *the psychological literature on intersectionalities needs to grow.* Recently, there has been some top-notch and promising work on intersectionalities that may serve as models for future research in this area. For example, Drazdowski and colleagues (2016) found that experiences of LGBTQ and POC discrimination—as well as the internalization of both kinds of oppression—are related to LGBTQ POC's illicit drug use, with LGBTQ discrimination seemingly more psychologically damaging. Consistent with these findings, Szymanski and Gupta (2009) looked at the intersections of internalized racism and internalized heterosexism and found that, although both are important for LGBTQ POC's mental health, internalized heterosexism may be more of a concern. In both of these studies, the interactions between racism and heterosexism (or LGBTQ discrimination) did not significantly predict mental health. However, other studies (e.g., Szymanski & Henrichs-Beck, 2014; Szymanski & Kashubeck-West, 2008; Szymanski & Owens, 2009) found that experiences of sexism and heterosexism—as well as the internalization of such forms of oppression—had unique and cumulative effects on sexual minority women's mental health. Indeed, this is definitely an exciting area of research and *future psychological work on multiple oppressed identities may shed further light on many remaining unanswered questions.*

You may have noticed that all the research recommendations we have mentioned so far (and frankly, a large majority of the book's content!) have focused on oppressed peoples and how oppression has negatively affected their psychological experiences. But as emphasized in Chapter 7, however, oppression and its damaging consequences (including internalized oppression) would not exist if there were not oppressors and oppressive systems! Therefore, *research attention and resources also need to be devoted toward improving our understanding of an important and huge component of the oppression issue: the psychology of the oppressors.* Indeed, although several theories have already been proposed—and although plenty of studies have already been conducted to test such theories—we know that oppression is a dynamic construct that is able to hide, adapt, and transform over time (as discussed in Chapter 4). Thus, continued research on why oppression continues to exist, how it adapts, and how it is able to survive across time and generations is still needed.

Similarly, although the vast majority of the literature on oppression (and the vast majority of the content in this book!) has been devoted to the psychological and health damages of oppression, and deservedly so, it is also definitely true that historically and contemporarily oppressed groups are resilient and that not all marginalized peoples suffer with poor health. For example, research suggests that having positive attitudes toward one's ethnic or racial group (i.e., racial or ethnic identity), being connected to and proud of one's group (i.e., cultural orientation), and understanding the historical and contemporary realities of one's group (i.e., ethnic/racial socialization) serve as protective factors against the harmful effects of ethnic or racial oppression (for a review, see Neblett, Rivas-Drake, & Umana-Taylor, 2012). Such findings may help us develop a more complete understanding of oppression, specifically in terms of what might we be able to do to combat it! Thus, *research on potential protective or resiliency factors that may operate to shield people from the negative effects of oppression is definitely welcome.*

As we move forward and attempt to answer specific research questions concerning any of the general areas of oppression (summarized in Table 10.1), we should also consider the methods that we subscribe to, value, and use in our studies. Currently, we see that researchers have employed both **quantitative** (e.g., surveys, experiments, many laboratory-based studies) and **qualitative** (e.g., interviews, focus groups, case studies) methods in their works on oppression, sometimes even using both in the same study (**mixed methods**), and this is great! Indeed, given the diversity of oppressive experiences between marginalized social groups and the complexity of oppression and its effects, *psychological research on oppression should definitely utilize both quantitative and qualitative methods.* However, we need to be aware of and guard against a general tendency to emphasize, value, and prefer quantitative research methods over qualitative ones, as there continues to be an overarching bias in the field of psychology toward quantitative methods (e.g., Enriquez, 1977, 1993; Kim, 2000; Shams, 2002; Yang, 2000). In other words, we need to make sure that we do not automatically privilege quantitative work on oppression—or research that seems to better satisfy conventional standards of "science" such as statistics, large sample sizes, hypothesis testing-oriented, highly controlled experiments in laboratories, or "objective" researchers who are detached from the topic and community of study—as inherently better, more rigorous, more significant, or more acceptable than qualitative work.

Keeping in check our tendency to automatically overvalue the standards of conventional science and unquestionably accept its assumptions,

TABLE 10.1 Ten General Recommendations for the Psychological Study of Oppression

1. **Diversity of Oppressive Experiences**: More research is needed on how various oppressed groups experience and are affected by oppression.

2. **Historical Oppression:** There is not so much psychological literature on historical, collective, or vicariously experienced oppression and their effects.

3. **Historical Trauma:** Continued research is needed to address serious conceptual limitations about historical trauma for it to remain a useful psychological construct.

4. **Contemporary Oppression:** There is still plenty we need to learn about directly experienced, contemporary forms of oppression (including subtle forms such as microaggressions) and how they influence peoples' psychological experiences.

5. **The Three "I"s of Oppression:** A more balanced research emphasis on all three levels of oppression (i.e., interpersonal, institutional, and internalized) is needed for us to move toward a more accurate and complete understanding of oppression.

6. **The Intersectionality Reality:** Psychological work needs to reflect the reality that multiple social identities exist simultaneously for many people, and such identities may interact in complex ways to influence their thoughts, emotions, behaviors, and health. The psychological literature on intersecting multiple identities needs to grow.

7. **The Psychology of Oppressors:** There is still plenty to learn about why oppression exists and persists, how it adapts, and how it survives across time and generations.

8. **Strengths-Informed:** Research on potential protective or resiliency factors that may operate to shield people from the negative effects of oppression is always welcome.

9. **The Value of Quantitative and Qualitative Methods:** Psychological research on oppression should equally value and utilize quantitative and qualitative methods.

10. **Other Ways of Knowing:** The field of psychology needs to be more critical of its research methods and be open to other ways of collecting information that may be more indigenous, natural, and empowering to marginalized communities.

values, and methods is especially important when we are studying oppression and working with oppressed social groups. This is because many oppressed groups have painful histories with conventional science, not only in terms of how science was used to inferiorize them (e.g., *The Bell Curve* by Hernstein & Murray, 1994; *The Barrow Alcohol Study*, see Foulks, 1989) and legitimize their oppression, but also because an overemphasis on Western scientific methods, assumptions, and values has contributed to the erasure of marginalized cultures' own epistemology or ways of knowing—a concept that scholars have called **scientific imperialism** (e.g., Diaz-Loving, 1999; Enriquez, 1993; Kim, 2000; Shams, 2002) or even **epistemicide** (de Sousa Santos, 2014). Thus, *we need to listen to the communities we are supposed to be serving and use research methods that may be more indigenous, comfortable, natural, and empowering to them.* In this regard, the growing interest in and use of **community-based participatory research (CBPR)** in the field of psychology is promising because this approach regards researchers and participants as equal stakeholders, the community of interest is engaged and involved in all aspects of the research process (e.g., decisions about topic, methods, funding sources), and the community has power over how the research is disseminated (e.g., journal articles, media coverage, conference presentations).

■ RECOMMENDATIONS FOR PSYCHOLOGICAL SERVICES TO ADDRESS OPPRESSION

Similar to how there is still plenty of room for growth regarding psychological research on oppression, the field of psychology also has plenty of work to do in terms of continuing to improve our psychological services to address oppression and its health effects. First, *clinical psychology work must incorporate a social justice framework to better identify oppression as a potential contributor to clients' distress and address it appropriately, sensitively, and effectively.* As we discussed in Chapter 6, oppression is consistently found to significantly influence the mental health of individuals who are members of marginalized social groups. However, as we discussed in Chapter 8, traditional clinical psychology approaches to helping tend to focus on factors within individuals—like how they think, feel, and act—in conceptualizing and explaining distress and psychopathology. Thus, *a potentially important "outside the individual" source of distress for marginalized social groups—oppression—may be missed, dismissed, or disregarded in conventional clinical work.* Incorporating a social justice lens into their existing clinical practices may help mental health service providers to ensure that they do not fall victims to simply teaching their clients to tolerate or become "well adjusted to a profoundly sick society."

According to Hall (2001), **culturally sensitive therapies** (CSTs) are clinical interventions that address and incorporate clients' cultural or sociopolitical contexts. Thus, when clients' cultural characteristics—including their experiences that are related to their social identities (e.g., experiences of oppression)—are taken into account in the conceptualization, design, and application of a clinical intervention, such an intervention may be regarded as a CST. One client characteristic that may be especially relevant to the mental health of individuals who are members of socially oppressed groups is oppression because oppression is an important contributing factor to marginalized peoples' mental health. Thus, adopting a social justice framework and becoming more "oppression-informed" in our practice is one way for us to become more culturally sensitive, supplement and "correct" for the inherent limitations of our conventional clinical orientations, and enhance the effectiveness of our clinical work.

The seemingly inherent limitations of conventional or dominant ways of clinical work bring us to our second recommendation for improved psychological services: *Clinicians must value—and be open to incorporating—other ways of healing (e.g., talking circles, sweats, storytelling, cultural immersion camps, hunting, berry picking) in their practice in order to more appropriately, respectfully, and effectively help individuals who are members of marginalized social groups.* A notable resource for different ways to do this is Moodley's and West's (2005) book *Integrating Traditional Healing Practices into Counseling and Psychotherapy.* This book provides a wide range of examples of incorporating indigenous ways of healing (e.g., Sahaja therapy, Maat, Morita therapy, herbalistas, voodoo, qigong, curandeiros) from various cultures around the world into clinical work. Incorporating other ways of healing and helping into our own clinical practices is one way in which we are changing clients' environmental contexts and structures, and making services more accommodating of their cultures, worldviews, and experiences, which helps in eliminating barriers to their seeking help.

In addition to making small changes in structures over which many clinicians have control, like our clinics and own theoretical orientations, more efforts are also needed toward changing larger systems or institutions (discussed in Chapter 9). This leads us to our third general recommendation for improved psychological services: *Psychologists and the organizations that represent psychologists (e.g., American Psychological Association) must work toward legitimizing and institutionalizing other ways of healing,* healing methods that are typically different from the **dualistic Cartesian view**—that the mind and body are two separate entities—that is followed by the dominant medical model (Moodley & West, 2005). Many of these other ways of healing are based on non-Western beliefs and worldviews, and emphasize a **holistic view** of health—a perspective that believes in the connection (instead of separation) and fluidity of the mind and the body (and spirituality). Psychology as a field must advocate for society and its institutions to regard other ways of healing as just as legitimate, valid, and potentially helpful as Western- or science-based practices. Some specific institutional-level changes that a social justice–informed field can work toward are requiring social justice or "oppression-informed" training in psychology graduate programs, including CSTs and other indigenous or traditional ways of healing in the list of Empirically Supported Treatments (Tolin, McKay, Forman, Klonsky, & Thombs, 2015) or Empirically Based Practices (American Psychological Association Presidential Task Force on Evidence-Based Practice, 2006), making health insurance companies recognize such practices as "reimbursable" and making health educational institutions, insurance companies, community agencies, hospitals, and clinics value the practitioners (e.g., elders, traditional healers) of these healing, helping, or intervention methods.

To assist in these efforts to legitimize and institutionalize other ways of healing, *we need more studies evaluating the effectiveness of CSTs and indigenous or traditional ways of healing when applied in the clinical context* for individuals who are members of oppressed social groups (Pomerville, Burrage, & Gone, 2016). The limited literature we have so far on this area, however, is promising in that findings seem to support the effectiveness of CSTs and indigenous or traditional ways of healing. For example, Fisher, Lankford, and Galea (1996) evaluated a treatment model for Alaska Natives in therapy for substance use disorders that were led by native counselors and included "cultural awareness activities" such as subsistence hunting trips, drumming, traditional dancing, creating traditional crafts (e.g., beading, sewing), making traditional foods, attending community cultural events, and education on traditional cultural practices. The researchers found that the culturally enhanced treatment program improved treatment retention for Alaska Native clients and helped in their recovery.

In addition to providing evidence to support the effectiveness of culturally enhanced clinical work, *we also need studies evaluating culturally tailored community-level interventions* (Pomerville et al., 2016). An example of this is the Our Life community mental health intervention (Goodkind, LaNoue, Lee, Freeland, & Freund, 2012a, 2012b), which was designed to help Navajo youth and their parents heal from historical trauma and its negative effects, reconnect to Navajo culture, increase self-esteem, and develop parenting skills that are appropriate for Navajo culture. The 6-month-long intervention (27 sessions) was shown to have helped participants enhance their feelings of belongingness to their community, their well-being, self-esteem, parent–child relationships, school grades, and quality of life. The promising results from the Our Life community mental health intervention, along with several other exemplary community-level wellness programs (for a review, see Gone, Hartmann, & Sprague, 2017), provide initial support for the effectiveness of culturally appropriate and collaborative work.

The community psychologists mentioned in the previous paragraphs like Joseph Gone, Jennifer Goodkind, and their collaborators (e.g., Burrage, Gone, & Momper, 2016; Gone & Calf Looking, 2015)—as well as others not yet mentioned like Gerald Mohatt, James Allen, and the rest of the People Awakening Project team (e.g., Allen, Mohatt, Beehler, & Rowe, 2014; Mohatt et al., 2004)—show how they have gone beyond the conventional walls of academia and clinical work to become more useful to the communities with which they work. Their examples bring us to our fourth general recommendation for improving our efforts to address oppression: *We must find and embrace other roles that will allow us to be more useful to the communities with which we work.* As mentioned in Chapter 9, mental health professionals must go beyond the walls of their clinics, therapy rooms, or hospitals and find other ways to be useful in their communities' efforts to become more fair, just, and healthy. In addition to developing, implementing, and evaluating community-level interventions, other roles that psychologists can fulfill to be more useful in our communities as we collectively try to address and eliminate social group oppression include **consultation** (assisting organizations, agencies, or community groups in some specific issues or projects), **community organizing** (bringing community members together in a joint action intended to improve their lives and well-being), and **coalition building** (bringing together diverse community groups, organizations, or stakeholders to address issues or create projects) (Rudkin, 2003).

Finally, and this last general recommendation may be applied to the others we have previously discussed (summarized in Table 10.2), *mental health clinicians, administrators, and policy makers must remain critical of current "standard operating procedures" or "best practices" and be prepared to stop their use when they may be oppressive. Instead, mental health professionals must work collaboratively in equal partnership with communities and listen to their ideas as to what might be more culturally appropriate, empowering, and effective for them.* As we alluded to earlier, a great example of this is the People Awakening Project (e.g., Allen et al., 2014; Mohatt et al., 2004), which is a collaborative community-level work that truly listened to—and incorporated—the community's voices in every step of the process (e.g., framing the issue or project, methods of intervention and evaluation) and one that equally valued the community as a stakeholder. In fact, even when tensions arose between the community's indigenous values and ways of knowing and the funder's Western-based worldviews and methodologies, the team did not simply bend to satisfy the funders. Instead, the team took time to carefully work with the community, build trust, and collaboratively develop a project that satisfied the values and standards of both stakeholders—the community and the funding agency. The People Awakening Project, therefore, is a great example of how psychologists (a) stopped their tendency to go to a "default" way of doing things simply because it was dictated by dominant institutions; (b) listened to the community's concerns about the "default" ways of doing things and the community's strong preference for methods that were more culturally appropriate; and (c) collaborated with the community to develop a project that satisfied the community's values and standards.

TABLE 10.2   Five General Recommendations for Psychological Services to Address Oppression

1. **Adopt a Social Justice Framework:** Clinical psychology work must incorporate a social justice framework to better identify and address oppression—a potentially important source of distress for individuals who are members of marginalized social groups.

2. **Incorporate Other Ways of Healing:** Clinicians must value—and be open to incorporating—other ways of healing (e.g., talking circles, sweats, storytelling) in their practice in order to more appropriately, respectfully, and effectively help individuals who are members of marginalized social groups.

3. **Legitimize and Institutionalize Other Ways of Healing:** Psychology as a field must advocate for society and its institutions (e.g., clinics, hospitals, community agencies, health insurance companies, schools) to regard other ways of healing as just as legitimate, valid, and potentially helpful as Western- or science-based practices.

4. **Be Useful in Many Other Ways:** Mental health professionals must go beyond the walls of their clinics, therapy rooms, or hospitals and find other ways to be useful in their communities' efforts toward becoming more fair, just, and healthy.

5. **Stop, Collaborate, and Listen:** Mental health clinicians, administrators, and policy makers must remain critical of current "standard operating procedures" or "best practices" and be prepared to stop their use when they may be oppressive. Instead, mental health professionals must work collaboratively in equal partnership with communities and listen to their ideas as to what might be more culturally appropriate, empowering, and effective for them.

■ OUR COLLECTIVE JOURNEY

In summary, more light needs to be shed in all areas of oppression and there remains an abundance of specific research questions within each of these areas that still need to be addressed. The same can be said about the clinical and community services we have as a field, in that more attention, resources, and effort need to be invested into making our tools and services more effective in addressing and eliminating social group oppression. Even further, we need to do work on our professional identities, challenge our conventional roles (e.g., professors, researchers, clinicians), and expand beyond the walls of academia, clinics, and hospitals in order to make ourselves more useful to society. The field of psychology can contribute toward the creation of a healthy society by helping to better understand social group oppression and to eliminate injustice, inequality, and bias at all levels of society. In our efforts to create a more just, fair, and healthy society, we need to make sure that the research methods, tools (e.g., testing and assessment materials), and services (e.g., therapy, advocacy, organizing) we use are not oppressive. Instead, we need to strive toward developing research methods, tools, and services that are liberating and empowering to the communities with which we are working. The field of psychology needs to be more critical of its conventions or "standard operating procedures," listen to communities the field is purportedly serving, and be open to ways of knowing, helping, and healing that may be more indigenous or natural to marginalized communities.

Beyond the field of psychology, we as a collective human society also have a very long and painful road ahead of us. For some of us, the road will be difficult because it requires that we evaluate our values and become aware of our privileged positions in society. It will require many awkward and worldview-threatening moments. It will require change. For others, the road will be difficult because the world remains treacherous, dangerous, and traumatizing—spiritually, psychologically, and even physically—as we continue to face oppression simply for being who we are. Yes, there is plenty of very tough, intimidating, and even depressing work to be done. And with this work, there are many aspects that are unknown and unpredictable, so there will be accompanying anxieties, tensions, and other devastating emotions. All of us will fumble, make mistakes, and repeat mistakes. Nothing is clear, except for the simple fact that we have plenty of work to do with ourselves, our immediate communities, and with the larger structures of society.

It's on us—all of us. Let's get to work.

REFERENCES

Allen, J., Mohatt, G. V., Beehler, S., & Rowe, H. L. (2014). People awakening: Collaborative research to develop cultural strategies for prevention in community intervention. *American Journal of Community Psychology, 54*, 100–111. doi:10.1007/s10464-014-9647-1

American Psychological Association Presidential Task Force on Evidence-Based Practice. (2006). Evidence-based practice in psychology. *American Psychologist, 61*, 271–285.

Brave Heart, M. Y. (2003). The historical trauma response among natives and its relationship with substance abuse: A Lakota illustration. *Journal of Psychoactive Drugs, 35*(1), 7–13.

Burrage, R. L., Gone, J. P., & Momper, S. L. (2016). Urban American Indian community perspectives on resources and challenges for youth suicide prevention. *American Journal of Community Psychology, 58*(1–2), 136–149.

Chae, D. H., Nuru-Jeter, A. M., Adler, N. E., Brody, G. H., Lin, J., Blackburn, E. H., & Epel, E. (2014). Discrimination, racial bias, and telomere length in African-American men. *American Journal of Preventive Medicine, 46*, 103–111.

David, E. J. R. (2010). Testing the validity of the Colonial Mentality Implicit Association Test (CMIAT) and the interactive effects of covert and overt colonial mentality on Filipino American mental health. *Asian American Journal of Psychology, 1*, 31–45.

David, E. J. R. (2013). *Brown skin, white minds: Filipino -/ American postcolonial psychology* (with commentaries). Charlotte, NC: Information Age Publishing.

David, E. J. R. (Ed.). (2014). *Internalized oppression: The psychology of marginalized groups.* New York, NY: Springer Publishing.

de Sousa Santos, B. (2014). *Epistemologies of the South: Justice against epistemicide.* New York, NY: Routledge.

Diaz-Loving, R. (1999). The indigenization of psychology: Birth of a new science or rekindling of an old one? *Applied Psychology: An International Review, 48*, 433–449.

Drazdowski, T. K., Perrin, P. B., Trujillo, M., Sutter, M., Benotsch, E. G., & Snipes, D. J. (2016). Structural equation modeling of the effects of racism, LGBTQ discrimination, and internalized oppression on illicit drug use in LGBTQ people of color. *Drug and Alcohol Dependence, 159,* 255–262.

Duran, E. (2006). *Healing the soul wound: Counseling with American Indians and other native peoples.* New York, NY: Teachers College Press.

Duran, E., & Duran, B. (1995). *Native American postcolonial psychology.* Albany: State University of New York Press.

Enriquez, V. G. (1977). Filipino psychology in the third world. *Philippine Journal of Psychology, 10,* 3–18.

Enriquez, V. G. (1993). Developing a Filipino psychology. In U. Kim & J. W. Berry (Eds.), *Indigenous psychologies: Research and experience in cultural context* (pp. 152–169). Newbury Park, CA: Sage.

Evans-Campbell, T. (2008). Historical trauma in American Indian/ Native Alaska communities: A multilevel framework for exploring impacts on individuals, families, and communities. *Journal of Interpersonal Violence, 23*(3), 316–338. doi:10.1177/0886260507312290

Fisher, D. G., Lankford, B. A., & Galea, R. P. (1996). Therapeutic community retention among Alaska Natives: Akeela house. *Journal of Substance Abuse Treatment, 13,* 265–271. doi:10.1016/ S0740-5472(96)00060-8

Foulks, E. F. (1989). Misalliances in the Barrow Alcohol Study. *American Indian and Native Alaska Mental Health Research, 2*(3), 7–17.

Gone, J. P. (2014). Reconsidering American Indian historical trauma: Lessons from an early Gros Ventre war narrative. *Transcultural Psychiatry, 51*(3), 387–406.

Gone, J. P., & Calf Looking, P. E. (2015). The Blackfeet Indian culture camp: Auditioning an alternative indigenous treatment for substance use disorders. *Psychological Services, 12*(2), 83–91.

Gone, J. P., Hartmann, W. E., & Sprague, M. R. (2017). Wellness interventions for indigenous communities in the United States: Exemplars for action research. In M. A. Bond, C. B. Keys, & I. Serrano-Garcia (Eds.), *APA handbook of community psychology: Vol. 2. Methods for community research and action for diverse groups and issues* (pp. 507–522). Washington, DC: American Psychological Association.

Goodkind, J. R., LaNoue, M. D., Lee, C., Freeland, L. R., & Freund, R. (2012a). Feasibility, acceptability, and initial findings from a community-based cultural mental health intervention for American Indian youth and their families. *Journal of Community Psychology, 40*(4), 381–405. doi:10.1002/jcop.20517

Goodkind, J. R., LaNoue, M. D., Lee, C., Freeland, L. R., & Freund, R. (2012b). Involving parents in a community-based, culturally-grounded mental health intervention for American Indian youth: Parent perspectives, challenges, and results. *Journal of Community Psychology, 40*(4), 468–478. doi:10.1002/jcop.21480

Hall, G. N. (2001). Psychotherapy research with ethnic minorities: Empirical, ethical, and conceptual issues. *Journal of Consulting and Clinical Psychology, 69*, 502–510.

Hatzenbuehler, M. L. (2009). How does sexual minority stigma get "under the skin": A psychological mediation framework. *Psychological Bulletin, 135*(5), 707–730.

Hernstein, R. J., & Murray, C. (1994). *The Bell Curve: Intelligence and class structure in American life.* New York, NY: Free Press.

Kim, U. (2000). Indigenous, cultural, and cross-cultural psychology: A theoretical, conceptual, and epistemological analysis. *Asian Journal of Social Psychology, 3*, 265–287.

Kirmayer, L. J., Gone, J. P., & Moses, J. (2014). Rethinking historical trauma. *Transcultural Psychiatry, 51*(3), 299–319. doi:10.1177/1363461514536358

Lau, M. Y., & Williams, C. D. (2010). Microaggressions research: Methodological review and recommendations. In D. W. Sue (Ed.), *Microaggressions and marginality: Manifestation, dynamics, and impact* (pp. 313–336). New York, NY: Wiley.

Mohatt, G. V., Hazel, K. L., Allen, J., Stachelrodt, M., Hensel, C., & Fath, R. (2004). Unheard Alaska: Culturally anchored participatory action research on sobriety with Alaska Natives. *American Journal of Community Psychology, 33*(3–4), 263–273.

Moodley, R., & West, W. (Eds.). (2005). *Integrating traditional healing practices into counseling and psychotherapy.* Thousand Oaks, CA: Sage.

Neblett, E. W., Rivas-Drake, D., & Umana-Taylor, A. J. (2012). The promise of racial and ethnic protective factors in promoting ethnic minority youth development. *Child Development Perspectives, 6*(3), 295–303.

Paranjpe, A. C. (2006). From tradition through colonialism to globalization: Reflections on the history of psychology in India. In A. C. Brock (Ed.), *Internationalizing the history of psychology* (pp. 56–74). New York: New York University Press.

Pomerville, A., Burrage, R. L., & Gone, J. P. (2016, October 13). Empirical findings from psychotherapy research with indigenous populations: A systematic review. *Journal of Consulting and Clinical Psychology.* Advance online publication. doi:10.1037/ccp0000150

Rudkin, J. K. (2003). *Community psychology: Guiding principles and orienting concepts.* Upper Saddle River, NJ: Pearson.

Shams, M. (2002). Issues in the study of indigenous psychologies: Historical perspectives, cultural interdependence, and institutional regulations. *Asian Journal of Social Psychology, 5,* 79–91.

Sue, D. W., Capodilupo, C., Torino, G., Bucceri, J., Holder, A., Nadal, K., & Esquilin, M. (2007). Racial microaggressions in everyday life: Implications for clinical practice. *American Psychologist, 62,* 271–286.

Szymanski, D. M., & Gupta, A. (2009). Examining the relationships between multiple oppressions and Asian American sexual minority persons' psychological distress. *Journal of Gay & Lesbian Social Services: Issues in Practice, Policy & Research, 21*(2–3), 267–281.

Szymanski, D. M., & Henrichs-Beck, C. (2014). Exploring sexual minority women's experiences of external and internalized heterosexism and sexism and their links to coping and distress. *Sex Roles, 70*(1–2), 28–42.

Szymanski, D. M., & Kashubeck-West, S. (2008). Mediators of the relationship between internalized oppressions and lesbian and bisexual women's psychological distress. *The Counseling Psychologist, 36,* 575–594. doi:10.1177/0011000007309490

Szymanski, D. M., & Owens, G. P. (2009). Group-level coping as a moderator between heterosexism and sexism and psychological distress in sexual minority women. *Psychology of Women Quarterly, 33,* 197–205. doi:10.1111/j.1471-6402.2009.01489.x

Tolin, D. F., McKay, D., Forman, E. M., Klonsky, E. D., & Thombs, B. D. (2015). Empirically supported treatment: Recommendations for a new model. *Clinical Psychology: Research and Practice, 22*(4), 317–338. doi:10.1111/cpsp.12122

Wong, G., Derthick, A. O., David, E. J. R., Saw, A., & Okazaki, S. (2014). The *What*, the *Why*, and the *How*: A review of racial microaggressions research in psychology. *Race and Social Problems, 6*(2), 181–200.

Yang, K. S. (2000). Monocultural and cross-cultural indigenous approaches: The royal road to the development of a balanced global psychology. *Asian Journal of Social Psychology, 3*, 241–263.

Index

Research paper

CPSIA information can be obtained
at www.ICGtesting.com
Printed in the USA
BVHW081802130722
642083BV00010B/55